NATIONAL GEOGRAPHIC

TRAVELER

ICELAND

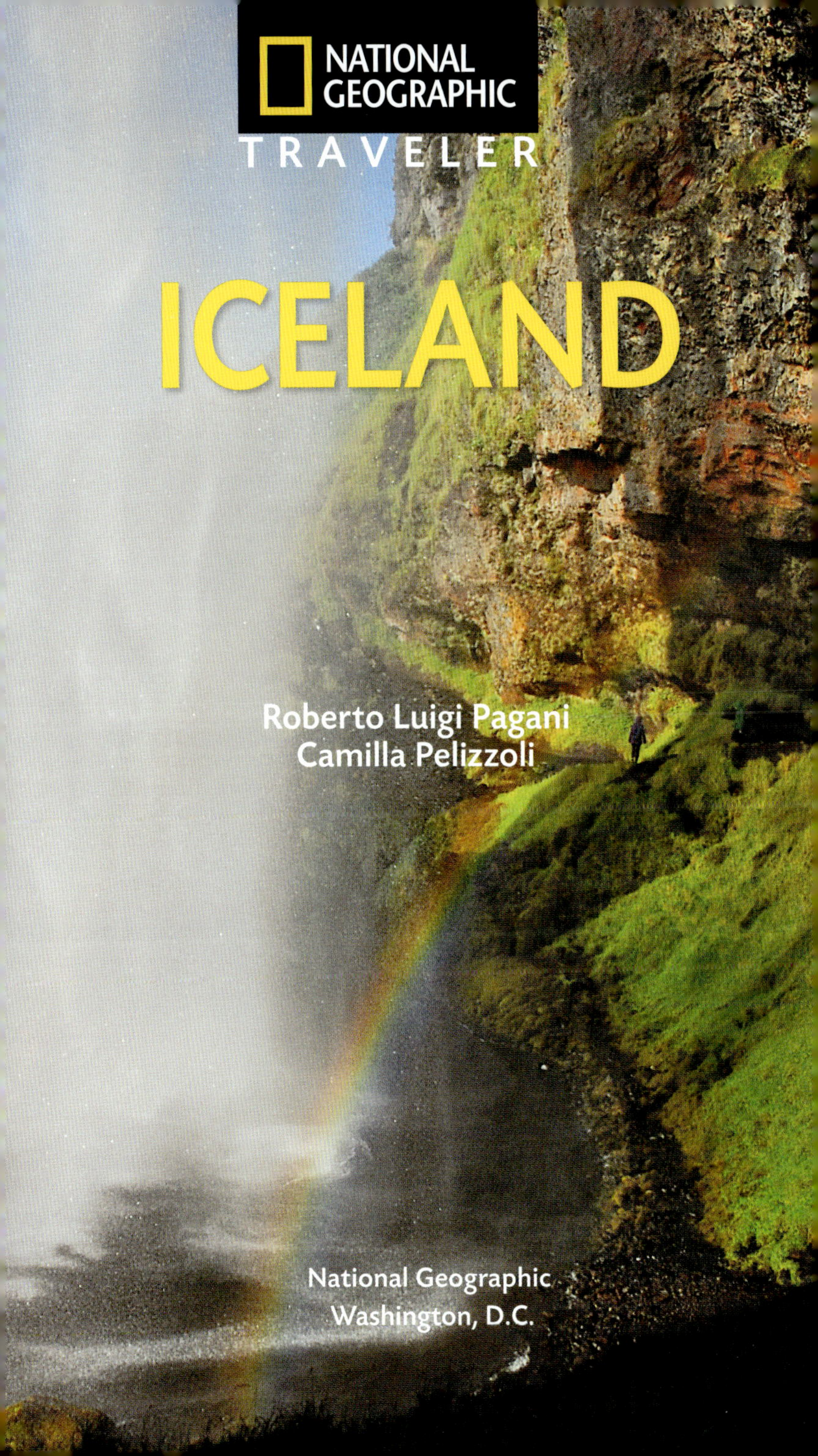

NATIONAL GEOGRAPHIC
TRAVELER

ICELAND

Roberto Luigi Pagani
Camilla Pelizzoli

National Geographic
Washington, D.C.

CONTENTS

Pages 2–3: Seljalandsfoss, a more than 196-foot-tall (60 m) waterfall in southern Iceland.

Page 4: A gravel road on the Vatnsnes Peninsula.

TRAVELING WITH EYES OPEN

Alert travelers go with a purpose and leave with a benefit. If you travel responsibly, you can help support wildlife conservation, historic preservation, and cultural enrichment in the places you visit. You can enrich your own travel experience as well.

To be a geo-savvy traveler:

- Recognize that your presence has an impact on the places you visit.
- Spend your time and money in ways that sustain local character. (Besides, it's more interesting that way.)
- Value the destination's natural and cultural heritage.
- Respect the local customs and traditions.
- Express appreciation to local people about things you find interesting and unique to the place: its nature and scenery, music and food, historic villages and buildings.
- Vote with your wallet: Support the people who support the place, patronizing businesses that make an effort to celebrate and protect what's special there. Seek out shops, local restaurants, inns, and tour operators who love their home—who love taking care of it and showing it off. Avoid businesses that detract from the character of the place.
- Enrich yourself, taking home memories and stories to tell, knowing that you have contributed to the preservation and enhancement of the destination.

That is the type of travel now called geotourism, defined as "tourism that sustains or enhances the geographical character of a place—its environment, culture, aesthetics, heritage, and the well-being of its residents."

NATIONAL GEOGRAPHIC
TRAVELER

ICELAND

ABOUT THE AUTHORS

Roberto Luigi Pagani was born in Cremona, Italy. He has been living in Iceland since 2014. He holds a master's degree in Icelandic medieval studies and is a doctoral candidate in the same subject. He is the author of the popular project "An Italian in Iceland" and collaborates regularly with some of Italy's major newspapers. He is a member of the boards of the Italian-Icelandic Chamber of Commerce and the Italian Association of Iceland. An adjunct lecturer at the University of Iceland since 2016, he has written for academic publications and translated Icelandic medieval sagas as well as a volume on the history and culture of Iceland. Since 2017, he has also been working as a tour guide in his adopted land, specializing in searching for the Northern Lights, and as a tour leader of specific cultural trips.

Camilla Pelizzoli was born outside the limits of Milan but has made a home in the big city. She has a degree in literature and is an editor by profession. She has been working for some time on updating National Geographic's Traveler and Walking Guides. She is passionate about Nordic mythology and loves to immerse herself in reading the *Edda*.

CHARTING YOUR TRIP

Iceland is perfect for those seeking an experience surrounded by nature. Whether it's a quiet trip exploring the rugged coastline or an adventurous vacation with excursions and hiking, the beauty of Iceland's regions is sure to impress. The capital city of Reykjavík is the perfect starting point for all forms of exploration.

Getting Around

Although Iceland's public transportation has a broad reach, moving around the country with ease is best done with a rental car. (You can arrive with your car but it's more complicated to arrange.) In recent years, thanks to an increase in charging stations, you can even choose an electric vehicle. There are no railways or trains. However, there is no shortage of domestic flights, scheduled buses, or boats and ferries to move between fjords or to the small islands near the coast. In Reykjavík, you can explore the city by bicycle.

Domestic flights take less than an hour, and at smaller local airports there are no more than a couple a day. Arriving from abroad, you almost certainly will pass through Keflavík Airport. Although the airports in Reykjavík, Akureyri, and Egilsstaðir see some international flights, they are mostly seasonal and fly to just a few specific destinations.

Public transportation on wheels is organized by Strætó (*www.straeto.is*); buses are recognizable by their dark yellow color. The service travels around the entire island along the Hringvegur, the 707-mile (1,339 km) Ring Road. In some areas of the island there are also local companies that have additional lines with shorter routes. In any case, it is good to pay attention to timetables. There can be radical changes in times and frequency between summer and winter. It's always worth checking the company's website.

The largest colonies of puffins can be found on the cliffs of southern Iceland.

For example, the so-called "Highland buses" or "Hicker buses" take hiking and mountain enthusiasts to the most popular spots but only in the summer season when the roads are passable.

The same goes for ferries that transport tourists and Icelanders between fjords and islands. It is good to inquire clearly about schedules because there may be only a few scheduled trips a day, especially in more remote regions.

In general, for complete independence and to visit even the most inaccessible villages, renting a car is probably the best option. At the car rental company, ask for a car suitable for your type of trip. Even in the summer, if you plan to get off the Ring Road and other paved roads, it is best to have four-wheel drive. Many roads, in fact, are still gravel and difficult for less prepared drivers or with an unsuitable car, which would also extend travel time quite a bit.

NOT TO BE MISSED:

Reykjavík & its museum circuit 79–96

Exploring Thingvellir National Park 119–121

Skaftafell area 162–163

Jökulsárlón glacial lagoon 165–166

Traveling the fjord circuit 202–217

Visiting the Glaumbær turf house 230

The region of Lake Mývatn 239–241

Askja caldera 294–296

Trip Plan

Exploring Iceland can be done in various ways. You can use the capital as a base for day trips or tackle the highway that encircles the island, changing scenery every day. It all depends on how much time you have and what you like. How adventurous are you? How interested are you in local folklore and history? As a general rule, have comfortable shoes (ideally hiking shoes) on hand, a raincoat, and an extra sweater just in case. The weather is really unpredictable and getting caught unprepared will certainly not contribute to an enjoyable trip.

The Golden Circle

One of the most popular routes is the Golden Circle, which is perfect if you have only a few days to spend in Iceland. You can easily add or remove legs to do it in one day, although of course, to fully experience it, the best approach is to take your time using Reykjavík as a base for day trips.

Over a long weekend, for example, you can spend the first day leisurely exploring the capital, immersing yourself in Icelandic hospitality, perusing the Art Museum and exhibits at the Árbær Anthropological Museum,

Icelandic National Tourist Board
Geirsgata 9, 101 Reykjavík, 535 5500, www.ferdamalastofa.is
Information office (Reykjavík)
Laugavegur 5, 551 3600, open daily 8:30 a.m.–9 p.m., www.whatson.is

or going to explore the island of Viðey by ferry. If you don't have your own vehicle, pick one up at a car rental.

On the second day, get ready for the first two-thirds of the circle. It takes about two hours to get to Geysir to admire the majestic jets of boiling water unique to this area. This is one of the few places in the world where you can observe this geothermal phenomenon so close-up. Although the main geyser doesn't always make an appearance, smaller Strokkur bursts into a 98-foot (30 m) column of water every 10 minutes or so. The entire area is active with hot springs, steams, and sulfurous mud pools to explore. When you're ready to move on, head to nearby Gullfoss Falls, a natural wonder of 26,400 gallons (100,000 L) of water from the Hvítá River falling 101 feet (31 m) every second into Gullfossgljúfur. To avoid being splashed by the icy water, come prepared with a raincoat. You can also plan the rest of the day so that you have time to pay a visit to one of the many geothermal springs where you can soak in the pleasantly warm water and stretch your muscles.

On the third day, finish off the Golden Circle with Thingvellir National Park. Whether you are a fan of local culture or more adventurous, there's something to tickle your fancy. Some major moments in Icelandic history took place in this park, such as the proclamation of independence from Denmark in 1944. The park is also home to the island's largest natural lake, Thingvallavatn. For diving enthusiasts the Silfra fissure is a must-see. Located between two tectonic plates, the water here is extremely transparent due to the lava rocks. On the fourth day, head back to the city before departing for home.

Hringvegur

If you have closer to two weeks, traveling the whole circumference of the island along the country's main road, Route 1 or the Ring Road, is a must. You can drive clockwise or counterclockwise, starting and ending in Reykjavík. If you choose the former, you will spend the first three days going north before reaching the coast.

On the first day, you will drive to the Snæfellsnes Peninsula, perhaps stopping at one of the many delightful villages along the coast.

Heading north on day two, you will arrive at the Tröllaskagi Peninsula, which is also part of the Arctic Coast Way, perfect if you have a few extra days and a passion for the landscapes of the far North.

The third day, drive toward Akureyri, a short distance away, and spend the day exploring the island's second largest city before heading out again on day four to wander Iceland's most geologically ancient region, Mývatn. It's impossible not to pass by Dettifoss, the second most powerful waterfall in Europe.

On the fifth day, proceed to the east coast, where, with luck, you might catch a glimpse of some whales and puffins. Seyðisfjörður tends to be the arrival point of choice for most travelers.

Driving in Iceland

Speed limits are 30 mph (50 km/h) in urban centers, 50 mph (80 km/h) on unpaved roads, and 55 mph (90 km/h) on paved roads. Pay attention to F-roads (mountain roads), which are unpaved and open only in the summer season. Gas stations are open until late in the evening, especially in summer. Always check online before you hit the road: *www.safetravel.is* for road conditions and *www.wet.is* for weather.

As you continue along the coast heading south, spend days six and seven enjoying the beautiful scenery of the vast Vatnajökull National Park, Europe's largest at 5,460 square miles (14,141 sq km). Here the intersection of volcanic activity and the ice cap, the fourth largest mass in the world, creates geological spectacles that cannot be found anywhere else. You could spend two to four days in this part of the island, depending on how much time you have, fully immersing yourself in the nature of Iceland.

As you head back to the capital, stopping at Selfoss along the way, you can choose to add on the Golden Circle route and the Borgarfjörður area. Don't forget a stop at a spa to recharge after your hiking sessions. Lastly, explore Reykjavík and all the conveniences of the capital. Climbing to the top of Hallgrímskirkja and taking in the view is a good way to bid farewell to Iceland.

Icelandic Currency

The current currency in Iceland is the Icelandic krona (in the local language *króna*, plural *krónur*; the official abbreviation is ISK, but in stores you will find it marked as kr). There are banknotes of 500, 1,000, 2,000, 5,000 and 10,000 kr, and coins of 1, 5, 10, 50 and 100 kr. There used to be coins worth less than one kr, called *aurar*, but they were taken out of circulation in the early 2000s.

HISTORY & CULTURE

A view of Reykjavík's rainbow street with Hallgrímskirkja church in the background.

ICELAND TODAY

Lapped by the water of the Gulf Stream, which mitigates its climate, Iceland is a land of contrasts, from the crimson lava to the stark white glaciers. It is struck by sudden changes, every year different from the last. Here, one must always be ready for the unexpected. In this harsh setting, Icelandic people have fought to survive for more than a thousand years, while managing to produce an extraordinarily flourishing culture.

A Land Forged by Ice & Fire

Iceland is a geologically young land. Located on a fault line that forms the boundary between the Eurasian and North American tectonic plates, it is constantly transforming. New matter continually emerges from below, expanding the land, and new lava flows reshape the landscape, constantly sculpted and smoothed by the erosion of water and ice. Glacier tongues have whittled out valleys and fjords, and rivers have carved the rock to create spectacular canyons, such as the one where the mighty Dettifoss waterfall spills over. Ice caps like Vatnajökull chisel the underlying rock then carry the dust toward the sea, depositing it on the coast to form the famous black beaches. The ground opens up and volcanic cones emerge, with lava molding new rocky terrain, the youngest on the planet, like Fagradalsfjall. Sometimes volcanoes erupt on the sea floor, surfacing and forming new islands, like the Vestmannaeyjar archipelago.

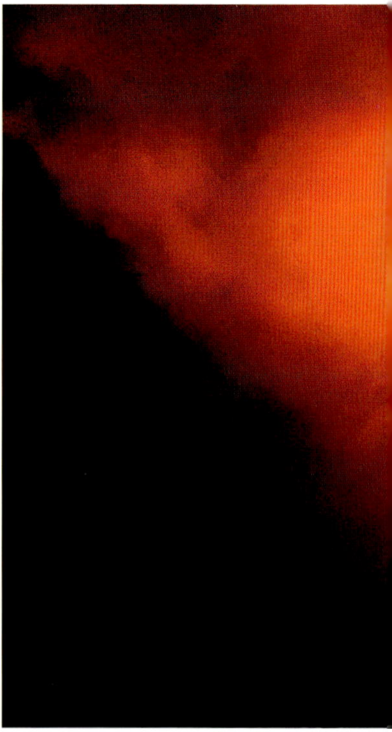

Icelanders

Living so close to this temperamental landscape has shaped the local people's mentality and attitude toward life. Nordic people are often stereotyped as being strict, rule-abiding planners, but Icelanders turn this idea on its head. In reality, they are not particularly prone to detailed planning and a literal observance of rules. This can sometimes cause misunderstandings for visitors, who perhaps wonder why services seem unprofessional compared to other places. The truth is that Icelanders are at their best in critical situations, demonstrating an unexpected capacity for improvisation and inventiveness under challenging circumstances. Even in social interactions, Icelanders are far from the cliché of cold, introverted, and taciturn Nordic people. They tend to be sociable, are often curious about foreigners, are fond of conviviality and social occasions, can be very blunt and direct, and are generally friendly and relaxed. Society is very informal and class differences have little value. People refer to each other by their first name, even when addressing institutional or higher-ranking figures. In work environments, the focus is on quality of life rather than efficiency and productivity.

Steam and red gas fumes billow from the top of Fagradalsfjall, which became active again in spring 2021.

Jökulsárlón, the glacial lagoon south of the Vatnajökull glacier.

Past & Present Society

Iceland finds itself torn between a traditional past, viewed with nostalgia, and the advancing future. The mentality and customs that were typical of Icelandic reality up until the mid-20th century, such as informality or flexibility in timing, often conflict with the demands of a society that is now highly urbanized and embedded in a dense network of international relations, in a context that has become globalized. Even today, there remains a certain tension between rural settings, seen as a repository of ancient values and traditions, and the urban one, concentrated in the Reykjavík metropolitan area, which is more innovative and forward-looking.

Demographically, things are skewed largely in favor of the city, with the capital region being home to about two-thirds of the population, but the electoral system is organized to balance this difference. A few families control large sectors of the economy, in some instances bordering on monopoly, and their strong influence on politics means that Iceland has the highest level of corruption of all the Nordic countries. Financial speculation without real fiscal control led to the colossal collapse of 2008, which was not followed by adequate structural reforms to prevent similar situations from occurring again. The unequally distributed income brackets place much of the tax burden on the shoulders of the average taxpayer. Overall, the gap between rich and poor in Iceland is getting wider. Large sectors of the population suffer from this situation, exacerbated by the crisis of the COVID-19 pandemic outbreak in 2020. Iceland has a very high GDP per capita (about

$74,000), which ranks eighth in the world. The most developed economic sector is the service sector, but industries (especially energy and aluminum processing) are also fairly well developed. The unemployment rate is low at 4.5 percent at the end of 2022.

One of the most serious problems that Iceland has been facing in recent years is the crisis in the real estate sector. Supply is scarce and house prices are skyrocketing, meaning it is impossible for families and young people to get out of the rent trap, exacerbated also by competition from alternatives like Airbnb. New construction is often acquired more as an investment by corporations than by people who intend to live there. The lack of political will to curb these dynamics or disincentivize them is creating an unsustainable situation for many.

Along with this increase in inequality is a rise in crime, but it remains a minor issue compared to other countries. Iceland is one of the safest destinations in the world. While there are shortcomings on the social justice front, Iceland boasts outstanding achievements in civil rights, which are seen as an important accomplishment for society as a whole, not just for minorities. The Pride parade, held annually in August, and a dense network

■ **Icelandic society is very open, creative, and inclusive.**

> **"According to statistics, Iceland has the highest number of writers per capita."**

of inclusion-themed events are not seen as a prerogative solely of the LGBTQ+ world but as a time for families and society as a whole to celebrate tolerance.

Besides Christmas and Easter, the main festivals are: Sumardagurinn fyrsti, the first day of summer, which falls on the first Thursday after April 18; Verkalýðsdagur (Labor Day) on May 1; Uppstigningardagur, the Ascension of Jesus, which falls 40 days after Easter; Thjóðhátíðardagur (National Day), on June 17; and Frídagur verslunarmanna (Merchants' Day), on the first Monday in August.

A Country of Writers & Readers

Living under the sometimes oppressive control of foreign kingdoms for most of their history, Icelanders value political independence and the preservation of their own identity. This explains the pronounced interest in history and culture, which generates an almost feverish production of books and publications. If you were curious about any aspect of Iceland, you are sure to find a book on the subject. Iceland's thriving publishing market is quite miraculous considering the total number of native speakers. According to statistics, Iceland has the highest number of writers per capita and regularly appears at the top of rankings about reading.

Language is another key element of local identity. Although Icelandic has undergone profound changes in sounds and grammar since the medieval period, it is the most conservative Nordic language and has been less subject to the influence of other languages. Where other European languages constantly have exchanged base words or created others from Greek and Latin roots that produce recognizable terms, Icelandic has preferred to coin new terms using its own roots. The result is that many words expressing complex concepts remain impenetrable to foreigners. For example, "satellite," a word that is the same in most European languages, is *gervitungl*, or "artificial moon," in Icelandic, whereas "psychology" and "diabetes" are *sálfræði* (science of the soul) and *sykursýki* (sugar disease) respectively. Many Icelanders identify the language as the most genuine expression of their national spirit.

A Fragile Identity

Although proud of their history and culture, Icelanders sometimes seem to suffer from a sense of fragility and insecurity. For this reason, they often twist representations of their past and identity, turning them into caricatures modeled on the stereotypes and prejudices of foreigners since they tend to be seen as more attractive to visitors. The most glaring examples involve Vikings, puffins, and elves. The image of the Viking, a noble and savage warrior, is an invention that emerged in the context of English and German Romanticism: the term *víkingr* in Old Icelandic simply referred to a "pirate" or "thug" and did not apply to entire Nordic populations. The settlers of Iceland were mainly Norwegians and Gaels, who were more dedicated to agriculture. The piracy that defined the Viking was practiced by a small percentage of the population, and only for short periods. However, since the romantic image of the savage warrior has become extremely attractive, Icelanders sometimes impersonate it, creating an aesthetic of their people and their history that has more in common with the imagination of TV directors than with their own culture. Even Icelanders themselves find the appearance of horns, furs, and amulets packed with anachronistic symbols excessive, finding it an oversimplification and distortion of their identity. These are, however, elements that are far too appealing to a large portion of visitors, and so the tourism and business sectors cannot resist them and continue to use them.

Puffins have always held a marginal role in Icelandic culture. At most, they were a source of food for communities located near nesting grounds. But tourist interest in these funny and colorful birds has unleashed a proliferation of themed merchandise mass-produced abroad, which has stifled local handicrafts. The souvenir stores are referred to in derogatory terms as *lundabúðir*, "puffin stores," and their commercial success has created unsustainable competition for small businesses in downtown Reykjavík, many of which have been forced to close or relocate.

The replica of an Iron Age village at Stokksnes is a famous tourist attraction.

Elves have also been to blame for the distortion of local culture. For centuries, Icelanders believed in their coexistence with elves, a people who had descended from Adam and Eve and who were made invisible by God, meaning they couldn't interact with humans. Their existence thus served as comfort for certain otherwise incurable sufferings. For example, the fate of a child with some disease could be explained by the elves exchanging the child in the cradle. It was easier to believe that a young man who had disappeared in the mountains had been kidnapped by a beautiful elf who would take him to her world to marry him than to accept the more realistic and terrible idea that he had died falling into a crevasse. Most of the population has legitimate suspicions about their existence, but there is a small minority who claim to communicate with these creatures, mostly individuals who identify as mediums or who are part of cultural and religious movements that have arisen with the New Age movement.

In the culinary sphere as well, persistence in sharing food as it was consumed in the past for survival, such as sheep head and entrails, is believed to be very attractive to tourists in search of the curious and the strange, meaning that today Iceland struggles to achieve the recognition as a top gastronomic destination that it deserves. Boiled sheep's head or fermented shark tend to monopolize people's ideas of Icelandic cuisine, sometimes even fostering a distrust and reluctance to experience the local dishes made of first-rate ingredients. However, the excessive proliferation of these false rep-

The puffin has sparked the interest of tourists and has become the subject of many low-quality souvenirs.

resentations has stimulated a desire to rediscover the authentic past, through a whole series of cultural initiatives and the emergence of museums and exhibitions devoted to aspects of local history and culture that had been cast off because they were mistakenly considered not attractive enough to tourists.

Katrín Jakobsdóttir was elected Iceland's prime minister in 2017.

People & Politics

Iceland's population is growing rapidly. While the birthrate stands at around 1.7 children per woman, the steady influx of foreigners, needed to meet the ever-increasing demand for labor, has contributed significantly to the increase. The population stands at about 376,000 people, two-thirds of whom are concentrated in the capital region. The largest demographic group after Icelandic is Polish, with around 8,000.

Iceland is a unicameral parliamentary republic. The political party with historically the most votes is the Independence Party (Sjálfstæðisflokkur), which is conservative, laissez-faire, and Eurosceptic; followed by the Progressive Party (Framsóknarflokkurin), which is ruralist, populist, and Eurosceptic; the Social Democratic Alliance (Samfylkingin); and the People's Party (Flokkur fólksins). Legislative power rests with Parliament, while executive power is vested in the various ministerial cabinets that make up the government, headed by the prime minister, which has been Katrín Jakobsdóttir since 2017. Iceland's president, since 2016 Guðni Thorlacius Jóhannesson, plays a largely symbolic role, although he has the right to appoint ministers, dissolve the House, and refuse to sign laws passed by Parliament, subjecting their approval to a popular referendum. In contrast, judicial power is exercised by an independent judiciary.

The official religion is Lutheranism, professed according to the rite of the National (or State) Church. The Constitution guarantees religious freedom. Although steadily declining in recent years, membership in the National Church remains quite high. More than two-thirds of Icelanders allocate part of their taxes to it, as stipulated by law. Of note is the presence of a sizeable group of neopagans who are followers of Ásatrúarfélagið, a religious movement born in the last decades of the 2th century and based on the recovery of Norse cults predating Christianity. It is primarily organized as a cultural association in which enthusiasts of ancient literature meet to read and discuss texts. It should not, however, be understood, as some sensationalist press has framed it, as a revival of ancient traditions.

Cutting-edge Energy

Iceland produces more energy per capita than any country in the world, almost exclusively from renewable sources, particularly geothermal power plants that harness the energy of steam generated by drilling pressurized aquifers at very high temperatures near magma pockets, and hydroelectric power plants. About 80 percent of this energy is used for industrial production, particularly that of aluminum and steel, which are processed here, where the cost of energy is very cheap, but with raw materials from abroad. No gas is used, not even for domestic ovens, which are also electric powered. In areas where there is geothermal activity, hot water from the ground is distributed to homes via a separate aqueduct from that of cold water. That hot water is then fed into radiators for heating. No need for boilers. In some parts of the East and Southeast, electric boilers are used instead. Energy costs for households are generally very low.

Svartsengi power plant was built on a geothermal field.

Bláa Lónið, known as the Blue Lagoon, is both a spa and a geothermal energy facility.

Tourism

Icelandic tourism has long been focused on the enjoyment of the natural landscape. Even today, cultural heritage is still often ignored by many visitors who, in the absence of ancient architectural wonders, believe that the country has nothing to offer from a cultural and historical point of view.

The widespread circulation of iconic photos on social media has also had a deleterious effect, leading to high concentrations of visitors in only a few places, resulting in a strain on local flora and the need to create parking lots, install security ropes, and provide services. This is the case at Gullfoss, Seljalandsfoss and Skógafoss waterfalls, on the beach at Reynisfjara, in the geothermal zone of Námafjall, and at various points around famous Lake Mývatn.

In reality, Iceland lends itself very well to different kinds of tourism experiences, tailored to each person's preferences. In addition to natural beauty, there is a dense network of interesting museums and exhibitions, small establishments where local crafts can be discovered, excellent restaurants, and much more. The capital city's museum network includes the Civic Museum of History (Borgarsögusafn) and the Colonization Exhibition (Landnámssýningin), the Reykjavík Art Museum (Listasafn Reykjavíkur, spread over several locations), the Árbær Anthropological Museum (Árbæjarsafn), and the Maritime Culture Museum (Sjóminjasafn), among others. In Húsavík, one can visit a museum about whales (Hvalasafnið), in Hvolsvöllur, one on volcanoes (LAVA), and in Hólmavík, one on local magic (Galdrasýning).

The fact that this is an island with a small population and one main road running around its perimeter often means visitors underestimate its size. Countless tours invite people to drive around the entire perimeter of the island in a week or less. This results in long drives, stops at busy spots, and little time to discover the authentic character of the island, when it should be sought in the less-visited corners, where one can enjoy the silence and solitude of immense spaces, and in the villages, which are too often seen exclusively as stopping points for supplies or overnight stays. They are precious little treasure chests of authentic reality.

The tourism explosion of recent years has led Icelanders to question the future of their country, particularly after destinations that became famous for their wild beauty have been profoundly altered by the need to be protected due to access by an increasing number of people. A mixture of economic interests and lack of foresight, however, has made the response to increased tourism extremely slow. This translates to difficulty managing flows and ensuring that they do not have a negative impact on the natural environment. Iceland's nature in fact is extremely fragile, and the tramping of millions of people is enough to turn vegetated areas into deserts.

The population, however, lacks the numbers and resources to be able to oversee the entire area and prevent irresponsible behavior. Therefore, when visiting Iceland, it is crucial to invoke individual responsibility. In addition to

Harpa auditorum looks out over Reykjavík Harbor.

The sculpture garden at the Einar Jónsson Museum in Reykjavík is open year-round.

the difficulty presented by the unpredictable climate and often inaccessible nature, a lack of proper preparation by visitors attracted to pretty postcard images can often lead to problems for them as well as for the natural environment. Respecting signs, closures, and restrictions is important for safety reasons, as well as for the integrity of the delicate local wildlife. ■

EXPERIENCE: Visit a Museum

A common misconception is that Iceland, famous for its unique nature, does not have as much to offer in terms of culture. This couldn't be further from the truth. Iceland's museum network, which consists of some 80 sites including accredited museums and historic buildings, chronicles the charm and richness of a history that is thousands of years old, focusing on countless aspects of local culture that add great value to one's experience in terms of personal enrichment.

Icelandic museums and exhibits are usually extremely well-maintained and state-of-the-art and, through technological tools and immersive methods, encourage learning about aspects of local history and nature that are entirely missed if focused solely on the visual enjoyment of the landscape.

HISTORY OF ICELAND

Little known abroad, Icelandic history is extremely rich and inextricably intertwined with European history. It has left less visible traces on the land: impressive buildings, witnesses to the splendors of the past, are missing, but knowing about the history makes the experience of a trip to Iceland more complete and profound and adds layers of significance to the natural landscapes.

Colonization

Archaeological finds have revealed that Scandinavian peoples were coming to Iceland in the summer to hunt seals, walruses and arctic foxes as early as the eighth century AD. True colonization began when these casual visitors found the island welcoming enough to settle there permanently. Icelanders,

In this 1850 painting, artist Johan Peter Raadsig imagines Ingólfur Arnarson's landing in Reykjavík.

however, have passed down a different version of their origin story: following a fortuitous discovery, the island was reportedly explored and renamed three times before the Norwegian Ingólfur Arnarson decided to colonize it, landing in 870 on the southeastern shores. Ingólfur threw his high seat pillars overboard, vowing to settle where they would land. They hit shore in the area of present-day Reykjavík, and here Ingólfur decided to stay.

Over a period of 60 years, numerous Norwegian and Gaelic men and women, mostly pagan but also Christian, occupied all the habitable land around the perimeter of the island. According to some scholars, this colonization can be traced to the centralization of power in Norway by King Haraldur Fairhair, which would lead to the unification of the country. However, there are no reliable sources that endorse this historical reconstruction. Today one is inclined to believe that the figure of this ruler was invented to create a founding myth that would justify Iceland's opposition to increasingly insistent Norwegian interference.

The Free State

In 930, according to ancient accounts, Icelanders decided to give themselves a legal system and founded a general assembly in Thingvellir, now a UNESCO-protected area. The assembly would meet every year for two weeks in July. However, we should not think of it as a parliamentary meeting in the modern sense, but rather as a sort of large festival in which people from all over the country would gather, pitch their tents, and collectively participate in a pivotal event in Iceland's political life. Marriages were arranged and honor duels fought, alliances were formed, lawsuits discussed, and amendments to laws proposed.

The body charged with the latter function was a small circle of influential local lords called Lögrétta, at the head of which was an elective office called lögsögumaður, a kind of jurisconsult whose job was to recite the entire body of law by heart and to act as an adviser or arbiter in the trickiest cases. The participants in the assembly

Eyrarland figurine (1000 AD) depicting Thór or Christ.

Reconstruction of a church from the medieval period.

were called *goðar*, notable men who held political and religious authority and were above the landowners. They could freely decide which lord they would submit and swear allegiance to. This system was crucial because the enforcement of legal rulings (and often even victory in disputes) depended largely on the size of one's following and allies.

Christianization

In the year 1000, an event completely reshaped the fortunes of the country: following discord due to the coexistence of two legal systems, one based on pagan morality and the other on Christian morality, the task of finding a solution was delegated to the lögsögumaður of that time, Thorgeir, a priest who was lord of a northern district. He recommended that the entire country adopt the Christian religion, as the presence of a single god would prevent religious conflicts from arising.

With the conversion to Christianity, the Icelandic Church became organized, and in 1056 the first diocese was founded in Skálholt, in the south, which served as the de facto capital of Iceland for centuries. Soon monasteries and convents sprang up. In these places a remarkable literary boom took place.

The Discovery of New Lands

It was during this period that Icelanders colonized Greenland, establishing several agricultural settlements along the mild and habitable west coast. There are two legends–albeit with some differing details–that tell the story of Erik the Red. Banished for killing a neighbor, he spent his exile exploring the coast of a land that had been spotted by accident and where he decided to settle. He named it Grænland (Green Land) because he believed that people would move there more willingly if its name sounded good.

A few years later, an Icelandic ship bound for Greenland was blown off course by a storm, sighting unknown lands to the west, which were partially explored, centuries before Christopher Columbus. It was the North American continent.

The Age of the Sturlungs

Beginning in the 12th century, power began to concentrate in the hands of a few powerful families, leading to an intensification of conflict. Each of the families had large followings, allowing them to launch decisive attacks against their enemies. This period of civil war was named the Age of the Sturlungs, after one of the most powerful clans of the time. Snorri Sturluson, a lord, lögsögumaður (the highest legal authority of the period), and writer, was one of the most prominent members of this clan. He had the idea to exploit the growing Norwegian authority to establish his own supremacy in Iceland.

He promised to submit to the authority of King Haakon IV in exchange for helping him subjugate all of Iceland. The plan failed because Snorri then took part in a plot against the king, who had him killed. Sturla Sighvatsson, a grandson of Snorri, later attempted to complete his plan but was defeated in a field battle in the north.

(continued on p. 32)

Statue of Leif Erikson, son of Erik the Red and first European explorer of North America.

MEDIEVAL ICELAND

The medieval period is often identified as Iceland's golden age, thanks largely to the flourishing cultural and literary movements of the time.

The Icelandic Middle Ages only partly overlap with the rest of Europe chronologically. Like all historical periodizations, this is only a convention. The Icelandic Middle Ages refers to the period between Christianization (1000 AD) and the execution of the last Catholic leader, Bishop Jón Arason (November 7, 1550).

The earlier period (793– 1000) was traditionally referred to as the Viking Age, but this designation is uncommon today because it reflects an outdated view of those centuries. Pirate raids from Scandinavia had begun in earlier centuries, but they mainly occurred along the Baltic coasts and continued sporadically well beyond the 11th century. Moreover, for Scandinavian society, it was a marginal occurrence. Those who engaged in pirate raids were a small minority of the general population, and even for them it was a seasonal activity. Despite the romantic idea of

"Sólfar," an elegant steel sculpture reminiscent of a Viking ship by Jón Gunnar Árnason, was unveiled north of Reykjavík in 1990.

the Viking as an indomitable warrior, these raids were frequently unsuccessful. They usually involved young upstarts, and a ship for this kind of activity was as valuable as an agricultural estate, therefore, certainly not very affordable.

With this in mind, to consider those centuries of Scandinavian history a period of piracy is reductive. Some archaeologists also point out that, from the point of view of the development of material culture, we cannot clearly separate the centuries of the supposed Viking Age from their predecessors and prefer to use the term Scandinavian Late Iron Age.

In the medieval period, Icelandic elites were part of the international cultural landscape of Europe. Studying abroad in countries such as England, Germany, France, and Italy was common. Shared religion bonded Europeans, as did widespread use of Latin and a cultural background rooted in the classical world.

Icelanders of the medieval period received an education similar to that of their counterparts in other areas of Europe, and cultural exchanges and relations were vibrant. Being Catholics at the time, they frequently made pilgrimages to holy places, such as Rome or Jerusalem, but they seem to have had a particular fondness for Bari, in southern Italy, as they were particularly devoted to St. Nicholas, the patron saint of sailors, to whom more churches were dedicated than to any other saint in the period before the Reformation.

Detail from the *Flateyjarbók*, a 14th-century illuminated manuscript.

> *Víkingur*, **in Old Icelandic, simply meant "pirate."**

It was one of the victors in this battle, Gissur Thorvaldsson, who was appointed *jarl* (high-ranking title of nobility) by the ruler of Norway and then succeeded in persuading the other lords to accept Norwegian authority, enshrined in an agreement signed in 1262 and called *Gamli Sáttmáli* (Old Covenant). From then on and until its independence, in 1944, Iceland would remain a dependent territory of other Scandinavian kingdoms.

The Norwegian & Danish Monarchies

One of the first acts of Iceland's annexation to Norway was the attempt to impose a new legal code, replacing the older Grágás (Grey Goose). The new code, which came into force in 1271 and was called Járnsíða (Ironside), did not find favor with Icelanders, and in 1281 it was replaced by another system, called Jónsbók after the name of its main author, Jón Einarsson, lögsögumaður at the time. The impact on Icelandic society was enormous. The Althingi, supreme national parliament established in 930, ceased to be a legislative assembly and assumed the role of supreme court; new official positions were established for administration and for the exercise and representation of Norwegian authority in Iceland.

In 1376, Ólafur Hákonarson, at just six years of age, ascended the throne of Denmark. His father was Hákon VI of Norway, who died in 1380, leaving him the Kingdom of Norway and the overseas territories of Føroyar (Faroe Islands), Iceland, and Greenland. Ólafur, however, died

The Term "Viking"

Víkingur, in Old Icelandic, simply meant "pirate." Sometimes, by extension, it was also used to mean "scoundrel" or "thug." Throughout Icelandic history, therefore, the name had a derogatory connotation. In the 19th century, however, it came into use in English-speaking countries, becoming inextricably associated with a romantic idealization that identified the "Viking" as a handsome, fearless and wild noble who was superior to other ethnic groups. "Viking" thus became tied to an ideal of racial hierarchy, rendering the term not only historically inaccurate but also highly problematic.

It is not the only misnomer used for convenience to define a historical population, but more than others, "Viking" is a term that elicits a number of erroneous associations in the public imagination, often generated by TV. Therefore, it's often better to use more neutral definitions such as "(ancient) Scandinavian," and "(ancient) Norwegian."

when he was only 17 years old, and his mother Margrete took the throne. In 1397, she managed to get herself elected queen even by Swedish nobles, creating a union of the Scandinavian world that would last until 1523. Norway would then remain part of the Danish Kingdom until 1814, when it was ceded to Sweden during the Napoleonic Wars. The overseas territories that had belonged to Norway in the medieval period, however, remained with Denmark, whose kingdom still includes the autonomous regions of Føroyar (Faroe Islands) and Greenland.

At the end of the 14th century, the plague, which had raged across Europe in previous decades, finally reached Iceland. Adding to the consequences of the Little Ice Age (the period in Earth's climatic history when there was a significant drop in temperatures), the plague made living conditions for the population extremely difficult. The cultivation of some grains, which had been practiced up until then, was no longer possible.

During the 15th and 16th centuries, trade relations with England and Germany were strengthened. At that time, Iceland was still a rural society, devoted mainly to animal husbandry, and lacked vessels suitable for intensive fishing. For this reason, its waters were frequently visited by foreigners who exploited its abundant fish resources undisturbed and indulged in acts of piracy, which Icelanders were not capable of fending off.

Reform

By the 16th century, the Roman Catholic Church had become the most powerful institution not only in Iceland but across northern Europe. Unlike in the southern part of the continent, the rulers were struggling to carve out some freedom of action. It was largely the excessive power and heavy influence of the Catholic Church that motivated support for the Reformation. In 1536, the Danish King Christian III decided to take direct control of the local church. Despite a small group of converts in the little port of Hafnarfjörður, due to German influence, and

Portrait of Christian III of Denmark by Jacob Binck.

The first Icelandic edition of the Bible was printed in 1584.

a handful of rebellious young students, almost the entire population of Iceland remained firmly anchored in Catholicism, and the two local bishops were still some of the most powerful authorities, even in the secular sphere.

The situation changed when a German representative of the Danish crown in Iceland decided, on his own initiative, to raid the monastery on the Island of Viðey, near Reykjavík, emboldened by the fact that the Danish king had begun to dissolve monasteries in Denmark. He then moved eastward, with the intention of attacking other monasteries, and went to Ögmundur Pálsson, an elderly and blind Catholic bishop, to assassinate him. He was however captured by a group of peasants and slaughtered.

Ögmundur's successor, Gissur Einarsson, pretended to be a fervent Catholic, but once in power he attempted to introduce Lutheranism to his diocese. The Catholic bishop of the north, Jón Arason, decided to take action. He succeeded in taking possession of the southern diocese, purging it of Lutheran reform efforts. He then wrote to the Pope and to the Danish king, asking to leave Iceland with its freedom to keep the Catholic faith. The king, in response, sent his own ships to Iceland. Even before the fleet arrived, Jón was ambushed by his enemies. He was beheaded along with two of his sons on November 7, 1550. The Icelandic Catholics thus found themselves without a leader. The following year, Denmark regained its control over the country and began the slow process of erasing Catholic customs, although its efforts were not complete and the Icelandic Lutheran tradition has retained several elements of its Catholic past.

The Commercial Monopoly

In 1602, King Christian IV established an exclusive monopoly over the Icelandic market. Each member of a small group of Danish merchants was assigned a trading post over which he held the exclusive right, and the inhabitants of the corresponding district were not allowed to do business in the other districts. This measure had the obvious effect of hindering the economic and social development of the country, keeping the population heavily subjugated to the wealthy landowners who managed trade with Danish merchants.

In 1627, Iceland was shaken by an event whose echoes are still felt today: the so-called *Tyrkjaránið* (Plunder of the Turks). The term "Turks" during this period referred to Muslims in general because of the Ottoman Empire's extensive control over the Muslim world. In reality, the pirates were of different nationalities, including Europeans who had converted to Islam. The raid was carried out by two fleets, one from the Moroccan city of Salé, the other from Algiers. The first struck the settlement of Grindavík and then attempted to attack the Danish government headquarters in Bessastaðir but was pushed back. The second one reached the eastern fjords first, and then pushed on to the Vestmannaeyjar. Several hundred women were kidnapped and then sold in slave markets in North Africa. A handful of these were bought back thanks to funds from the Danish government. Among them was Guðríður Símonardóttir, who would become the wife of Reverend Hallgrímur Pétursson, Iceland's leading poet during the Baroque period.

In the 17th century, witch hunts took hold. In various regions, and especially in the Westfjords, numerous individuals were accused by secular authorities of having committed some crime in service of evil and were burned at the stake. These were mostly men, probably because Icelandic magic was based heavily on written texts, since it made extensive use of

Iceland as depicted in a 1590 map by Ortelius.

seals derived from the Renaissance demonological tradition, and at that time largely only males were literate.

In 1661 absolutism was established in the Kingdom of Denmark, and the organizational structure of local government was also overhauled: a governor-general was joined by two or sometimes three regional governors. The office of *fógeti*, a kind of minister for finance and economic development, was established.

The Odyssey of Manuscripts

The precious manuscripts with which Iceland's abundant medieval literature was handed down were largely lost, destroyed to recycle the parchment for other uses or simply thrown away because they were too damaged. Since all Icelanders, regardless of class, lived in damp peat houses, the conditions for preserving these artifacts were not ideal. Nevertheless, there are around a thousand preserved manuscripts and fragments from the medieval period, many more than the medieval codices preserved from the entirety of mainland Scandinavia. This is due to the work of Árni Magnússon between the 17th and 18th centuries.

Magnússon was an Icelandic professor of philology at the University of Copenhagen and an antiquarian for the king. While conducting a census of his native country, he took to collecting and collating all the ancient texts he could get his hands on, even having some of them copied. His impressive collection was then transported to the Danish capital, where he lived. Several medieval texts survived exclusively as a single, invaluable manuscript copy.

The Issue of Manuscripts

Icelandic manuscripts are considered the most important national monuments. Embedded with Icelandic pride, they offer testimony of a people who have always found ways to create high cultural expression in spite of difficult external circumstances.

The issue with the manuscripts was particularly thorny from a legal point of view because they had been bequeathed to the University of Copenhagen in 1730 by the Icelandic scholar Árni Magnússon, who could hardly have imagined that the capital of the kingdom of which he was a subject would one day become the capital of a foreign state. The Danish court ruled that the government could not freely surrender the manuscripts because it did not have the power to annul the legally valid will of a private citizen. A solution was found through a semantic loophole: the collection was divided, and one half of it was brought back to Iceland as a "permanent loan" while remaining the property of the Danish university.

The great scholar Árni Magnússon.

In Denmark, the manuscripts had better conditions for preservation, but they were in danger of being obliterated forever by the outbreak of the Great Copenhagen Fire in 1728. Magnússon did not immediately perceive the threat of the fire and only later took action to save the texts with the help of some friends. Although he was extremely thorough in noting the circumstances under which he obtained each text, Árni never created an inventory of his collection. It is believed that most of the manuscripts were saved, and that mostly printed books burned in the flames, but the scholar was convinced that several unique items were lost in the fire. Upon his death, Magnússon bequeathed the collection to the university by establishing a fund for the preservation and study of this heritage.

The Rise of Reykjavík

According to medieval sources, Reykjavík was the country's first settlement, but for a long time it held no particular importance, mainly because the shallow waters of its bay gave it no natural harbor. This forced ships to moor at offshore islets and reach the coast in dinghies. The situation changed in the mid-18th century when the then fógeti Skúli Magnússon came up with the idea of reviving the country's economic and social fortunes in the spirit of the Enlightenment. The initiative, called Innréttingar (Enterprises), included founding a wool-processing industry. Skúli Magnússon had built his residence on the Island of Viðey. When he asked the Danish king for a grant, he was given the land of an estate that was owned by the Crown, located a few minutes by boat on the mainland: Reykjavík.

A row of wooden shacks soon sprang up on either side of an unpaved road, which would be named Aðalstræti (Main Road). The emergence of this economic activity–which would later fail–spurred population growth. A further boost occurred between 1783 and 1784, when a series of earth-

"In 1783, one of the most devastating catastrophes in Icelandic history occurred: an eruption of enormous scale that would alter the climate of the entire Northern Hemisphere."

quakes destroyed the diocese of Skálholt and the Latin school associated with it. These institutions were moved to Reykjavík and were followed in 1806 by the governor's office, leaving its historic residence in Bessastaðir. In 1845, the new parliament was established in Reykjavík, on the site of the Latin school and not in Thingvellir, where the tribal assembly and supreme court had met for centuries.

The Fires of Síða

In 1783, one of the most devastating catastrophes in Icelandic history occurred: an eruption of enormous scale that would alter the climate of the entire Northern Hemisphere. It occurred in the area of the mountain known as Laki, in the highlands region. The flow covered an area of 218 square miles (565 sq km) and spewed toxic substances that poisoned the air, land, and water, causing widespread deaths of animals and livestock and killing thousands of people. The episode is known as *móðuharðindin* (mist hardships). The hardest hit district was the one closest to the eruption, Vestur-Skaftafellssýsla, and in particular the area of Síða, hence the name of the eruption: Síðueldar, "Fires of Síða."

One event became legend: the local parish priest, Jón Steingrímsson, summoned the surviving population for what everyone believed would be the last mass before their demise. With lava advancing and the view obscured by ash, people went to the celebration. When the rite was completed, the Kirkjubæjarklaustur church was still intact and the lava front had stopped, sparing the settlement. The miracle was attributed to the religious ceremony, which took the name *eldmessa*, "fire mass."

The eruption lasted about two years. In 1784, the effects of colossal earthquakes that destroyed hundreds of farms in the south were added to

Depiction of the god Loki from an 18th-century manuscript.

the heavy toll. The situation was so catastrophic that the Danish government considered evacuating the entire population of Iceland to the Jutland Peninsula.

Jón Sigurðsson, a key figure in the awakening of Icelandic national consciousness.

Romanticism & Autonomy

The Romantic ideals that began to seep their way into Europe in the early 19th century contributed to the development and strengthening of an Icelandic national consciousness. Some intellectuals of the time, in the wake of the nationalism that had taken hold across the continent, began to promote a sense of identity that was strongly rooted in medieval culture. In particular, four Icelandic students at the University of Copenhagen founded the journal *Fjölnir*, through which they promoted their ideas, most significantly, a spelling reform that would bring the spelling of the modern Icelandic language closer to that of the 13th century, the golden age of sagas, and the establishment of an Icelandic parliament within the Kingdom of Denmark.

For centuries, although they recognized their own linguistic and cultural tradition, Icelanders did not question Danish authority. During the 19th century, however, political demands for greater autonomy began to arise, which would eventually result in the birth of parliament. At the forefront of these initiatives was the philologist Jón Sigurðsson, who attempted to awaken national pride through the rediscovery and study of medieval literary heritage. When the Danish king abolished absolutism in 1848, Sigurðsson suggested that political authority be returned to the Icelanders since, in his view, the "Old Covenant" of 1262 vested authority over Iceland to the king but not to his successors.

By that time, Thingvellir had become an isolated place, and so the seat of the new parliament was established in Reykjavík. Initially, this assembly had a purely advisory role; only with the issuing of the constitution in 1873 did it assume legislative powers as well. Romantic intellectuals established historical continuity between the medieval institution of the Althingi and the new parliament to give it greater prestige.

The Herring Era

The period between the late 1800s and the late 1900s is known as the "herring years." Iceland had for centuries been a society of peasants at the mercy of landowners, who had done everything they could to prevent their subordinates from achieving any economic freedom, keeping the country severely underdeveloped. Toward the end of the 19th century, however, some reforms enabled many workers to break free from dependence on landowners and seek new opportunities in the emerging fishing industry, or by emigrating to the Americas.

The 19th century also represented the culmination of the Little Ice Age, which had begun in the mid-14th century: Iceland's glaciers reached their peak. This led to a deterioration in the living conditions of the population, about 20 percent of whom emigrated to the United States and especially Canada, where today a thriving community of descendants of Icelandic settlers lives, particularly in the Winnipeg area.

> **"Toward the end of the 19th century ... some reforms enabled many workers to break free from dependence on landowners."**

In Iceland, meanwhile, new boats allowed fishermen to spend long periods on the open sea, maximizing the yield of their labor and helping the fishing industry to flourish. In the early 20th century, the advent of motors and trawlers led to unprecedented economic development. Iceland exported large quantities of fish at competitive prices, even to Catholic Mediterranean countries, such as Spain and Italy, tapping into the demand of the custom of eating fish on Fridays. Fishing thus became the most profitable economic activity, surpassing livestock farming, and created unprecedented wealth in Iceland, subsequently triggering major changes in politics and social reforms, such as the establishment of compulsory schooling and the creation of the first trade unions.

Independence

In 1918, after a difficult, decades-long process, Denmark agreed to grant Iceland autonomy, while keeping it dependent on the Danish crown and considering foreign policy matters still the prerogative of the government in Copenhagen. Thus, the Kingdom of Iceland was born.

At the outbreak of World War II, the country attempted to remain neutral, which proved unrealistic given its important geographic position halfway between Europe and America. In response to Germany's occupation of Denmark, the British invaded Iceland.

The following year, they would be replaced by an American contingent of 60,000. Although the military occupation was not appreciated by many people, who would have liked to have seen their neutrality respected, the foreign presence led to the construction of important infrastructure, such as roads and airports, as well as an enormous influx of money into the Icelandic economy, which expanded as a result and brought unprecedented prosperity to the population. However, there was no shortage of problems. Numerous Icelandic women and the children they had with American soldiers became the subject of scorn and were considered traitors to the homeland.

In 1944, the Icelandic government felt it could permanently sever the island's relationship with Denmark, whose government was in exile due to the German occupation and unable to fulfill its functions. On June 17 of that year, the date of Jón Sigurðsson's birth, huge crowds gathered in Thingvellir, and the republic was proclaimed following a referendum.

As early as the Romantic period, in the early 19th century, Icelanders identi-

The Icelandic Parliament today.

American soldiers in Iceland, 1943.

fied with symbols of their national identity in the literary tradition, and thus in the ancient manuscripts in which it was preserved. Up until then, it had not been a problem that these texts were kept in Copenhagen, but after gaining independence, the so-called manuscript issue, *handritamálið*, exploded (see sidebar p. 36). There was an insistence that these be returned to Iceland. The issue was resolved with a compromise: the collection was divided, and half of it was returned to Iceland. In 1971, a large crowd of Icelanders was present at the handing over of the first two volumes, which belonged to the Danish royal collection, at the port of Reykjavík, where the figures in charge of the task disembarked. It was a truly important moment for Icelandic identity.

The Cold War & Codfish

When the war ended, the United States expressed its intention to maintain a military presence on the island—despite complaints from a large part of the population—guaranteeing the country substantial aid under the Marshall Plan. In 1949, Iceland was among the signatories of the Atlantic Pact, joining NATO. Protests led by the Socialist Party had to be contained by law enforcement. In 1951, Parliament passed a measure authorizing the establishment of a U.S. military contingent at the Keflavík base. However, the soldiers' presence was heavily regulated: interactions with Icelandic women were limited, as was access to premises in the capital, and, until 1960, soldiers of African American descent were prohibited. In 2006, the American military left the island. Protection of Icelandic airspace is still provided by NATO countries to this day.

During the 20th century, with the technological improvement of vessels and the expansion of the fishing fleet, possibilities opened up for the exclusive exploitation of an ever-widening area of ocean around Iceland's coasts, which were particularly rich in cod. In 1952, a decision was made to extend the exclusive economic zone to 4 nautical miles, with no major consequences, despite some British objections. However, in the years to follow, Iceland further extended the zone: first to 12 nautical miles and then to 50 miles in 1972. Clashes between Icelandic and British fishing vessels prompted the U.K. to send military ships to defend its fishermen. The government in London agreed to the new territorial limits, provided it allowed British fishing boats to fish in some agreed-upon areas. In 1974, a further extension of Iceland's exclusive economic zone caused a diplomatic rupture between the two countries that was barely reconciled thanks to NATO intervention.

The year 1975 was a watershed in Icelandic history: the female population went on strike en masse, paralyzing the nation, to demand more rights in both the domestic and labor spheres. A few years later, in 1980, Icelanders would elect their first president and the world's first democratically elected female head of state, Vigdís Finnbogadóttir. It was the beginning of greater female presence in political institutions.

Vigdís Finnbogadóttir, the first democratically elected woman president in the world.

The End of the Cold War: Expansion & Collapse

In 1986, Reykjavík was chosen as the location of a summit between U.S. President Ronald Reagan and General Secretary of the Communist Party of the Soviet Union Mikhail Gorbachev. The meeting, which aimed to strike an agreement on a gradual reduction of nuclear warheads, is usually identified as one of the pivotal moments that led to the end of the Cold War.

Over the next two decades, the Icelandic economy veered decisively toward neoliberal policies. Privatization and other operations ostensibly transformed a small nation into a financial behemoth: investors from all over the world bought Icelandic bank securities, driven by strong demand and their success on the stock markets. It would later emerge that the banks themselves had purchased the debt securities through front companies to artificially inflate their value and entice foreign investors to buy them. Some big players in the financial market discovered the scam and started selling those securities, no longer deeming them profitable and casting doubt on the ability of Icelandic banks to manage the situation. This set off a chain reaction, and in 2008, when creditors demanded to collect their dues, three of Iceland's largest banks were unable to pay and went bankrupt. The total debt amounted to seven times the country's GDP.

Ronald Reagan and Mikhail Gorbachev discuss arms control at the Reykjavík Summit in October 1986.

The eruption of the Eyjafjallajökull volcano in 2010 created serious problems for air traffic throughout Europe.

Encouraged by banks to take out high-risk loans without concern for the resilience of the economy, many Icelanders fell into heavy debt to afford a lifestyle well above their means.This led to drastic social consequences, with a substantial part of the population unable to deal with their debts. Despite the strong reformist demands of the short-lived political administration of the Social Democratic government (between 2009 and 2013), which had to make unpopular decisions to cope with the economic disaster, citizens returned to supporting the same parties that had governed in the years before the crisis.

Recovery & Recent Developments

In 2010, the eruption of the Eyjafjallajökull volcano created major disruptions for European aviation. The event put a spotlight on Iceland, paradoxically contributing to the beginning of a period of huge expansion in the tourism industry. This mitigated the economic downturn to some extent, creating numerous economic and job opportunities, but in the long run it would also lead to serious problems due to the uncontrolled development of the industry.

The Prime Minister's Office in Reykjavik

In 2016, the Icelandic government became embroiled in the Panama Papers scandal, which involved Prime Minister Sigmundur Davið, who during an interview admitted to hiding capital in offshore companies. Although trampled by the allegations, he refused to resign, triggering large protests in Parliament Square. Protestors repeatedly threw food at police officers and the walls of Parliament. Forced to resign, the prime minister was replaced by a coalition government of the Green Party and the center-right Independence Party, which had dominated the Icelandic political scene throughout the 20th century. The coalition marked a gradual shift of the Green Party, led by Prime Minister Katrín Jakobsdóttir, to the right, causing a collapse in support and growing disaffection among the party's electorate.

During the COVID-19 pandemic, Iceland implemented a very strict policy on arrivals from abroad, while maintaining milder domestic measures. This, along with a strict testing campaign and extensive vaccination coverage, made the pandemic otherwise bearable for the population, even with the severe hardships caused by the freeze on tourism.

As the emergency comes to an end, the country is having to cope with significant inflation, as well as a severe crisis in the real estate sector, with the cost of housing and rents increasingly eroding citizens' purchasing power and driving many families below the poverty line. These problems are accompanied, however, by unemployment at historic lows and data indicating a mild economic recovery.

ARTS & CULTURE

Surprisingly, given its small population size and relative geographical isolation, Iceland exhibits an artistic and cultural production on par with far larger and more populous countries. Having internationally renowned writers and musicians is of great pride to the island, and Icelanders place significant value on their nation's cultural and artistic development.

Runes & Magic

A sequence of letters representing the sounds of the language, runes probably derived from Latin alphabet around the third century AD. This alphabet, which has undergone modifications over the centuries, has never been widespread in Iceland, where traces of it can be found mainly on a few objects dating to the earliest centuries, usually to indicate the owner's name, or in cemeteries, where it was sometimes used for inscriptions on tombstones from the Christian period.

Runes are not to be confused with *galdrastafir*, magical symbols that first appeared in manuscripts in the 15th century, likely European in origin, although the two are often confused in tourist merchandise. Magical symbols are often presented as combinations of different runes, but the identification of runes within them is more likely due to the fact that they are often geometric symbols with many intersecting lines. Runes are simple juxtapositions of a few strokes and, therefore, can be easily "extrapolated" from any fairly complex symbol.

The magic documented in Icelandic Renaissance and modern texts should not be taken for an ancient tradition that survived through the centuries because there is no trace of it in the medieval period. It seems to have emerged suddenly in the 16th century

A mysterious staff displayed at the Witchcraft Museum in Hólmavík bears a runic inscription.

and bears very strong similarities to the European esoteric tradition that is traced back to King Solomon. Some scholars speculate that its emergence was due to the suppression by Danish authorities of the rich and flourishing cosmos of Catholic superstitions associated with the cult of saints, which Icelanders turned to with various forms of popular superstition to receive intercessions. No longer able to turn to the saints, they turned to magic, sparking a parallel occult tradition. The magical symbols used are often accompanied by Christian prayers, and the cosmology of these texts is also similar to the Christian one, with an opposition between good and evil, angels and demons, contrasts that did not belong to pagan culture. The rare times that names of pagan deities appear, they are added to lists of demons from the Jewish tradition, with whom they were thus associated.

The Church & the Culture of Books

With the arrival of the Catholic Church in Iceland came the technology for making books along with the Latin alphabet, which was adapted to the Icelandic phonological system with the addition of specific letters for sounds not found in Latin, such as Þ (Th) and ð, or through the modification of already existing letters, as in the case of á or æ. The earliest texts produced in Iceland, around 1100, must have been copies of books on religious subjects necessary for conducting liturgy. In general, Ari Thorgilsson is considered the first to have written in the vernacular. A collection containing a compendium of Icelandic history from colonization is attributed to him. His stories are the inspiration for the creation of the *Íslendingasögur*, "sagas of the Icelanders," prose narratives about the lives of the first generations of Icelanders. These texts, a diverse group of more than 40, began to be written around the 13th century, the century in which many of the most important, and successful, epic narratives of the Icelandic Middle Ages took shape.

Detail from a medieval illuminated manuscript.

It is common to imagine Iceland of centuries past as a remote place largely ignored by the cultural movements of the rest of Europe. The Nazis believed they would find a kind of oasis of perfectly preserved ancient Germanic culture before realizing that this was not the case. With conversion, Iceland effectively

The stone statue of Bárður portrays the troll protagonist of the *Bárðar saga Snæfellsáss.*

became part of the community that constituted medieval Western Christianity. The pagan past was soon abandoned, and whatever remained, such as the Eddic carols or the mythographic work of Snorri Sturluson, was heavily influenced by Christian thought. Far from being an isolated world, as some Romantic propaganda often tried to portray it, Iceland was fully embedded within the cultural and political currents that affected medieval Europe. Not only was it fully integrated into the ecclesiastical apparatus of the Church, with tax collection going all the way to Rome, but many Icelanders often made pilgrimages to Rome, Bari (St. Nicholas was one of the most venerated saints on the island), and even Constantinople and the Holy Land. Icelandic clergy members were trained in important study centers in Italy. And numerous influences from medieval continental literature have been traced by scholars in Icelandic texts of the period.

The Sagas

One of the most popular literary genres in medieval Europe was hagiography, or the didactic and celebratory biography of saints. Soon, the lives of Christian saints were also being composed in Icelandic. These are the so-called *heilagra manna sögur*, "sagas of the saints." According to some scholars, it was hagiographies that inspired Icelanders to compose texts centered on the lives of their ancestors (see above).

In Iceland, the term "saga" has a different meaning than it has in many modern languages. It is not necessarily an articulate and wide-ranging narrative, but a largely prose text written mainly, though not exclusively, in the medieval period. The term "saga" is related to the verb *segja*, which means "to tell or narrate," valid for both a tale and a succession of supposedly real events. In fact, historical reality and fantastic narrative seem inextricably intertwined. For a long time, they had been considered reliable historical sources, whereas today the events narrated in them are considered credible only when they are corroborated in independent sources or by archaeological evidence, otherwise they are treated with skepticism. External literary influences are recognized in the sagas, and political and cultural interests must have had no small influence in their writing, not to mention they recount events that took place at least two centuries earlier.

Another important group of sagas are the *samtíðarsögur*, "contemporary sagas," which include the lives of Icelandic bishops (*biskupa sögur*) as well as sagas and stories about Icelandic history between the 12th and 13th centuries. The *riddarasögur*, "sagas of knights," are a large group that includes texts derived from the European chivalric tradition, particularly the Carolingian cycle, centered on the figure of Charlemagne, and the Breton cycle, centered on King Arthur, but also includes texts about the classical world, particularly Rome, Troy, and the figure of Alexander the Great.

Literature

In the medieval period, considered a golden age due to the flourishing of sagas and skaldic poetry, written histories began to be produced, such as the *Íslendingabók* (*Book of Icelanders*), a compendium of history from colonization to the beginning of the twelfth century, and the *Landnámabók* (*Book of Colonization*), a catalog of the colonizers of Iceland with brief biographical and genealogical notes. There are also numerous religious texts, in prose and poetry, as well as scientific texts, usually (but not exclusively) translated from Latin and containing treatises on mathematics, astronomy, and medicine.

The first printed text in Icelandic was the translation of the New Testament by Oddur Gottskálksson in 1540, followed by the complete Bible in 1584 by the Bishop of Hólar, Guðbrandur Thorláksson. This transla-

The writer Halldór Laxness, Nobel laureate in 1955.

tion provided an authoritative model for the Icelandic language, contributing to its preservation through the centuries.

One 17th-century writer was Hallgrímur Pétursson, the greatest exponent of the Icelandic Baroque period, who was particularly famous for the *Passíusálmar* (*The Passion Hymns*), sacred hymns dedicated to the Passion of Christ, which are still widely recited during Easter season. Another curious work from the same century is the *Travelogue* by Reverend Ólafur Egilsson, which recounts the events he endured following his capture by a crew of Saracen pirates in 1627 and his journey across Europe to implore the Danish king to ransom his enslaved countrymen in the Muslim world.

The 18th century saw the rise of Enlightenment literature, such as the *Report* by Eggert Ólafsson, a treatise written in Danish on behalf of the king in which he listed information about the flora, fauna, geological formation, agricultural production techniques, most prevalent diseases, diet, language, and character of the inhabitants of Iceland.

National consciousness awakened with Romanticism in the 19th century, leading to the rediscovery of medieval literature, as well as a literary boom. Worthy of mention are the poet Jónas Hallgrímsson and the novelist Jón Thoroddsen. It was in the 20th century, however, that Icelandic literature experienced a flourishing moment comparable to medieval times, with internationally known novelists such as Gunnar Gunnarsson, Thórbergur Thórðarson, and Halldór Laxness (Nobel Prize winner in 1955), and, in the second half of the century, Thor Vilhjjálmsson, Hallgrímur Helgason, Jón Kalman Stefánsson, Auður Ava Ólafsdóttir, Bergsveinn Birgisson, and Steinunn Sigurðardóttir, to name a few. One genre that has experienced significant development is crime novels, thanks to Arnaldur Indríðason, Yrsa Sigurðardóttir, and Ragnar Jónsson.

Keldur, which means "bogs" in Icelandic, is the site of the country's oldest peat farm, now under the responsibility of the National Museum of Iceland.

Architecture

For much of its history, Iceland had no real architecture apart from peat houses and churches. The earliest buildings constructed by settlers from the eighth or ninth century onward were the so-called longhouses, typical of the Nordic world of the late Iron Age. They consisted of wooden frames, either imported or made from driftwood originating mainly from Siberia and carried by sea currents to the shores of Iceland. The walls and roof around each longhouse were built with peat bricks. Inside, the walls could be covered with wooden panels, and planks were placed near them as beds. In the center was a hearth with an opening in the ceiling above where the smoke could escape

With the disappearance of birch forests as the Middle Ages progressed came a shortage of wood. Since peat, unlike wood, was not a great heating fuel, as it produces a lot of smoke and little heat, significant changes in the construction of buildings were necessary. Ceilings became lower to better retain heat in more confined spaces. Houses now had a space for livestock on the first floor and rooms for the family on the upper level to take advantage of the heat produced by the animals. Much of domestic life took place in a multipurpose room called the *baðstofa*, "bathing room," which had evolved from the room where the bath was originally located. The space had beds arranged in rows. People could sleep two or four to a bed, head to toe, reaching as many as 30 people in a single room, which helped keep the temperature more comfortable. During the day, people

The major works of Icelandic architect Guðjón Samúelsson include the University of Iceland building and the National Theater (above).

Hallgrímskirkja Cathedral, in Reykjavík, is the last and best-known work of architect Guðjón Samúelsson.

worked and ate while sitting on the edge of the beds after removing the carved rails that were placed during the night to prevent falls. These boards were called *rúmfjalir* and were often finely carved with geometric patterns or writing. When placed on the lap, they served as a work surface.

Food was eaten out of a sort of pot-bellied, wooden keg with a lid, like a wide, squat beer mug: the *askur*. The most common dishes were soups, rather valuable cuts of meat, and dried fish with butter and *skyr* cheese. Kitchens were located in a separate space because cooking with peat produced a lot of smoke. There were other rooms, sometimes side by side and sometimes with a separate entrance, which served as workshops, stables, or storerooms.

People from all walks of life lived in these types of houses. The difference was usually in the quality of the furnishings. These buildings were usually damp and often infested with fleas. They were also very costly to maintain because the peat would crumble and collapse over time, meaning it had to be completely replaced after a few years. Nowadays, very few peat buildings remain, partly because of the high cost of maintenance.

It was not until the 18th century that the first brick-and-mortar buildings were constructed, such as Viðeyjarstofa, Bessastaðir (the present presidential

The farmhouse in Glaumbær, northern Iceland, dates back to the 1800s.

residence), and Hólar Cathedral, while prefabricated wooden houses, usually painted with pitch, became more popular. Throughout the 19th century and into the early 20th century, these prefabricated wooden houses, clad in corrugated sheet metal dipped in a special rustproof zinc paint applied vertically, were imported from abroad. This is the type of building most commonly associated with Iceland. In the early twentieth century, however, concrete became widespread, and it is still the preferred building material today, in part for earthquakeresistance.

The rise of concrete paved the way for local architecture, its earliest exponent being Rögnvaldur Ólafsson, who designed the old post office building in Reykjavík and the agricultural colleges in Hvanneyri and Hólar. However, Guðjón Samúelsson was the first great Icelandic architect, destined to leave his mark almost everywhere: the main building of the National Hospital, the Catholic Cathedral in Reykjavík, the Sundhöllin public swimming pool, the prestigious Hótel Borg, the main building of the University of Iceland, the National Theater, and the Church of Akureyri, among others. In his early period Samúelsson tried to follow the example of the traditional architecture of peat houses, producing buildings whose facades echoed its modular layout. They look like multiple constructions in rows. Examples are the District School, Héraðsskóli, in Laugarvatn; the building next to the church in Thingvellir, Thingvallabær; or the house in Straumur, on the northern side of the road from the capital to the airport, past the steel mill industrial complex. Later, the currents of functionalism and modernism arrived in Iceland, and these perhaps have had the most visible and aesthetic impact on the urban layout of Icelandic cities.

Art

Iceland did not experience a significant artistic movement until the 19th century. It was then that two prominent artists arrived on the scene: Thórarinn Thorláksson, famous for Icelandic landscapes in the naturalist and Romantic style, and Jóhannes Kjarval, who was also particularly esteemed for his landscape depictions and his studies on the application of paint to render the shapes and colors of lava soils. The latter was perhaps the most beloved Icelandic painter. One of the buildings of the Reykjavík Museum of Art is dedicated to him.

The greatest Icelandic exponent of pop art is undoubtedly Guðmundur Guðmundsson, known as Erró, a pseudonym acquired during a period of study in Italy. There are numerous contemporary artists as well as art events, museums, and art galleries, such as the national one, Listasafn Íslands, and the civic one in the capital, Listasafn Reykjavíkur. Worthy of mention is the

A mural created by Erró decorates the Lisbon subway.

Björk Guðmundsdóttir, aka Björk, is an international icon of alternative music.

Korpúlfsstaðir venue in eastern Reykjavík, where exhibitions are held and where the Association of Icelandic Figurative Artists organizes workshops for artists.

Music

Despite some attempts at reconstruction, we do not have a clear idea of what Icelandic music was like in the pre-Christian period because there were no forms of musical notation that would allow melodies to be recorded graphically. The oldest known music in Iceland is medieval sacred music, initially monodic and then polyphonic. With the Reformation, religious hymns in Icelandic gained prominence.

As for instruments, the *fiðla*, a name referring to the English fiddle, is mentioned in ancient sources. In Icelandic, this is the term for the modern fiddle, whereas the native *fiðla* is today called *íslensk fiðla*; it consists of a sound box across which strings are stretched and is played with a bow. Notes are produced by picking the strings from below with the fingernails, the wrist facing upward. From the 18th century on, there are definite records of the *langspil*, an instrument in the family of the board zithers that is very important in Icelandic folk music. It has a melodic string and several drone strings, similar to many other instruments in the European tradition, but different because it is also played with a bow. The publication of a small volume on the basics of music theory and performing religious hymns from the mid-19th century refers to the *langspil* for practical study. This volume criticizes the state of Icelandic music, saying that people learn by ear and distort melodies in oral transmission (like a wireless telephone), that instruments are badly tuned, and there is a generalized ignorance of notation and music theory.

This situation changed dramatically during the 20th century. At the beginning of the century, Bjarni Thorsteinsson published a monumental collection of Icelandic folk songs, *Íslensk Thjóðlög*, and in the following decades the importance of music in Icelandic society continued to grow. The Symphony Orchestra of Iceland was founded in 1950. Five years later, Italian singer Vinzenz Maria Demetz, later renamed Sigurður, came to the country and was a major figure to advance the teaching and promotion of opera singing. In 1995, he helped found a music school in the capital, which was later named after him. In general, at least one opera a year is performed at Harpa auditorium, as well as numerous classical concerts. There are many chamber or baroque choirs and orchestras in the area, and the calendar of events is quite full.

In the realm of pop music, there is a wide variety of genres; from the alternative rock of Björk, Sigur Rós, and Emilíana Torrini to the pop-folk of Of Monsters and Men. On the current scene, Hildur Guðnadóttir is making waves, the winner of numerous prestigious international awards, including two Grammy Awards, a Golden Globe, and an Academy Award. Other notable musicians are Páll Óskar, perhaps Icelands' most beloved singer; Daði Freyr, who rose to international prominence at the 2021 Eurovision Song Contest; and Bríet, a new rising star on the local scene, whose debut album *Kveðja* in 2021 won the *Íslensku tónlistarverðlaun*, which is the most important music award in the country.

Nanna Bryndís Hilmarsdóttir during a concert of her folk band Of Monsters and Men.

Film

The long Arctic nights lend themselves to putting sagas and novels on the page or composing dreamy post-rock tunes, somewhat less so to filming a movie complete with crew and actors. Perhaps this is also why film has historically been the least practiced of the seven arts in Iceland. That was until 1979, when the state established the Icelandic Film Fund. It paid off just a dozen years later with *Children of Nature* (*Börn náttúrunnar*, 1991), which was nominated for an Oscar for best foreign film. The movie was directed by Friðrik Thór Friðriksson, the the founder of Iceland's first film criticism magazine, the country's first film festival, and a major production company. He made many other films, like *Angels of the Universe* (*Englar alheimsins*), that laid the foundations of Icelandic film poetics, characterized by a frustrated longing to escape and light-hearted, bitter humor that mellows out the tone of dramas, turning them into comedies.

Another director, Baltasar Kormákur, made his debut in 2000 with *101 Reykjavík*, a portrait of a somewhat lost and indolent generation inspired by Hallgrímur Helgason's 1996 book of the same name. Soon after *101 Reykjavík*, Kormákur was called up to Hollywood. Since then he has alternated between films with international appeal and small Icelandic productions, often hinging them on a struggle against the forces of nature, another common theme in Icelandic culture. In *The Deep* (2012), Kormákur reconstructed a 1984 news story in which a fisherman survived a shipwreck off Vestmannaeyjar, enduring the icy ocean waters against all odds.

A contemporary of Kormákur, Dagur Kári made his debut with the unsettling *Nói albínói* (2002), which recounts the events set in motion by young Nói as he attempts to escape once and for all from the icy Westfjords. More recently, Kári brought another quirky character to life in *Virgin Mountain* (*Fúsi*, 2015), the story of a man employed at the Icelandic airport who is bullied by his colleagues for being naïve.

Quirky characters are a leitmotif of Icelandic cinema. Halla,

the protagonist of *The Electric Woman* (*Kona fer í stríð*, 2018) directed by Benedikt Erlingsson, is a music teacher who wages a lonely war against the steel industry as it claims land on the island, defacing its landscape. *Stories of Horses and Men* (*Hross í oss*, 2013), by the same director, is set in a remote Icelandic province and depicts a surreal microcosm of spiritual symbiosis between men and horses. Grímur Hákonarson's *Rams - A Story of Two Brothers and Eight Sheep* (*Hrútar*, 2015) is also about humans and animals. The protagonists are Gummi and Kiddi, two shepherd brothers who live in the middle of nowhere and have not spoken to each other for 40 years. It won the Un Certain Regard prize at Cannes. The film mentions every sheep in the film one by one in the credits. Continuing with the "humans and animals" theme is Valdimar Jóhannsson's *Lamb* (*Dýrið*, 2021), a kind of fantasy horror in which a farming couple adopts a hybrid being, half child, half lamb, taking it away from the sheep that gave birth to it.

It's as if the extreme latitude and distance from everything adds an eccentric flair to human stories. Icelandic cinema is captivating because of its ability to come up with such original stories. One example is *The Neighbor's Tree* (*Undir trénu*, 2017), a dark comedy by Hafsteinn Gunnar Sigurðsson about a feud between neighbors over a tree whose foliage reaches over the fence. Also by Sigurðsson, *Either Way* (*Á Annan Veg*, 2011) tells the story of a long summer for two road maintenance workers with silences rather than words. Or there's *Echo* (*Bergmál*, 2019) by Rúnar Rúnarsson, which depicts Christmas on the island in 56 episodes that are like minimal *tableaux vivants*.

But in Iceland, strange stories happen off the set as well. The latest cinematic discovery is Hannes Thór Halldórsson, a former national soccer team goalkeeper who managed to block a penalty shot by Messi in the 2018 World Cup. Before being recruited to play soccer, Halldórsson was involved in music videos, so when he hung up his cleats, he returned to his old love and filmed *Cop Secret*, which was presented in competition at the 2022

Locarno Film Festival. A sort of parody of star-studded action movies, the film feeds on the irreverent Nordic humor that pervades much of Icelandic cinematography. Also from 2022 is the historical film *Godland* (*Volaða land*), a sort of Western among the glaciers by the award-winning director Hlynur Pálmason. It is captivating first and foremost for the beauty of the landscapes it depicts.

Religion

According to the belief that Irish hermits were present in Iceland before the arrival of the Norsemen, Christianity has been rooted in Iceland for many centuries. The Norse population, however, was majority pagan, and for 70 years, from the end of colonization in 930 AD, the society had mixed religions. No reliable and accurate accounts on aspects of Norse pagan religion have survived, but recently some neopagan groups have developed new religious forms inspired by literary suggestions contained in medieval texts written by Christian authors. In the year 1000, Christianity became the official religion, and from the mid-16th century Iceland adhered to the Lutheran denomination.

Today the prevailing religious denomination, albeit in sharp decline, according to official data from 2022, is the Protestant National Church, followed by the Catholic Church and the Free Church of Reykjavík.

Dómkirkjan Cathedral in Reykjavík is the main house of worship for the National Church of Iceland.

Although Mass attendance is low, for many Icelanders the National Church still plays a crucial role in some important life moments like baptisms, confirmations, weddings, and funerals.

Language

The official language is Icelandic, *íslenska*. It is a Germanic language of the northern group, most closely related to the mainland Scandinavian languages, namely Danish, Norwegian, and Swedish, and more distantly to English and German, as well as to the other Indo-European languages.

It developed from the Old Norwegian spoken by early settlers; however, it differs quite significantly in phonology as well as in many of its grammatical and lexical features.

Although it is often claimed that Icelandic is the same language as that of the ancient Nordic peoples, since it too has undergone major evolutions and modifications, this is incorrect. Compared to the medieval period, it has been no more preserved than other European languages, such as Italian or Spanish, and reading the sagas is not always that easy for a modern-day Icelander.

One feature that makes Icelandic even more difficult, compared to other European languages, is that it has rejected most of the lexical characteristics borrowed from classical and Romance languages (especially Greek, Latin, and French), which greatly facilitate the learning

Agnes M. Sigurðardóttir, the first woman bishop of Iceland.

National Icelandic Language Day is celebrated on November 16, the birth date of Jónas Hallgrímsson, Iceland's foremost Romantic poet.

EXPERIENCE: Learn Icelandic

Although some discourage learning Icelandic, it is far from impossible, as evidenced by thousands of foreigners living in the country who use it on a daily basis. However, it is true that Icelandic has maintained a more complex grammatical system than many of the more widely spoken European languages, and it requires a considerable amount of effort at the start. It is then repaid by giving you access to an extremely vibrant and diverse cultural world that produces astonishing numbers of incredible books and music each year. There are digital and print resources available, and bookstores in the capital are usually stocked with them. Even for those who do not want to have a go, learning at least some basic expressions, such as greetings or thanks, will get a much friendlier reception from locals, who will appreciate the effort in speaking their language.

of vocabulary in languages that share these characteristics. Icelandic, on the other hand, prefers to coin new terms from its native roots. This has helped prevent the use of terms that don't fit the grammatical rules of the language, causing confusion. ■

Although it may seem like a difficult language, many resident foreigners speak Icelandic.

THE NATURAL LANDSCAPE

Icelandic nature is quite diverse. Ice tongues alternate with valleys rich in the vegetation typical of these latitudes, black deserts give way to bucolic agricultural scenes and austere cliffs are often replaced with pleasant beaches. Throughout the country, lakes, rivers, waterfalls, islands, and mountains make up a color palette that changes across spaces as well as over time, changing dramatically with the seasons.

Located on the shores of Lake Mývatn, Leirhnjúkur is one of Iceland's major volcanic regions.

Iceland can be divided in different ways depending on what you're looking at. The Icelandic Meteorological Institute, for example, subdivides the territory differently than the road authority, and the regions often referred to in tourism do not correspond to those used by the National Institute of Statistics. All this can cause confusion when trying to locate certain areas, which might be included in different regions depending on the various institutions. The division into regions of the National Institute of Statistics has no real legal significance. Regions are merely territorial portions that consist of associations of municipalities aimed at cooperation and the pursuit of common goals and projects, but they do not play an administrative role, which is the prerogative of municipalities, the only administrative level in the country apart from the central government.

The regions in question, understood as loose associations of municipalities, are: *Höfuðborgarsvæðið* (Capital region), *Suðurnes* (Southern Peninsula), *Vesturland* (Western region), *Vestfirðir* (Westfjords), *Norðurland vestra* (Northwest region), *Norðurland eystra* (Northeast region), *Austurland* (Eastern region) and *Suðurland* (Southern region). Regions generally denote the territory under the jurisdiction of the *sýslumenn* (prefects), state officials in charge of special tasks in the area, such as issuing licenses, documents and permits.

In ancient times, the territory was divided into four major areas (*fjórðungar*): South, West, North, and East. These however did not correspond precisely to a division that strictly followed the cardinal directions. For example, the Eastern area began at the River Jökulsá á Sólheimasandi, just before Vík, and

The volcanoes of the Leirhnjúkur region.

continued to Langanes in the far Northeast. Even the division into geographical regions made according to the cardinal directions tends to differ according to practical needs. Sometimes the South is merged with the Southeast or the Southwestern half into a large Southern area; other times, for example in the case of the meteorological office, the Southeast is treated as a separate region, or is formally included in the Eastern region. Even with district courts and healthcare organization, territorial division does not match official division.

“The Icelandic landscape is considerably shaped by volcanism and tectonic activity. It features one of the highest summits of the Mid-Atlantic Ridge.”

Glaciers & Volcanoes

The Icelandic landscape is considerably shaped by volcanism and tectonic activity. It features one of the highest summits of the Mid-Atlantic Ridge, a mostly underwater mountain range that marks the point of separation between two tectonic plates, North American and Eurasian. Iceland is roughly traversed by the rift, running southwest to northeast. New rock emerges from it, pushing the plates apart at a rate of almost one inch (2 cm) a year. The uniqueness of Iceland's location on the ridge is that it is above sea level. Normally, the oceanic ridges from which new land emerges are completely underwater. Experts believe that Iceland has emerged because it is located above an area where primordial material in the Earth's mantle rises due to a hydrostatic buoyancy caused by its lower density. The upward buoyancy would have caused the ocean floor to bulge, making it emerge. In ancient times, the western and eastern fjords, which geologically are the oldest parts of the island, were two parts of a considerably smaller Iceland; the emergence of new material caused them to gradually recede and the island's land to expand. Of note are the more than 30 volcanic systems and about 130 volcanoes that run along the continental fault, about 20 of which are currently active.

Until the end of the last ice age, Iceland was entirely covered by an ice cap and was connected to continental Europe by sea ice. This was how the arctic fox, the only native species, managed to get there. The presence of ice has profoundly shaped the landscape: the fjords are nothing more than furrows carved by colossal tongues of long gone ice replaced with seawater. The melting of the ice cap and still existing glaciers that cover about 10 percent of the land caused the phenomenon of the post-glacial rebound; in other words, the land swells once it is relieved of the weight of the ice. Today, the rebound from the melting of Vatnajökull seems destined to make the waters at the southeastern port of Höfn too shallow and unnavi-

Lake Mývatn.

gable, resulting in the extinction of the local fishing industry, an important source of livelihood for the community.

Rivers & Lakes

Iceland has countless rivers, though they are generally quite small. The longest ones are Thjórsá (143 mi, 230 km), Jökulsá á Fjöllum (128 mi, 206 km), and Ölfusá (115 mi, 185 km), which has the greatest flow. Iceland's largest lake is Thórisvatn (32 sq mi, 83 sq km), located inland, followed by Thingvallavatn (31.5 sq mi, 82 sq km), in Thingvellir National Park; Lögurinn (20.5 sq mi, 53 sq km), in the east; and Mývatn (14 sq mi, 37 sq km), in the northeast. Fish species such as salmon and trout are found in the rivers and lakes. Fishing requires the purchase of a license or permit from the owner of the land on which the stream or body of water is located.

Flora

Iceland's flora is similar to that of mainland Scandinavia, although it also shares some with that of the British Isles and Greenland. In total, there are more than 1,500 classified species, just under a third of which are vascular plants. New species arrive all the time, carried by the wind or migratory birds or imported by humans.

About two percent of the territory is covered by boreal forest. At the time of colonization, this percentage must have been between 20 and 40 percent. The sensitivity of the ecosystem and the thinness of the soil have made it subject to severe erosion and desertification due to logging for firewood. Dwarf birch, arctic willow, and rowan are the native tall tree species, whereas poplars, larches, firs, and pines have been introduced since the 19th century in a series of experiments aimed at restoring forests. The largest of these, Hallórmsstaðaskógur, lies to the east, on the eastern shore of Lake Lagarfljót (also called Lögurinn).

There are numerous wildflowers, such as arctic thyme, used as a spice for meat or herbal teas, and mountain avens, a favorite food of partridges, as well as various species of berries, such as blueberries, currants, and black crowberry. Also very common are sorrel (excellent in salads), rhubarb, dandelion, caraway, yarrow, and angelica. Icelandic lichen is also consumed, put in soups or chopped and mixed with flours. Also of note is the presence of numerous species of edible mushrooms.

Icelandic lichen is taken for its many beneficial properties.

A humpback whale breeches off the coast of Húsavík.

Land & Marine Mammals

The only native land mammal is the arctic fox, whose fur can be bluish-gray, brownish, or white. Feeding on birds, eggs, and rodents, these foxes live in intricate underground tunnels and can be spotted in many parts of the country. Reindeer were introduced in the 18th century in an attempt to create a new source of economic activity, but that experiment was unsuccessful; only a few herds survive today, confined to eastern areas. In recent years a population of mink, escaped from fur farms, spread across the country and survived by preying on birds. In the sea there are numerous seal colonies, some 20 cetacean species, including the fin whale, blue whale, humpback whale, pilot whale, orca, and beluga.

Birds

Birds are the most numerous animals in Iceland. The gyrfalcon, while rare, is the national bird. Other species include the loon, arctic tern,

EXPERIENCE: Bird-watching

Bird-watching is one of the most popular activities among visitors in Iceland. Seventy-five species of birds have been recorded in the country, but several others are occasionally spotted despite not being permanently established on the island, totaling more than 400. Some of these birds are quite rare, such as the gyrfalcon, which is the national symbol, or the sea eagle; others are more common, but only in specific areas, such as the puffin, skua, and gannet. Several species can only be spotted in the summer season, such as the aforementioned puffin, as well as the tern and woodcock, when they return to Iceland to nest.

There are 121 Important Bird and Biodiversity Areas (IBAs) throughout the country. It is possible to join a wide variety of tours that take you to areas where you are likely to spot certain species of birds, but with a little luck you might also have a chance sighting on your trip.

gannet, skua, puffin, woodcock, golden plover (a favorite of many Icelanders, as a harbinger of the warm season), sea eagle, raven, and starling. There are numerous colonies, particularly in the summer season, with many species using the cliffs to nest and breed and taking advantage of the abundance of food like plankton and small crustaceans that proliferate in the coastal waters.

Human Geography

In addition to the capital region, the island's largest urban centers are Reykjanesbær (pop. 20,000), where Keflavík International Airport is located, and Akureyri (19,000), the main town in the north. Other important towns are Selfoss (10,000), Egilsstaðir (3,000), Ísafjörður (3,000), Höfn í Hornafirði (2,000), and Borgarnes (2,000). The rest of the settlements are small villages and isolated farms, scattered along the coasts or in flat inland areas. The inland region is almost uninhabited, inaccessible in winter and open in summer only to special vehicles. The Hringvegur, or Ring Road, runs around the perimeter of the island, cutting through the Westfjords, the Snæfellsnes Peninsula, and part of the northeast (as well as some peninsulas). Road transportation, in some remote areas, can be problematic during winter, and supplies, as well as travel, are done by plane or ship. ■

FOOD & DRINK

There is a certain misconception about Icelandic cuisine that has developed over the years, exacerbated by marketing. It emphasizes the strange and grotesque, spreading the false notion that foods consumed in the past are still the basis of today's local diet. In reality, the situation is quite different. Icelandic cuisine has experienced miraculous growth, making the island a respectable gastronomic destination.

Fermented shark, lamb's head, mutton testicles, and black pudding were once indispensable foods in a land of limited resources. Today, however, the availability of premium local ingredients, products from the international market, and the creativity of chefs has a truly interesting evolution in Iceland's gastronomic scene. The main course of an Icelandic meal generally consists of a meat or fish dish, accompanied by potatoes and various vegetables. In restaurants, there is no cover charge and water is always free. The courses tend to be plentiful and very carefully presented.

Fermented shark, a dish for adventurous eaters, is best accompanied with several shots of Iceland's most potent brandy, *brennivín*.

The famous shrimp soup, accompanied by grilled shrimp, bread, and salad.

The basis of local cuisine is fish and lamb, with which a myriad of dishes of varying degrees of elegance are cooked. With the exception of a couple of traditional dishes, such as *plokkfiskur*, a cod and potato pie, and *kjötsúpa*, a lamb soup, there are not many classic, strictly codified recipes or dishes that can be found in any restaurant, as is the case in other countries. Instead, one finds an endless array of culinary offerings designed around basic ingredients, the freshness and quality of which are some of the cuisine's strong points. Instead of focusing on classic and canonical dishes, Icelandic cuisine tends to favor creativity, developing dishes from raw materials that are as local as possible. A large number of restaurants cater to vegetarians and vegans, particularly in the capital region, and virtually every establishment provides at least one meatless alternative.

Seafood

Fish is a staple of Icelandic cuisine. Cod and salmon are very common in Icelandic cooking, along with haddock, wolffish, and ling. The most common shellfish is langoustine, which is put in a famous soup often available in restaurants. Due to a translation error, langoustine soup is often presented as lobster soup in English, the two species being quite similar. Only rarely offered on restaurant menus, whale meat is not a traditional food because for centuries Icelanders did not have vessels suitable for hunting them. If they happened to eat the meat, it was because they had traded for it with foreign sailors and whalers. Consumption of it is discouraged because it is rarely fresh, quality meat. There is almost no domestic demand for it, which is why whaling products largely end up in foreign markets (such as Japan) or are destined for tourists.

Meat

Icelandic meat in general is extremely healthy because it comes from animals fed almost exclusively on local hay and often raised outdoors. Although excellent quality beef, pork, horsemeat, and poultry are available, sheep meat predominates in the local diet. Dishes made from lamb can be found in almost every restaurant, and most of the lamb meat that is served is from animals that were slaughtered when they were almost adult age. The flavor of this meat is strong but still milder than that of sheep or mutton. A must-try is the smoked lamb, called *hangikjöt* ("hung meat"), which is eaten boiled year-round but especially at Christmas time. It is cut into thin slices and laid on a folded flatbread called *flatkökur*, an essential part of sack lunches.

Fruits & Vegetables

Despite what you might think, Iceland produces most of the vegetables it consumes, thanks to the harnessing of geothermal energy for greenhouse

EXPERIENCE: Try Icelandic Lamb

Lamb has been the true staple of Icelandic cuisine for a millennium. Before the "explosion" of the fish industry in the 19th century, sheep meat dominated the local diet. Even today, lamb meat is almost always on restaurant menus, and is a traditional, healthy ingredient sustainably produced by local farmers and on family farms (there are no industrial sheep farms in Iceland). There is no standard recipe, only endless variations subject to the creativity of the cooks.

In restaurants, it is commonly presented as steak, but it is also worth tasting the smoked ham (*hangiálegg*), which is a traditional staple in Icelanders' sack lunches, stuffed inside buttered *flatkökur*.

cultivation, which began as early as 1924. The ultrapure water used for irrigation and hydroponic greenhouse technology yield surprisingly tasty vegetables. Local production focuses on tomatoes, cucumbers, peppers, mushrooms, carrots, turnips, potatoes, bok choy, broccoli, and various cabbages. Recently, there has also been a substantial cultivation of garlic. Fruits, on the other hand, are largely imported, with only berries being grown enough to be sold commercially, particularly strawberries, blueberries, and raspberries. Some experiments with other fruits, from bananas to apples, have been successful, but have not achieved a significant enough yield to be a potential commercial interest.

Dessert & Drinks

Iceland's most traditional sweets are quite diverse: *kleinur* (*kleina* in the singular), deep-fried dough braids; *ástarpungar* ("love balls"), round pancakes decorated with raisins; *hjónabandssæla* ("happy marriage cake"), a rhubarb tart; and *pönnukökur*, sweet crepes that can be decorated with sugar and rolled or garnished with whipped cream and jam and folded over. Icelanders are also fond of licorice, which can be found in numerous forms, including chocolate-covered candies.

Popular beverages include *brennivín*, a spirit spiced with caraway; local beer, available in a myriad of brands, many from microbreweries scattered around; and malt, a very sweet and fizzy soft drink. Spirits above three percent proof are available for purchase only in state-owned stores, where an extremely rich selection can be found. Wine, imported from all over the world has lately become much more popular than beer. ■

The *kleinur* is a typical fried twisted dessert made of puff pastry.

An urban island rich in culture and leisure, surrounded by pristine nature

REYKJAVÍK & THE SOUTHWEST

Ingólfur Arnarson, the first settler of Iceland, is said to have founded Reykjavík in the year 874 AD.

REYKJAVÍK & THE SOUTHWEST

The world's northernmost capital city, Reykjavík, is home to two-thirds of Iceland's entire population. It is also the gateway to the Reykjanes Peninsula, located between the city and the airport, which offers a taste of the wildest and most remote Icelandic landscapes.

Medieval sources identify Reykjavík as the oldest settlement in the country. Between 870 and 874 AD, a Norwegian nobleman named Ingólfur Arnarson is said to have settled here. For a long time Reykjavík remained on the fringes of society, an agricultural estate like any other with no particular political or economic significance. Its disadvantage was due to the forma-

tion of the coast, having extremely shallow waters that prevented ships from docking, forcing passengers to shift to dinghies to reach the shore. The town's fortunes changed in the mid-18th century, almost by accident. The first Icelander to hold the position of *fógeti*, a kind of minister of economic development, obtained the land that would become Reykjavík from the Danish king to establish a small wool-processing plant there (see History & Culture, p. 37). Soon, a handful of wooden homes arranged in rows sprang up along a dirt road: the foundations of the fledgling wool industry. This was the original nucleus of the town. The little road would later be called Aðalstræti (Main Road). Today it retains its former name, although it is essentially the side of a square. Only one building remains, at No. 10. It houses the city's history museum, Borgarsögusafn.

Though small, the wool industry sparked significant population growth and prompted the relocation of the bishop's seat and the Latin school to Reykjavík. The main building of the Latin school still stands on the eastern side of Lækjargata, one of the city's main streets. Around the middle of the 19th century, having obtained the right to have their own parliament from the Danish government, Icelanders decided to establish its seat in Reykjavík, permanently sealing its status as the capital city.

Since then, the city has seen tremendous, albeit chaotic, growth. Today, the municipal area covers 105 square miles (273 sq km). Reykjavík offers very diverse attractions. The small historic center is packed with various museums and art galleries, and in the outer districts one can visit the Kjarvalsstaðir Art Museum, Laugardalur Park with its botanical garden and zoo, the open-air museum Árbær, Viðey Island, and the Heiðmörk Reserve, a walking and hiking destination.

Home to more than two-thirds of Iceland's entire population, Reykjavík is the beating heart of Iceland, embodying the cosmopolitan and innovative nature typical of capital cities, without abandoning traditions. The year is chock-full of

NOT TO BE MISSED:

The National Museum of Iceland 91–92

The Árbær open-air museum 98

The art museums of Reykjavík 86–87

The Reykjavík City History Museum 83

The Island of Viðey 96

Icelandic geology exhibits at the Perlan 93–94

The region around Lake Kleifarvatn 107

The solfataras of Gunnuhver 109–110

art events, film festivals, music and literary festivals, exhibitions, and concerts. Numerous restaurants make Reykjavík a respectable gastronomic destination, where the tradition of utilizing local ingredients (especially meat and fish) is combined with contemporary creativity.

The rest of the Southwest consists mainly of the Southern Peninsula region (*Suðurnes*) and provides a valuable opportunity to sample wild vistas typical of remote areas in central Iceland. Formed by volcanic activity along the fault that bisects the island before sinking into the ocean, the Reykjanes Peninsula is a young land dominated by black lava and green moss. Volcanic eruptions are constantly forming new rock and altering the landscape as waves sculpt the cliffs creating unique shapes; solfataras emit endless clouds of steam; ancient craters dot the landscape; and water fills chasms in the land creating lakes with ancient contours. Along the coast, numerous villages and lighthouses add a human dimension to the lunar landscapes that characterize the peninsula. Its proximity to the capital and relatively small area make Reykjanes an ideal option both for those who want to take on challenging hikes or day trips by car, and for those looking for something to do before heading to the airport to catch their flight home. ■

The cliffs of Krýsuvíkurberg, on the Reykjanes Peninsula.

REYKJAVÍK

Colorful, quirky, and surreal, Reykjavík is a unique combination of nature and culture and is full of surprises, from its museums and art galleries, music festivals and exhibitions, restaurants and cafés to the natural landscapes that surround its urban limits.

Historic Center

The small historic center of **Reykjavík** (particularly the area called Kvosin, between Tjörnin Lake and the sea) has long been considered the oldest settlement in the country. An agricultural estate stood here for centuries starting in the mid-18th century, before evolving into what would become the present-day city. Some 20 years ago, an archaeological excavation uncovered ruins that some have sought to identify as Ingólfur Arnarson's farm. How-

Reykjavík – Tourist office ✉ Laugavegur 5 ☎ 551 3600
🕒 Open daily 8:30 a.m.–9 p.m. **www.whatson.is**

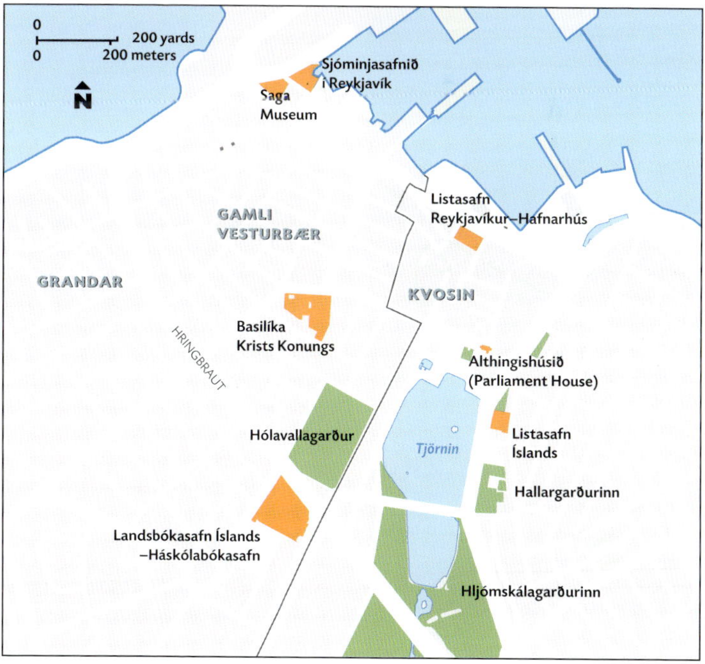

ever, some scholars have disputed this reconstruction. Ingólfur was believed to have landed in the southeast, at Ingólfshöfði, where he threw decorative wooden pillars overboard, vowing to settle where they would hit shore. An experiment was conducted in 1970: dozens of numbered logs were thrown into the sea near the southeast coast, and none of them made it as far as Reykjavík. Moreover, the city's historic center lies in a natural depression and on a low coastline that make it impossible for ships to reach land. For this reason, the small settlement of Reykjavík held no particular importance in the Middle Ages and for most of the modern age.

Hallgrímskirkja Lutheran Church, one of the symbols of the Icelandic capital.

Another curious aspect is that the bay where the present old harbor is located is called Rauðarárvík, and it is unclear what portion of the capital's waterfront was in the past called Reykjavík, meaning "bay of smoke." Some believe that it was the portion between the present-day Höfði building (where the summit between Reagan and Gorbachev was held in 1986) and the Laugarnes Peninsula, a small promontory that was home to an influential local family in the Middle Ages. It is mentioned in the *Njáls saga* (see pp. 129–131), perhaps the most important of Icelandic sagas. This thesis would be supported by the fact that the coast here has deeper waters that allow ships to moor (Reykjavík's new harbor was built just beyond it, down the coast) and by the presence of a stream of warm water coming from the Laugardalur springs, from which steam would have risen, giving the bay its name. It is unclear, however, how the name of the bay was later transferred to the agricultural settlement farther west, where the center of the capital stands today.

South of Reykjavík, on the Álftanes Peninsula, was Bessastaðir, a

Reykjavík in the mid-1800s.

center of power in the Middle Ages and later the seat of representatives of the Danish crown. This today is the residence of the president of the republic. Farther south, the present harbor of the small town of Hafnarfjörður was the favored landing place for those arriving by ship in what is now the capital area.

The evolution of the small settlement of Reykjavík was decreed by a series of events that occurred between the 18th and 19th centuries, after Skúli Magnússon established his wool industry there. A further boost to the development of the city came with the relocation of the bishopric of Skálholt and its Latin school. Then when Icelanders were allowed to have their own parliament in 1844, Reykjavík was chosen as the seat, establishing its prominent role once and for all.

Today, Reykjavík is Iceland's only major urban center. Despite its continued growth, it retains a relaxed, small-town feel but with all the services and entertainment one would expect to find in a capital city.

Old Reykjavík

Old Reykjavík mainly comprises the area of Kvosin, between the Old Harbor and Tjörnin Lake, and Gamli Vesturbær (Old Western End), which is the neighborhood between the western part of the Old Harbor to the north and Hringbraut Street to the south, beyond which is the university campus. A large number of museums and tourist attractions are concentrated here. In Parliament Square, Austurvöllur, you can find the Parliament building, Althingishúsið, built in 1881, and the **Dómkirkjan í Reykjavík** cathedral. The interior of Parliament cannot be visited, but its garden in the back is open to the public. In the heart of the square is a statue depicting Jón Sigurðsson, an important 19th-century politician.

On the street that passes in front of Parliament, Kirkjustræti, is a small square, Fógetagarður, where there is a statue of Skúli Magnússon, considered the "father" of the city. There was formerly a cemetery here, near which stood the old Reykjavík church, before the cathedral was completed in 1796. The original church was turned first into a vegetable garden, then into a public park. It still houses the oldest tree in the city, a rowan tree planted in 1884. In the southwest corner of the square is the entrance to **Landnámssýningin:**

Dómkirkjan í Reykjavík Kirkjustræti 520 9700
Open Mon.–Fri. 10 a.m.–2 p.m. **www.domkirkjan.is**

The colorful rooftops of Reykjavík.

Iceland's National Holiday

Thjóðhátiðardagurinn is Iceland's national holiday and it falls on June 17, the birthday of Jón Sigurðsson (1811), one of the most important leaders of the Icelandic independence movement who fought for cultural and political autonomy from the Kingdom of Denmark, which would later be granted in 1848. A professor of Literature at the University of Copenhagen, he worked to revive national pride through the glorious literary heritage of the medieval period. For the celebration, the bishop officiates a mass in the cathedral that faces Parliament Square, then the country's leaders address the nation. This is followed by the recitation of a poem from memory by a woman dressed in national costume. She is called *fjallkona* (mountain woman), the personification of Iceland. Between ceremonies, musicians perform traditional music from the small balcony of the Parliament building.

Reykjavík 871±2, an exhibition built around the archaeological excavation of a building dating to the early years of colonization.

The west side of the square is lined by Aðalstræti (Main Street), on either side of which rose the buildings of the small wool industry founded by Skúli Magnússon. Only one remains today, at No. 10, a wooden house that looks like a large bungalow, painted entirely with brown pitch around white-framed windows. It initially served as a warehouse and office, then was used for different purposes, including as housing for families of various classes and as a workshop. Behind Aðalstræti 10 stands a larger building that is part of the complex that forms the **Borgarsögusafn Reykjavíkur** (City History Museum), connected to the Landnámssýning: Reykjavík 871±2 via an underground tunnel. The two exhibitions can be visited with a single ticket.

On the eastern side of Aðalstræti is Ingólfstorg Square, a monument that pays tribute to Ingólfur Arnarson: two basalt columns bear the section of the *Landnámabók* (*Book of Colonizations*) that recounts how he is said to have settled in the area.

Behind the square, on the west side, is the Grjótathorp which may have been the city's first "suburb." Time seems to stand still here with cobblestone streets and historic buildings built mostly of wood

Landnámssýningin: Reykjavík 871±2 & Borgarsögusafn Reykjavíkur
Aðalstræti 10 & 16 · 411 6370 · Closed Dec. 24, 25 · $$
reykjavikcitymuseum.is

INSIDER TIP:
In Grjótathorp, time seems to stand still. Visit the cobblestone streets and historic buildings dating from the 19th and 20th centuries.

—ROBERTO LUIGI PAGANI
Author of the guidebook

and sheet metal dating to the 19th and 20th centuries. East of Ingólfstorg Square runs the tourist street Austurstræti, which comes out on Lækjargata, the road that leads from Tjörnin Lake to **Harpa** auditorium and along which stands the main building of Reykjavík High School, a neoclassical building from 1846. The Icelandic parliament met in its auditorium until the current building was completed in 1881.

On the same side of the street, but closer to the sea, stands Stjórnarráðshúsið, the Government Palace, originally built as a prison between 1761 and 1771, one of the very first stone buildings in the country. Two statues were placed in front of it depicting Danish King Christian IX (who granted Iceland its own constitution, albeit under the Kingdom of Denmark) and Hannes Hafstein (poet and first to serve as prime minister, in 1904). In what was the home of Hafstein is now a museum and private art exhibition, as well as a venue for talks and concerts, with an adjoining café and restaurant, called **Hannesarholt.**

To the north of the Government Palace stretches a grassy hill called Arnarhóll, a busy outdoor space in the summer season. Sometimes it also serves as a grandstand for events: the street facing it is closed off and stages and big screens are set up. On the top is a statue by sculptor Einar Jónsson depicting Ingólfur Arnarson, placed here in 1924.

Behind this area, on the corner of Hverfisgata and Ingólfsstræti, the **Safnahúsið** (Collections Building) puts on many types of temporary exhibitions. Designed by a Danish architect and completed in 1908, the building housed the National Library until 1994 (see p. 91). The facade is decorated with effigies of important figures in Icelandic literature. Next to it stands **Thjóðleikhúsið,** the National Theater. Inaugurated in 1950, the building was designed by Guðjón Samúelsson, who also devised its

Harpa ✉ Austurbakka 2 ☎ 528 500/528 5050 (to buy tickets) **www.harpa.is** • **Hannesarholt** ✉ Grundarstígur 10 ☎ 511 1904 **www.hannesarholt.is** • **Safnahúsið** ✉ Hverfisgata 15 ☎ 515 9600 🕒 Closed Mon. Oct.–April & Dec. 24, 25, 31, Jan. 1 $ $ **www.listasafn.is**

exterior, a mixture of quartz, obsidian, and Iceland spar that covers the concrete structure.

At the foot of the hill, east of the intersection of Austurstræti and Lækjargata, is the steep street Bankastræti. On the south side, underground, is **Pönksafn Íslands** (Museum of Icelandic Punk), a small exhibition devoted to the history of the musical genre. At the southern corner, just behind the staircase leading to the museum, stands a historic building: a black wooden house with a red roof. Built in 1834, this structure housed the country's only bakery until 1868, when a second one opened in Akureyri. Today the inside of the building has been renovated and reopened as a bakery, bar, and restaurant.

At the point where the hill stops and the road becomes flat, you encounter a fork in the road that diverges into Laugavegur and Skólavörðustígur streets. The former is the main tourist street, filled mainly with stores, cafés, and restaurants, and leads to Hlemmur Square, an important hub for public transportation. Skólavörðustígur, whose lower half is often painted in rainbow

Thjóðleikhúsið ✉ Hverfisgata 19 ☎ 585 1200 **leikhusid.is** • **Pönksafn Íslands** ✉ Bankastræti 2 🕒 Open daily 10 a.m.–6 p.m. $ $

Harpa, Reykjavík's auditorium and convention center, opened in 2011.

colors, leads instead to the top of Skólavörðuholt Hill, where you can find the imposing **Hallgrímskirkja,** a church designed by Guðjón Samúelsson completed in 1983. The bell tower is 244 feet (74.5 m) high and can be visited with the purchase of a ticket. From the top you have the best view of the city and its surroundings. In front of the church is a statue donated by the American people to Iceland in 1930 to mark 1,000 years from the founding of Iceland's General Assembly. It depicts Leif Erikson, son of Erik the Red, famous for exploring Greenland. Leif was among the first Europeans to venture into North American territory around the year 1000. He attempted to coordinate settlements but failed due to fierce opposition from the local Indigenous peoples. At least, this is the story we find in Icelandic sagas.

On the west side of the square is **Listasafn Einars Jónssonar** (Einar Jónsson Museum), dedicated to the important Icelandic sculptor from the 19th and 20th centuries. In 1909, Jónsson donated all his works to the state on the condition that they be displayed in a museum, which was completed in 1923. The artist and his wife lived in the penthouse above the museum, which has been preserved and can be visited today.

Overlooking Tjörnin Lake is the **Fríkirkjan í Reykjavík** church, built in 1903 according to designs by Rögnvaldur Ólafsson. It's recognizable by the bright green color of its roof. Next to the church, the National Art Gallery, **Listasafn Íslands,** holds works by Icelandic and foreign artists. The building that houses it was designed by Guðjón Samúelsson and was built in 1916.

The Icelandic Flag

The Icelandic flag was designed by Matthías Thórðarson in 1906. In documents from that time, no mention is made of the symbolic meaning of the colors, but in the public imagination, the idea was to portray the role of elements of Icelandic nature. While most believe the red represents lava and the white is the ice, there's less of a consensus about the blue, with some seeing a reference to mountains observed from a distance and others associating it with the sea and still others with the sky.

Hallgrímskirkja ✉ Skólavörðuholti ☎ 510 1000 🕒 Closed during services $ $ (bell tower) **www.hallgrimskirkja.is • Listasafn Einars Jónssonar** ✉ Hallgrímstorgi 3 ☎ 551 3797 🕒 Open noon–5 p.m. (closed Mon.) $ $ **www.lej.is • Fríkirkjan í Reykjavík** ✉ Fríkirkjuvegur 5 ☎ 552 7270 **frikirkjan.is**

The Reykjavík Cathedral, Dómkirkjan.

It was originally a refrigeration plant until it became the gallery's home in 1987, when the collection was moved there. South of Tjörnin Lake is Hljjómskálagarðurinn public park, named after the Hljómskálinn, a small octagonal pavilion built in 1923 to serve as a rehearsal hall for the city's marching band.

Across from the western shore of the pond, Hólavallagarður is the oldest cemetery in the city still in use, established in 1838. Gravestones and grave monuments can be found there, but it is also a botanically interesting place, as it is home to about 200 species of plants. It is crisscrossed by several footpaths for a pleasant walk. Turning back to the lake, you will find a nice view of downtown Reykjavík.

On top of a knoll in the middle of the town stands the neo-Gothic **Basilíka Krists Konungs** (Basilica of Christ the King), the town's Catholic cathedral. Beginning in the mid-16th century, Catholicism and its traditions were gradually

Listasafn Íslands ✉ Fríkirkjuvegur 7 ☎ 515 9600 🕒 Closed Mon. Oct.–Apr. & Dec. 24, 25, 31, Jan. 1. $ $ **www.listasafn.is** • **Basilíka Krists Konungs** ✉ Túngata 13 ☎ 552 5388

Laugavegur, Reykjavík.

eradicated by the Danish authorities, but in the 19th century freedom of worship was restored. The first Catholic missionaries bought the property of Landakot. At the time, it was just outside the town of Reykjavík, but now sits in the center of town. In 1855, the Catholic Church established the North Pole Apostolic Prefecture, and a few years later French missionaries Bernard and Jean-Baptiste Baudoin arrived. Later, Iceland was incorporated into the Apostolic Prefecture of Denmark, eventually becoming the Apostolic Vicariate of Iceland in 1929 and finally being elevated to the diocese of Reykjavík in 1968. In the meantime, religious orders, especially female ones, arrived in Iceland and became part of the social fabric by founding schools and hospitals. To this day, Catholicism has the second-highest number of adherents in the country and continues to grow.

The original basilica was a prefabricated wooden building (now preserved in the Árbæjarsafn; see p. 98). The whereas the present church was designed by Guðjón Samúelsson and consecrated in 1929. At that time, it was the largest building in the country. Inside is a wooden statue of the Virgin Mary, which dates from the 14th century and comes from Reykhó-

EXPERIENCE: Cafés and social life

Iceland's capital is distinguished by an abundance of cafés, bars and clubs, from wine bars, and beer gardens to clubs where nightlife comes alive. These play an important role in the winter season, providing places to meet and socialize when temperatures outside are harsh. Several clubs offer occasional live music and host cultural events.

In addition to chains such as Te & Kaffi, Kaffitár, and Reykjavík Roasters, there is a dense network of independent coffee shops, with very different characteristics and atmospheres.

The coffee ritual, which has become increasingly popular in Iceland, generally involves enjoying a cup slowly while socializing. All of Iceland's major coffee shop chains have their own roastery and carefully selected blends and preparations, offering a wide selection worth exploring during your stay.

Basilíka Krists Konungs.

lar, in the northwest, where it was preserved by a local family.

Overlooking the street on the old harbor is **Listasafn Reykjavíkur – Hafnarhús,** the largest of the buildings that make up the Reykjavík Art Gallery, which houses numerous works by contemporary artists. In particular, exhibitions dedicated to Erró (a pseudonym for Guðmundur Guðmundsson), Iceland's foremost pop artist, are regularly held there. On the west side, exhibitions of contemporary or vintage photography are held in the **Ljósmyndasafn Reykjavíkur** (Museum of Photography). The **Saga Museum,** on the other hand, allows visitors to relive some of the pivotal stories chronicled in the Icelandic sagas, medieval epics about the lives of the first generations, between the period of colonization until shortly after the conversion to Christianity in the year 1000. Audio guides describe and explain the episodes immortalized in the retellings.

Listasafn Reykjavíkur – Hafnarhús ✉ Tryggvagata 17 ☎ 411 6410 $ $$ **listasafnreykjavikur.is • Ljósmyndasafn Reykjavíkur** ✉ Tryggvagata 15, 6. Hæð ☎ 411 6390 🕒 Closed Dec. 24–26, 31, Jan. 1, Easter, May 1, 13, 23, 24, June 17 $ $ **borgarsogusafn.is • Saga Museum** ✉ Grandagardi 2 ☎ 511 1517 🕒 Open daily 10 a.m.–5 p.m. $ $$ **www.sagamuseum.is**

Sculptures preserved in the Saga Museum.

A short distance away stands the **Sjóminjasafnið í Reykjavík,** overlooking the old harbor. It is part of the City History Museum circuit and is dedicated to the relationship between man and the sea, the development and construction of the old harbor and how it had a profound impact on the history of the city, and the lives of its inhabitants. It offers a wealth of information on boats, the tools and techniques used for fishing, the lifestyle of fishermen and their families, the fish caught, and the methods of preservation.

The waters surrounding Iceland are populated by numerous cetaceans. The interactive **Whales of Iceland** exhibit reproduces them in life-size forms, hanging from the ceilings of the exhibition rooms so visitors can see the colossal scale of these animals.

One of Reykjavík's most popular attractions is **FlyOver Iceland,** a 360-degree cinema where the viewer is suspended on a row of moving seats with the illusion of flying

Sjóminjasafnið í Reykjavík ✉ Grandagarður 8 ☎ 411 6340 🕒 Closed Dec. 24, 25, Good Friday $ $$ **borgarsogusafn.is • Whales of Iceland** ✉ Fiskislóð 23-25 ☎ 571 0077 🕒 Closed Dec. 25 $ $$ **www.whalesoficeland.is • FlyOver Iceland** ✉ Fiskislóð 43 ☎ 527 6700 $ $$, **www.flyovericeland.com**

through Iceland's iconic natural landscapes. Scents and sprays of steam make the experience highly realistic. Not far away is the **Lava Show,** which demonstrates what real lava looks like up close.

Vesturbær & Seltjarnarnes

The new part of Vesturbær district, south of Hringbraut Road, is home to three important institutions: Háskóli Íslands (University of Iceland), **Landsbókasafn Íslands** (National Library), and **Thjóðminjasafn Íslands** (National Museum of Iceland). The National Library is free to access; a card is required for lending purposes only. The main floor houses exhibitions devoted to a wide variety of aspects of Icelandic publishing, writing, and literature. The National Museum, on the other hand, houses a chronological exhibition on the country's history, starting

Lava Show ✉ Fiskislóð 73 $ $$$ **icelandiclavashow.com** • **Landsbókasafn Íslands** ✉ Arngrímsgötu 3 ☎ 525 5600 🕒 Closed Sat.–Sun. mid-Dec.–Jan. 8 (bar closed Dec. 17–Jan. 4) **landsbokasafn.is** • **Thjóðminjasafn Íslands** ✉ Suðurgata 41 ☎ 530 2200 🕒 Closed Mon. Sept. 16–April 30 $ $ **www.thjodminjasafn.is**

The waters surrounding Iceland are populated by numerous species of whale, which you can see in life-size form at the Whales of Iceland exhibit.

Preserved in the National Museum of Iceland, the Valthjófsstaður Gate depicts a version of the legend of the knight and the lion.

with the oldest excavated artifacts (which include some Roman coins from the third century) and ending with the modern era.

To the east of the museum, beyond the university campus, is Vatnsmýri, a small protected area in the heart of the city. It is prohibited to pass there in the summer because it becomes an important nesting ground for some bird species, such as the arctic tern. On the south side of the protected area, next to a body of water, **Norræna húsið** (Nordic House) serves as a cultural center, exhibition space, and conference hall. Opened in 1968, it was designed by the celebrated Finnish architect Alvar Aalto.

The farthest tip of the peninsula on which Reykjavík sits is an independent municipality named after the peninsula itself, Seltjarnarnes. There are several points of interest here, including the lighthouse located on the tidal Island of Grótta, a protected area, which can be reached on foot at low tide (it is important to consult the tide chart posted at the access point of the peninsula). In June, access to the island is prohibited so as not to disturb nesting birds. A number of walking trails around the surrounding natural areas start south of the parking lot. **Nesstofa,** one of the oldest stone buildings in the country, is located here. Finished in 1767,

Norræna húsið ✉ Sæmundargata 11 ☎ 551 7030 🕒 Closed Mon. **nordichouse.is • Nesstofa** ✉ Neströð 5 ☎ 595 9111 **visitreykjavik.is**

it once housed a pharmacy and the headquarters of the directorate of health, a still-existing state institution responsible for coordinating and managing the national health system. Inside, a museum tells the story of health care and medicine in Iceland in the 19th and 20th centuries.

Hlíðar & Laugardalur

Just east of the center, the Hlíðar and Laugardalur districts were part of the first stage of expansion of the urban fabric of the city. One of the main points of interest in the Hlíðar district is Klambratún Park, where one of the three buildings of the Reykjavík Museum of Art stands: **Kjarvalsstaðir.** Completed in 1973, it was the first to be built expressly with the intention of housing artwork. It houses the permanent collection of artist Jóhannes Kjarval in one wing and exhibitions of various contemporary Icelandic artists in the other.

On the south side of the district, atop the forested hill of Öskjuhlíð, stands **Perlan** (Pearl), a building initially used to store the city's water supply. In 1991, the dome that gives the building its name was inaugurated. It houses the Wonders of Iceland Museum of Natural His-

Kjarvalsstaðir ✉ Flókagata 24 ☎ 411 6420 🕒 Closed Dec. 24, 25, 31, Jan. 1 $ $ **listasafnreykjavikur.is • Perlan** ✉ Öskjuhlíð ☎ 566 9000 🕒 Open daily 9 a.m–10 p.m. $ $$$ **www.perlan.is**

Panoramic view of the glass dome of Perlan, located on the hill of Öskjuhlíð, in Reykjavík.

Interior view of Perlan's restaurant.

tory, as well as a planetarium and an artificial ice cave. The museum features exhibits on Icelandic wildlife, the geology of the area, and earthquakes. The artificial ice cave, designed as a 328-foot-long (100 m) immersive exhibit, faithfully recreates the interior of a glacier, with typical formations, trapped layers of volcanic ash, and a simulation of a vertiginous crevasse. The planetarium, on the other hand, offers an educational show on the Northern Lights and a realistic projection of the phenomenon filmed at different locations around the country. An observation platform over the entire capital can be accessed from the upper floors, and inside the dome is a café and bistro on a rotating platform around the inner perimeter, giving visitors the chance to enjoy a 360-degree view without getting up from their table.

Öskjuhlíð Hill is crisscrossed by numerous paths, suitable for walking or mountain biking, with several picnic areas. At the foot of the hill, on the southern slope, is the geothermal beach Ylströndin (*Ylströnd, 411 5330, ylstrond@itr.is*), around the small artificial bay of Nauthólsvík, which is partially heated due to the geothermal water pumped into it. The temperature is a few degrees higher than that of the ocean, but it remains cold year-round, at a maximum of 61°F (16°C). There is free access to a heated pool at 100°F (38°C) on the beach, and the facilities include changing rooms and showers.

The neighborhood of Laugardalur is built around the city's largest green area, a park of the same name, which is home to numerous sports clubs as well as the stadium where the national soccer team plays. To the south, on the corner of Reykjavegur and Sigtún, stands **Ásmundarsafn,** another building of the Reykjavík

Museum of Art, dedicated to the sculptor Ásmundur Sveinsson, who set up his home and workshop here. The building design was inspired by the domes typical of Mediterranean architecture and the Egyptian pyramids. Next to the stadium, **Laugardalslaug** is the city's largest public geothermal pool, with numerous outdoor and indoor hot pools, two Olympic-size pools, and a children's area. In the middle of the park are a zoo (*Reykjavík Múlavegur 2, mu.is*) and the Grasagarður Reykjavíkur Botanical Garden, which transforms in summer into an oasis of greenery decked with the colors of thousands of species of flowers. At the center of the garden are a greenhouse, a pond, and numerous plant species typical of warmer climates, including grapes. Along the waterfront stretches the town of Laugarnes, just down from the new harbor. A hiking trail starts here, next to **Lista-safn Sigurjóns Ólafssonar,** an art gallery dedicated to sculptor Sigurjón Ólafsson, who died in 1982.

Ásmundarsafn ✉ Sigtún ☎ 411 6430 🕒 Open May–Sept. 10 a.m.–5 p.m., Oct.–April 1 p.m.–5 p.m.; closed Dec. 24, 25, 31, Jan. 1 $ $ **listasafnreykjavikur.is** • **Laugardalslaug** ✉ Sundlaugavegur 30 ☎ 411 5100 🕒 Open Mon.–Wed. and Fri. 6:30 a.m.–10 p.m., Thur. 6:30 a.m.–midnight, Sat.–Sun. 8 a.m.–10 p.m. $ $ **reykjavik.is** • **Listasafn Sigurjóns Ólafssonar** ✉ Laugarnestangi 70 ☎ 553 2906 🕒 Closed Dec.–Jan. (times of special exhibitions on the website) $ $ **www.lso.is**

A reindeer and two starlings at the city zoo in Laugardalur, Reykjavík.

From Skarfabakki pier in the north, you can catch a ferry for the 3-minute crossing to Viðey Island. **Viðeyjarstofa,** the house that once belonged to Skúli Magnússon, considered the "father" of Reykjavík, finished in 1755, still stands here and is part of the city's Museum of History. It was the first stone building erected in Iceland. Next door, at the rear of Viðeyjarkirkja church, is the archaeological excavation of an Augustinian monastery founded in 1225, which was to become one of the wealthiest and most influential institutions in the country.

Viðey Island is very popular with Reykjavík residents for outdoor activities and offers several options for walking (a detailed map of the island can be requested when buying a ferry ticket). On the southeastern side, the ruins of an old fishing village abandoned in the mid-20th century can still be found. You can also visit the building that housed the local school. On the western side of the island is the Imagine Peace Tower, an installation created by Yoko Ono in 2007 in memory of John Lennon. The monument projects a beam of light into the sky from October 9 to December 8, the dates of the former Beatles singer's birth and death. ■

Viðeyjarstofa ✉ Viðey ☎ 411 6360/519 5000 🕒 Open Sept. 1–May 14; ferries 1:15 p.m.–3:15 p.m. (weekends only) $ $ **reykjavikcitymuseum.is**

Viðey Island and the base of the Imagine Peace Tower, created by Yoko Ono.

THORRAMATUR

This Icelandic buffet for adventurous eaters will take you back to the ancient traditions of a diet that was meant to help people survive the winter.

Every year, the Friday between January 19 and 25 begins the month of *thorri*, according to the lunar calendar used in Iceland before the introduction of the Gregorian calendar. To mark the occasion, for just over a century various associations have held convivial evening celebrations that consist of a dinner with speeches, traditional songs, and most importantly, the celebration of Icelandic culinary history through the consumption of food that was once indispensable for surviving the last and most difficult part of winter, the so-called *thorramatur* (food of thorri). Here are some examples:

Blóðmör: "blood fat," black pudding made from lamb's blood, oatmeal and rye flour.
Bringukollur: "top of breast," fat extracted from the sheep's chest.
Flatbrauð: "flatbread," unleavened bread baked on the back of a pan.
Hákarl: fermented shark.
Hangikjöt: "hung meat," lamb meat smoked and then boiled.
Harðfiskur: stockfish, usually cod, haddock, or wolffish.
Hrútspungar: "mutton testicles," preserved in jellied buns.
Lundabaggi: "packed fillet," rolled sheep fat preserved in whey.
Lifrarpylsa: "liver sausage," composed of liver, oat, and rye flour.
Rófustappa: mashed turnips.
Rúgbrauð: rye bread, rather sweet.
Saltkjöt: salted lamb meat preserved in salt.
Súrhvalur: whale blubber preserved in whey.
Súr sviðasulta: "sour burnt jam," like Sviðasulta, but to preserve it better, it is dipped in whey. The flavor of Simmental (a breed of cattle) overlaps with the sour flavor of whey.
Svið: "singed," sheep's head, so called because the hairs are burned with a flame, then it's sawn in two and boiled.
Sviðasulta: "singed jelly," sheep's head, emptied of the brains, boiled for two hours until the meat comes off the bone; the mixture is then poured into a vessel and, as it cools, it turns into a kind of jelly.

These foods, especially those preserved in whey, are rarely eaten these days. Exceptions are stockfish, liver sausage, black pudding, flatbread, and smoked lamb. Some of these preparations, such as fermented shark, were once scarcely available, but now they are even readily available in supermarkets because of the interest they arouse for tourism.

NEARBY

Outside the historic center are suburbs and independent municipalities whose territory merges seamlessly with that of the capital into a single urban area. Here, too, there is no shortage of both cultural and natural attractions.

The open-air museum in Ábær.

Árbær

The neighborhood of Árbær, a suburb of Reykjavík, owes its name to an old farm that stood on the site. Today you can visit **Árbæjarsafn,** an open-air museum that is part of the city's Museum of History. It houses historic buildings transported here from various parts of the country and preserved with period interiors and furnishings. The museum illustrates the private and working lives of Icelanders, particularly during the 19th and 20th centuries. The highlight of the museum is Árbær Farm (a stately building made of peat, stone and wood that once served as a place for rest and refreshment for travelers), which was in a state of disrepair until it was renovated in 1957 and the land around it used as a museum. A short distance away, Elliðaárdalur is a valley completely surrounded by the urban sprawl of Reykjavík. A public park of dense wooded areas is intersected by

Árbæjarsafn ✉ Kistuhyl ☎ 411 6320 🕒 Open Sept.–May 1 p.m.–5 p.m., June–Aug. 10 a.m.–5 p.m.; closed Dec. 24–26, 31, Jan. 1, Good Friday, Easter $ $ **reykjavikcitymuseum.is**

the Elliðaár River, one of the most popular waterways for salmon fishing. Along it, there are a number of waterfalls and trails.

Kjalarnes

A hamlet of Reykjavík located on the peninsula north of the city across the bay, Kjalarnes is the setting of the capital region's only saga, the *Kjalnesinga saga* (see pp. 100–101). A short distance from the settlement stands a black church, Brautarholtskirkja. The existence of a place of worship at this location is mentioned in texts from as early as the 13th-century. In 1823, the church was rebuilt in peat, like the previous building. Entirely rebuilt in 1957, restoration began in 1987 to remodel it with the same characteristics as those of the oldest documented church. Inside, some valuable works can be found, including a painting of Christ in Gethsemane dating from the mid-19th century by a German painter; a red chasuble, the work of an Icelandic seamstress; a silver- and gold-plated, Gothic-style chalice; a wooden pulpit from the mid-17th century; and a marble baptismal font, purchased in the 1950s in Genoa by Hálfdán Bjarnason, who was Icelandic consul in Italy.

Útialtari

Since 2016, an association based in Kjalarnes has been working to create an outdoor shrine at Esjuberg Farm. It was here, according to the *Kjalnesinga saga*, that the first church in Iceland was built in the early ninth century. The shrine consists of a circular stone wall covered with grass, with openings on all four sides. In the center, there is a boulder that serves as an altar, above which a cross has been erected with motifs typical of Gaelic sacred art. As of 2021, the shrine, consecrated by the bishop of Iceland, Agnes Sigurðardóttir, can be reached from Route 1 by following the sign "Útialtari" along a turnoff for a few hundred yards.

Kópavogur

Although it is a separate municipality, Kópavogur is fully connected to the urban fabric of the capital. A natural history museum, **Náttúrufræðistofa Kópavogs,** which hosts exhibits on Icelandic flora and fauna, as well as an art museum, **Gerðarsafn – Listasafn Kópavogs,** can be visited. On the end of the Kársnes Peninsula, **Sky Lagoon,** a spa located on the seashore, offers swimming in an infinity pool and unmatched views of the Reykjanes Peninsula.

(continued on p. 102)

Náttúrufræðistofa Kópavogs ✉ Hamraborg 6a ☎ 441 7200 🕒 Closed Mon. $ Free admission **natkop.kopavogur.is** • **Gerðarsafn – Listasafn Kópavogs** ✉ Hamraborg 4 ☎ 441 7600 🕒 Open daily 10 a.m.–5 p.m. $ $ **gerdarsafn.kopavogur.is** • **Sky Lagoon** ✉ Vesturvör 44 ☎ 527 6800 $ $$$ **www.skylagoon.com**

THE *KJALNESINGA SAGA*

Despite being considered the island's first permanent settlement, Reykjavík does not appear much in ancient sources, and the only saga set in the area is a late text that mixes vague historical memories with late medieval literary taste.

Mount Esja inspired the name of a character of the saga.

The only saga that takes place in the capital area of Reykjavík is the *Kjlanesinga saga* (*Saga of the Inhabitants of Kjalarnes*), also called *Búa saga Andríðssonar* (*Saga of Búi Andríðsson*). It is derived from a tradition dating back to the second half of the 15th century and is one of a group of sagas sometimes referred to as "post-classical" sagas, which mix elements and motifs typical of Icelandic sagas (such as local feuds and fratricide) with those of chivalric romances (magic, supernatural creatures, and impossible quests for the main hero).

The story goes that Helgi bjóla was a powerful lord who lived in Hof on the Kjalarnes Peninsula. He was the son-in-law of the famous Ingólfur Arnarson and had two sons, Thorgrímur and Arngrímur. Helgi is presented as a heathen who was not particularly devout; for this reason an Irish bishop named Patrick suggested that one of his relatives, Örlygut, move to Iceland to live with him.

Having gone to live near Helgi, Örlygut erected a church on Helgi's land. A number of immigrants from Ireland then arrived in Iceland, including a woman named Esja and two men names Kolli and Andríður, who became close friends with Helgi's sons. Helgi then donated land to Andríður, who built the house where he lived with his wife.

When Helgi died, he was succeeded by his son Thorgrímur, who was extremely overbearing as well as devoted to pagan gods, to the point of having a large temple built. Andríður had a son, Búi, who was raised by Esja, who had settled on the farm that had belonged to Örlygur, who was elderly and heirless. Búi was also a Christian and refused Thorgrímur's demand that he pay homage to pagan gods. When Thorgrímur and his son Thorsteinn tried to kill him, Búi defended himself with a simple slingshot, receiving magical help from his adoptive mother Esja, who caused an impenetrable darkness to fall, allowing him to emerge from the ambush unscathed. Búi retaliated by killing Thorsteinn and setting fire to the pagan temple. Thorgrímur, after failing to capture Búi, who had been hidden by Esja in a cave, was overcome with rage and killed his father Andríður.

Considering the affront over, Búi returned to society to ask for the hand of Ólöf, a beautiful girl and daughter of Kolli. The girl was claimed by another boy, Kolfinnur, who challenged Búi to a duel. Esja again used magic to help Búi, offering him an impenetrable shirt and a dagger, which helped him prevail. Búi took the girl with him to the cave, but Esja, fearing that her adoptive son would be killed in revenge, urged him to flee abroad.

When Búi arrived in Norway, the king, who had heard about the fire Búi had set in the pagan temple, charged him with an impossible mission: to steal a magic chessboard from the mountain king Dofri, a giant. Búi was taken in by the giantess Fríður, Dofri's daughter, a beautiful girl who helped him and spent several nights with him. Before Búi left again, Fríður revealed to him that she was expecting a child and asked him to swear that if it was born a boy, Búi would take care of it. Returning to the king with the chessboard, he was again tested in a fight with a "blue man." He successfully defeated him.

Back in Iceland, Búi discovered that Ólöf had given birth to a girl, his daughter, but also that his rival in love, Kolfinnur, had kidnapped her. Kolfinnur ambushed him, but Búi managed to kill him. He refused to take Ólöf back, however, marrying Thorgrímur's daughter Helga instead. Years later, a young boy presented himself to Búi. His name was Jökull, son of the giantess Fríður, and he demanded to be recognized as Búi's son, but Búi refused. The situation came to a head when the two challenged each other to a duel; Jökull killed his father, then escaped. Búi was buried, and his descendants are considered some of the noblest in the country.

Garðabær

The municipality of Garðabær includes the Álftanes Peninsula, where **Bessastaðir,** the residence of the president of the republic, is located (*visit by reservation only and for groups, 540 4400, forseti@forseti.is*). The main building dates from the mid-18th century, but Bessastaðir has been a center of power since the medieval period, first as the seat of local lords, then as the residence of representatives of the Danish government. It was unsuccessfully attacked by Saracen pirates in the 17th century. It became the presidential residence in 1941. On the south side of the peninsula, Garðakirkja church, built in the mid-20th century, stands on the foundations of a medieval religious building. In the heart of Garðabær, **Hönnunarsafn Íslands** (Museum of Design and Applied Arts) is dedicated to the protection and study of Icelandic design, and a small park next to the modern Vídalínskirkja church houses the archaeological excavation of a ninth-century longhouse, Hofsstaðir, the second largest ever found. The site is always open and can be visited for free.

Hafnarfjörður

This pretty municipality is particularly known for its traditional architecture, which is more conspicuously present than in downtown Reykjavík, where it is often overshadowed by more modern buildings. Two museums are of particular interest: **Hafnarborg,** a building that houses the local art museum, and **Byggðasafn Hafnarfjarðar** (Hafnarfjörður Museum of Local History). The public park, Hellisgerð, is located in the heart of the town. According to local folklore, a number of elves live hidden in it. ■

Hönnunarsafn Íslands ✉ Gardatorg 1 ☎ 512 1525/512 1526 🕒 Open Tues.–Sun. noon–5 p.m. $ $ **www.honnunarsafn.is** • **Hafnarborg** ✉ Strandgata 34 ☎ 585 5790 🕒 Open Mon, Wed.–Sun. noon–5 p.m. $ Free admission **hafnarborg.is** • **Byggðasafn Hafnarfjarðar** ✉ Vesturgata 6 ☎ 585 5780 🕒 Open June–Aug. daily 11 a.m.–5 p.m., Sept.–May Sat.–Sun. 11 a.m.–5 p.m. $ Free admission **byggdasafnid.is**

Hafnarfjörður at sunset.

WALKING & DRIVING ROUTE: NEARBY REYKJAVÍK

One of the advantages of Iceland's capital city is that it is surrounded by natural landscapes of great beauty, with hiking trails, photographic points of interest, and views of unparalleled magnificence.

Sunset from the small lighthouse at Garður.

This route can be done over several days, depending on how much time you want to devote to each individual destination. As you head down Route 41 toward the airport, take the exit toward Kaldársel to reach Route 410. After 1.5 miles (2.5 km), you pass two roundabouts and then reach an intersection: turn right and follow the dirt road to the parking lot on the shore of **Hvaleyrarvatn** 1, considered one of the most beautiful lakes near the capital. Local lore claims it was inhabited by a water demon, Nykur, who allegedly killed a girl from a nearby farm by dragging her into its depths. You can stop briefly to admire the scenery, take a walk on the paths that run along the lake, or climb the surrounding hills.

Returning by car to the same road, take the first exit at the roundabout and continue for about 1.8 miles (3 km) until you reach the intersection with Route 408. Turn left and you will come to the parking lot next to **Maríuhellar caves** 2, a protected area where you can see the "tubes" that were formed by lava flowing through a now solidified vault. Once the lava had flowed out, the tubes were left empty and became tunnels. The caves were used in the past as shelters for livestock.

Continue then on the 408 for 2.2 miles (3.5 km) to the parking lot at **Búrfellsgjá** ❸. From here you can take the hiking trail along the valley formed by lava flow. Following the channel through the rock, take the easy path that runs for 1.5 miles (2.5 km) past lava formations and the dry stone walls of the former sheep sorting pen, Gjáarrétt. The last section of the trail runs slightly uphill and leads to the top of the volcanic cone of **Búrfell** ❹, where you get an incredible view of the Reykjanes Peninsula. Formed as a result of an eruption

See also map p. 76
➤ Hvaleyrarvatn
22 miles (35 km)
1–2 days
➤ Bjarnarvatn

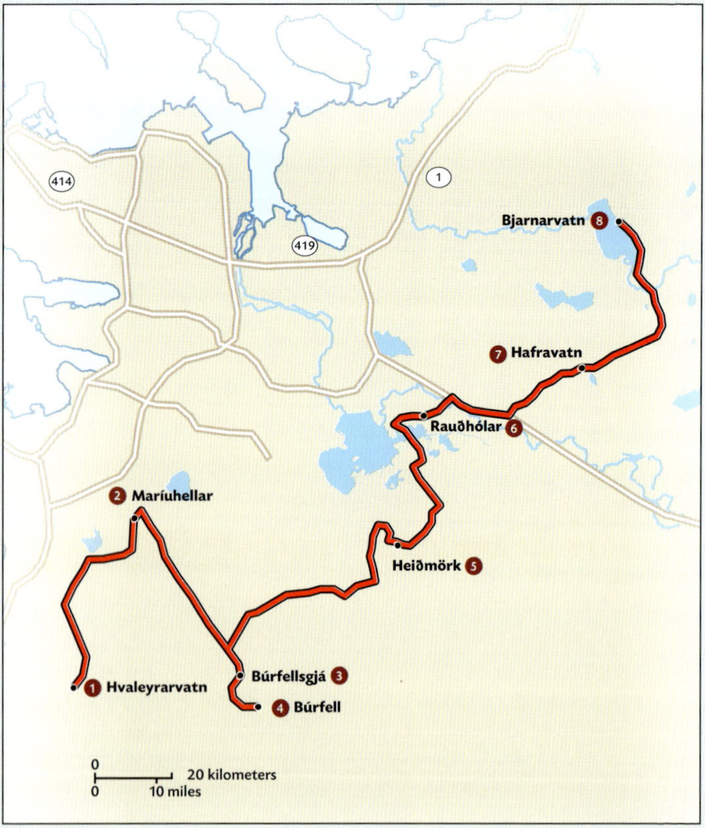

some 8000 years ago, the volcano reaches a height of 262 feet (80 m) and a width of 196 feet (60 m). It is the northernmost point of the Krýsuvík volcanic system, which cuts diagonally across the peninsula.

After returning to the parking lot, drive down the 408 until you cross **Heiðmörk Reserve** ❺. Opened in 1950, it covers an area of 7,900 acres (3,200 ha) and includes more than 4 million trees of 26 species and more than 150 species of plants and wildflowers. There are numerous rest stops, picnic areas, and forest trails.

Continue on until you reach Route 1, which skirts the **Rauðhólar** ❻, "Red Hills," which owe their name to the oxidation of the iron in the soil. They are the remains of an aggregate of pseudocraters formed 5000 years ago by the flow of lava over the waters of a lake. At one time there were more than a hundred craters, then the area was used as a quarry to supply gravel used in various construction projects, including Reykjavík Airport.

NOT TO BE MISSED:

Hvaleyrarvatn lake • Búrfell crater • Heiðmörk Reserve • Hafravatn lake

When you reach Route 1, turn right and continue for 0.9 miles (1.5 km). Turn right onto 431 and follow it for 2.8 miles (4.5 km). Turn left on dirt road 8045 to the shores of **Hafravatn lake** ❼, also believed to be the home of a water demon. You can stroll around the lake, or take the 3-mile (5 km) circuit from the southeastern shore up the hills to **Bjarnarvatn** ❽, a lake set on a plateau overlooking the Esja mountain range.

The Rauðhólar, red-colored lava rock hills.

REYKJANES PENINSULA

Although often ignored by visitors arriving and departing from Keflavík International Airport, on its western end, the Reykjanes Peninsula offers some of the most beautiful scenery in all of Iceland. It is also home to the UNESCO-protected Reykjanes Geopark, one of two in the country.

The infernal spectacle of Fagradalsfjall.

The Reykjanes Peninsula, which is shaped like an inverted boot, is a continuation of the Mid-Atlantic Ridge and is thus divided between the North American and Eurasian tectonic plates. Here the ridge dips into the ocean and acts as an extension of the Icelandic landscape typical of the central highlands, traversed by geological faults and dotted with volcanic systems.

Unlike other coastal areas of the country, which are geologically much older and where centuries have allowed human colonization, Reykjanes is a relatively young and inhospitable land, constantly reshaped by volcanic eruptions, such as the one that began in March 2021 at Fagradalsfjall. Lava fields where water percolates into the depths, becoming inaccessible to plant or animal life, solfataras, volcanoes, and moors where gray moss dominates: these are the most common sights. However, even here man has managed to carve out space, and all along the perimeter little villages have sprung up.

The entire peninsula is furrowed by volcanic systems, arranged in parallel from northeast to southwest. Along them, fissures open from time to time from which effusive eruptions gush, as happened between March and September 2021, and in August 2022. Because of tectonic activity and volcanism, earthquakes in this area are frequent, although most are not felt by people.

Kleifarvatn

Kleifarvatn is a lake reminiscent of the typical landscapes of the central highlands. Formed by the filling of a geological fault, it is one of Iceland's deepest lakes (nearly 330 ft, 100 m). Surrounded by barren, wild mountains and bordered by long stretches of black beaches, it is a popular excursion and hiking destination for residents of the capital. Legend has it that a monster lurks in its depths. The lake also gives its name to a novel by mystery writer Arnaldur Indriðason *Kleifarvatn*, published in English in 2004 as *The Draining Lake.*

Krýsuvík

The Krýsuvík area is most famous for the Seltún sulfataras. A short distance away, on the opposite side of the road, is Grænavatn (Green Lake), the name coming from its sulfur-rich waters. At 138 feet (42 m) deep, it is a crater of volcanic origin. The Krýsuvíkurkirkja church, on a knoll south of the sulfataras, has a troubled history. Built in the 19th century, it was remodeled again and again until 2010, when a boy set it on fire with a can of gasoline. The church was rebuilt by students from Hafnarfjörður Technical College according to its original appearance: wood covered with pitch.

Bláa Lónið spa complex, also known as the Blue Lagoon.

Fagradalsfjall

Interest in this site is mainly due to the eruption that occurred in 2021. After weeks of earthquakes (more than 50,000 tremors were recorded), a rift along one of the volcanic systems on the Reykjanes Peninsula opened in a small valley between the mountains at the hill known as Fagradalsfjall. An eruption began on March 19 and continued until September. Its mostly effusive nature (slow lava flow from the rifts) makes it easily accessible to visitors. The main risk is the occasional emission of toxic gases, which are monitored by the Civil Defense. Another smaller eruption occurred in August 2022. The site is of great interest because visitors can observe the young lava rocks and newly formed parts of the land. When it rains, the water that seeps through the rocks of the crust down to the warmer layer below evaporates, rising to the surface and creating an otherworldly atmosphere. The area is accessible on foot via trails of medium difficulty that start from the parking lots next to the road.

Grindavík

Grindavík is a small town with a thousand-year history. Founded in 934 AD, it was the scene of a pirate raid in the 17th century. Recently, it has become a thriving center, with its economy focused on fishing and tourism. It is also within easy reach of the site of the volcanic eruption at Fagradalsfjall and the famous Bláa Lónið (Blue Lagoon) spa, which sits on the lava field north of Grindavík and is one of Iceland's most popular attractions. It developed by accident following the construction of the Svartsengi geothermal plant, which produces electricity by harnessing the energy of water and steam extracted from underground at a very high temperature and pressure. The recovered water cannot be used for domestic purposes because of its high mineral content and deposits, and is therefore dispersed into the surrounding lava field. Over time, the deposits accumulate in the fissures of the lava, blocking them and causing the water to surface. In 1981, a man with psoriasis discovered that soaking in the pools that had formed relieved his

EXPERIENCE: Unique Snacks

In any supermarket or gas station in Iceland, you will find unique snacks. These typical snacks are not sweets, but rather various types of dried fish such as cod, haddock, or wolffish packaged in bags similar to those used for candies. They can contain long fillets or smaller pieces. The best way to enjoy these traditional Icelandic delicacies is to eat them with the local salted butter, *smjör*. The strong taste of the fish is considerably muted by the butter for an irresistible flavor.

The Gunnuhver geothermal area.

symptoms, and the site soon became famous. The spa opened in 1987. Scientific studies have proven the beneficial value of the waters for psoriasis, and as of 2016, admission for Icelanders with the condition is free.

Gunnuhver

The Gunnuhver geothermal area lies near a power plant. It has boiling hot springs; water perpetually sprays and bubbles in the open crater in the ground.

According to one legend, the name Gunnuhver (Gunna Hot Springs) comes from the presence of the ghost of a woman named Guðrún Önundardóttir, also known as Gunna, who allegedly lived in the employ of a lawyer, Vilhjálmur Jónsson, who took away her only possession, a cooking pot, when she could no longer pay her rent. This drove the woman mad and she died. While the grave was being dug for burial, the lawyer's lifeless body was found, swollen and with broken bones. It was thought to be Gunna's revenge. Unexplained events began to happen, and many of the inhabitants went mad or died after claiming to have seen the woman's ghost. Reverend Eiríkur of Vogsósar offered a solution: he gave the villagers a ball of yarn and explained that the ghost would have to chase to rewind the

The NATO Base

During World War II, Iceland was occupied first by the British and then by the U.S. military. It served as a strategic and logistical base in the Atlantic, midway between the United States and Europe. When the war ended, the Americans were granted permission to maintain the base, and in 1949 the Icelandic parliament ratified the country's membership in NATO. The decision was highly contested and met with protests from a large segment of the population, which was very attached to the idea of neutrality. Today, the integrity of Iceland's airspace is guaranteed by the other NATO countries, which take turns fulfilling this role.

string. The ball of yarn was unwound into a solfatara and once the ghost chased it in, the curse ceased.

Southwest of Gunnuhver, beyond the hill where the Reykjanesviti lighthouse stands, stretches the Valahnúkar cliffs. Sea stacks emerge from the waves that change color with the seasons. The stack off the coast, Karl, is what remains of an ancient volcanic eruption and is home to colonies of seabirds. Eldey Island, also born of an underwater eruption, can be seen on the horizon in the distance. The last two known examples of great auk lived there, the only species of the genus *Pinguinus* that survived until the modern age and then disappeared around the mid-19th century. Similar to penguins, great auks inhabited the North Atlantic and reached 33 inches (85 cm) tall. They were a source of food and feathers and were thus hunted to extinction. A life-size statue of this animal can be found on the seashore at Valahnúkar Reef.

Farther down the coast, closer to Grindavík, a short path next to the road leads to Brimketill, a saltwater pool naturally carved by the waves. Legend has it that a troll woman named Oddný bathed in it. The natural pool is visible from an observation platform on top of the cliff above it, which can be reached from the parking lot adjacent to the road.

The Víkingaheimar (Viking World) in Keflavík.

Suðurnesjabær

This scattered municipality includes the settlements of Garður and Sandvík. The former is located on the northern end of the peninsula. Just outside the town, heading north, you can find a prime spot for watching the Northern Lights. Sometimes you can also spot whales a short distance from the coast, attracted by the plankton that is stirred up by the combination of gulf and ocean currents. Two lighthouses stand out over the sea: a smaller one (41 ft, 12.5 m) from 1897, closer to the ocean, and a taller one (92 ft, 28 m), farther back from the beach, built in 1944.

South of the small settlement of Sandvík stands the Hvalsneskirkja church, built of basalt stone with a wooden tower painted yellow, red, and green, consecrated in 1887. It holds the tombstone of Steinunn Hallgrímsdóttir, daughter of Iceland's greatest poet from the Baroque era, psalmist Hallgrímur Pétursson, who was pastor at the church. Lost for centuries, the tombstone was rediscovered in 1964.

Reykjanesbær

Formed from the merging of the two adjacent towns of Keflavík and Njarðvík, Reykjanesbær is the municipality with the largest population after the capital.

Keilir Mountain, inland on Reykjanes Peninsula.

Although not usually frequented by tourists, it offers several points of interest that warrant a visit. **Rokksafn Íslands** (Icelandic Rock Museum) tells the story of Icelandic music from 1830 on. You can listen to local music on provided tablets and try out musical instruments. The **Víkingaheimar** (Viking World) houses a faithful reproduction of a Norse ship from the medieval period, *Íslendingur* ("the Icelander"), which can be boarded. A permanent exhibit is devoted to the exploration of the American continent by Scandinavian peoples in the medieval period. A short distance away is the local history museum, **Byggðasafn Reykjanesbæjar – Stekkjarkot,** located in the reconstruction of a small peat cottage like those that were used as homes. Its special feature is to show the living conditions of the lower classes of the population. On the other hand, **Slökkviliðsminjasafn Íslands** (Icelandic Fire

Rokksafn Íslands ✉ Hjallavegur 2 ☎ 420 1030 ⏲ Closed Dec. 24, 25, 31, Jan. 1, Good Friday, Easter $ $ **www.rokksafn.is** • **Víkingaheimar** ✉ Víkingabraut 1 ☎ 422 2000 ⏲ Open daily $ $ **www.vikingworld.is** • **Byggðasafn Reykjanesbæjar – Stekkjarkot** ☎ 865 6160 ⏲ Open by appointment **sofn.reykjanesbaer.is** • **Slökkviliðsminjasafn Íslands** ✉ Njarðbraut 3 ☎ 899 0557 ⏲ Reservations can be made by phone

Museum) is dedicated to the history of firefighting in a country where, due to the extensive use of wood for construction in past centuries, the risk of fire was very high.

Hafnir, a hamlet of Reykjanesbær, is a small town overlooking the wild Kirkjuvogur Bay. In addition to the pretty local black church, Kirkjuvogskirkja, rebuilt in the late 20th century, an archaeological excavation in the early 2000s uncovered a building believed to have been the home of Herjólfur Bárðarson. Herjólfur is mentioned in the *Landnámabók* as the sworn brother of the first settler Ingólfur Árnarson, who is said to have granted him land here. The latter was the grandfather of the eponymous Herjólfur Bárðarson who moved to Greenland (along with Erik the Red), who in turn was the father of Bjarni Herjólfsson, who according to the *Grænlendinga saga* was the first European to sight the American continent following a storm that had blown him off course on a voyage to Greenland.

Vatnsleysuströnd

The northern coast of the Reykjanes Peninsula is largely formed by extensive lava fronts that have reached the sea as a result of eruptions that occurred in the volcanic systems. Along the semicircular road 420, off Route 41 that connects the airport to the capital, one encounters **Kálfatjarnarkirkja,** a church consecrated in 1893 on a site that had housed a church since at least the 13th century. When it was built, it was the largest of Iceland's churches, excluding Reykjavík, a testament to the wealth of the thriving local fishing industry. Inside, an altarpiece depicts the Resurrection.

About 2 miles (3 km) south of the church, in the middle of the lava field, stands **Staðarborg,** a circular dry stone wall, 6.5 feet (2 m) high and 26 feet (8 m) in diameter. Several centuries old, it was probably used as a cattle pen. Folk legend, however, tells of a sharecropper named Guðmundur who wanted to build a great structure, but when the priest in Kálfatjarnarkirkja realized that the building would be taller than the church, he ordered him to stop.

Trölladyngja & Grænadyngja

In the heart of the Reykjanes Peninsula lies an area where the landscapes mirror those of the central highlands. The two groups of hills, Trölladyngja and Grænadyngja, were formed as a result of volcanic eruptions that occurred below the ice cap that covered the region toward the end of the last ice age.

They are surrounded by geothermal areas and, in addition to the views they offer of the entire peninsula, are famous for their brilliant colors (shades of green, ochre, and red) due to the composition of the soils and rocks. The area can be reached from Djúpavatn lake, along dirt road 428. A parking lot is present near the northern shore. The trail to visit the site is of medium difficulty and about 6 miles (10 km) long. ■

Geysers and waterfalls, farms and towns, volcanoes and islands: here you'll find everything that makes Iceland so unique

THE SOUTH

The autumn colors make Thingvellir National Park even more striking. The park has been protected as a heritage site since 2004.

THE SOUTH

Its proximity to the capital has helped make this the most visited region, but it is truly rich in history and natural wonders, such as the UNESCO site of Thingvellir, volcanoes, glaciers, the must-see Strokkur geyser, and the Vestmannaeyjar archipelago.

The *Landnámabók* (*Book of Colonizations*) calls the Southern region (Suðurland) "the most flourishing in all Iceland because of its resources and because of the lords who lived there, both the learned and uneducated." It consists of a vast area surrounded by mountains, except in its southern half, which is instead lapped by the ocean. Due to its geography, it is the only region where roads crisscross in multiple directions, intersecting each other. Over the years, it has become the most heavily visited region, by virtue of its cultural and scenic wealth,

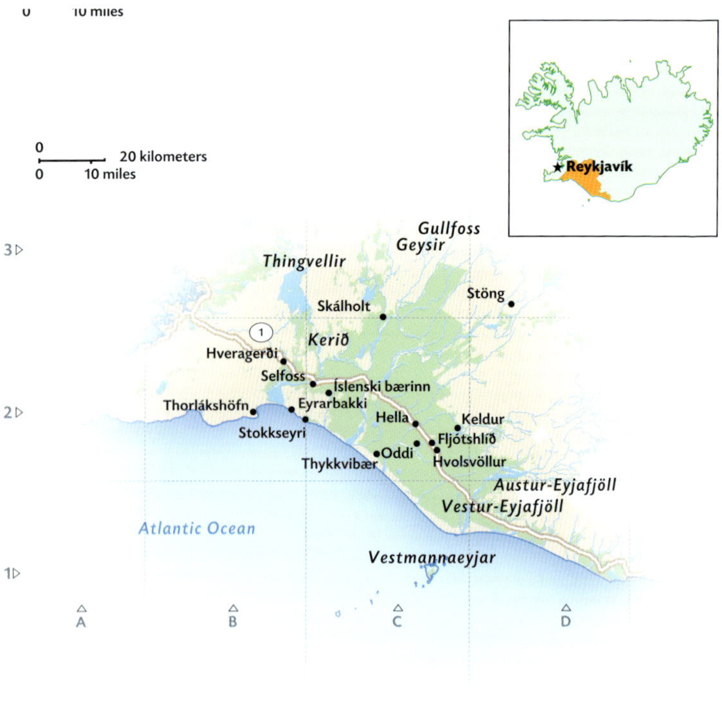

but some areas have suffered from these high concentrations of people. However, most tourists who visit the area don't stay long, exploring only a few hot destinations, such as the UNESCO site of Thingvellir Valley, the southern waterfalls, and the Geysir area.

In reality, the region is peppered with many points of interest that can easily be incorporated into your itinerary. For example, Selfoss, the region's primary town, is gaining popularity for its downtown area, created from the ground up as a faithful reconstruction of historic buildings dating to the 19th and 20th centuries that had been destroyed. Moving to the southern coast, the small towns of Eyrarbakki and Stokkseyri are home to interesting museums of local culture and are located next to Friðland í Flóa, one of the country's most important bird sanctuaries.

In the heart of the region, Iceland's first bishopric, Skálholt, was founded in 1056. This would remain, for centuries, a kind of de facto capital of the country. There is also no shortage of hot springs, such as those at Laugarvatn, Flúðir, or Seljavallalaug, and there are numerous businesses producing vegetables and berries in hydroponic greenhouses, some of which can be visited, like those at Friðheimar. In addition, there are sites of great historical significance. Notable among these are Thjóðveldisbærinn, or the reconstruction of a farm from the Free State period (930–1264), the peat houses of Keldur, and the caves of Hella.

NOT TO BE MISSED:

Downtown Selfoss 133–134

The village of Eyrarbakki and its local history museum 141–142

The medieval farm of Stöng 125

Keldur peat houses 135–136

LAVA Centre in Hvolsvöllur 136

The museum in Skógar 140

Seljalandsfoss & Skógafoss waterfalls 138–140

The Golden Circle 126–128

Another point of interest is the Eyjafjöll mountain range. Here, numerous waterfalls, such as Seljalandsfoss and Skógafoss, plummet from crags that once formed steep cliffs. Also worth mentioning are the Anthropological Museum in Skógar, one of the most famous and popular in Iceland, and LAVA in Hvolsvöllur, a museum about volcanoes.

Lastly, from the pier at Landeyjahöfn, you can get to the Vestmannaeyjar archipelago, a series of islands arranged along the arc of an underwater volcanic system, created by the emergence of lava from ancient and recent eruptions. The main island, the only inhabited one, houses museums devoted to local culture, as well as a sanctuary for belugas, and it is home to one of the most important music festivals of the year: Thjóðhátíð. ■

INLAND

The inner part of the region contains some of the country's most important and popular destinations, more specifically, the iconic destinations of the Golden Circle. However, it would be a mistake to believe that these destinations are all that the inland area has to offer.

The Öxará River flows through Almannagjá Gorge in Thingvellir National Park at sunset.

The area farthest from the sea includes vast spaces such as Thingvallasveit, around Thingvallavatn lake; Grímsnes, between the Sogið and Brúará rivers; Laugardalur, farther north, where the village of Laugarvatn and its hot springs are located; and Biskupstungur, a vast area between the Brúará and Hvítá rivers, where the famous Strokkur geyser is located. Unlike in other regions of the country where one main road traverses a strip of land lying between mountains and the sea, the South is mainly flat with a few hills.

Thingvellir

It is hard to overstate the importance of Thingvellir, a national park and UNESCO site of both historical and ecological value. It is a sort of spiritual heartland for the Icelandic nation. In 930 AD, at the end of the age of colonization (which began around 870 AD), Icelanders founded their general assembly, the Althingi. The story of its founding is recounted in the *Íslendingabók* by Ari Thorgilsson the Wise (12th century). According to the story, the owner of the area was found guilty of murder and executed. His estates became public property and were chosen to host the general assembly because of their relative accessibility from anywhere in the country. The journey, for those coming from the Northeast, could take more than two weeks, and was done through the interior highlands, along trails such as the Sprengisandur. The area provided the necessary resources during gathering, such as birch forests for wood fuel as well as abundant pastures for horses.

Throughout the medieval period, the ancient Althingi held a distinct centrality in the lives of Icelanders: numerous pivotal episodes in the sagas take place here, but perhaps the most significant was the conversion to Christianity, which occurred only 70 years after the assembly was founded. The highest legal authority of the time, the jurisconsult Thorgeir Ljósvetningagoði, devised a solution to the difficulty of coexistence between pagans and Christians at the assembly's instruction, suggesting that the whole country convert to Christianity so that they would all be united under the banner of a single religion.

The modern Icelandic parliament bears the same name and is often referred to as "the oldest parliament in the world," despite the fact that there is no real historical continuity between the two institutions. The present-day Althingi is a modern single-chamber parliament founded under grant from the Danish monarchy in 1844, whereas the ancient version, to modern eyes, would probably have seemed more like a big music festival.

At the time of its inception, the assembly was held for two weeks every July, and Icelanders from all corners of the country traveled there, pitching tents in the area overlooking the Almannagjá Gorge. Merchants, minstrels and street performers, artisans, nobles, and ordinary people would all gather there. This was the centerpiece of Icelandic cultural life. It was an opportunity to cement or forge alliances and arrange marriages. Against this backdrop, an assembly of powerful oligarchs, the Lögrétta, debated the passage of new laws and issued rulings on the most complex legal cases. After 1262, with the annexation to Norway, the Althingi

Thingvellir – Visitor Center ☎ 482 2660 🕘 Open May–Oct. 9 a.m.–6 p.m., Nov.–May 9 a.m–5 p.m. (reduced hours Dec. 24, 25, 31, Jan. 1) **www.thingvellir.is**

essentially became a supreme court without legislative authority, only to be finally dissolved in 1798.

For much of its history, this institution maintained great symbolic importance for the Icelandic people. The year of its founding is considered the birth year of the nation, and the 1944 declaration of independence was made here because of its historical importance.

Geologically, the park is one of the best spots to get a close-up view of the place where the North American and Eurasian tectonic plates meet. The Almannagjá Fissure is often reported to be the point of separation between the two tectonic plates. You can walk down inside of it on trails; the entire length is about 5 miles (8 km) long (only part is marked by trails), and its walls reach a max height of about 131 feet (40 m). But in reality, this canyon is only a small fracture on the rim of the North American plate, marking its boundary. The Eurasian continental plate, on the other hand, is marked by the Hrafnagjá fissure, about 3 miles (5 km) to the east, across a plain, which is the tectonic trench between the continental plates. The two plates are separating at an average of 0.4 inch per year. The plain is crisscrossed by numerous fissures, some of them filled with water, where visitors can snorkel in the crystal clear water.

The easiest way to visit Thingvellir is tostop at the park visitor center, located at the Hakið overlook. In addition to the tourist information point, the center also houses an exhibition on the history and geology of the place. The overlook offers a view of the entire

In Thingvellir National Park, you can dive in the waters of the Silfra fissure, along the tectonic trench.

valley and Thingvallavatn lake farther south. From here, you can descend into the Almannagjá fissure and follow the trail northward. At some point you will cross Lögberg, a rocky outcrop that is believed to have been the point from which the jurists delivered their judgments back when the assembly was active. The exact spot is marked by a flagpole in front of a small wooden platform. Not far away on the west side of the canyon is Drekkingarhylur, a pleasant little pool fed by small waterfalls flowing off the rock face. In it, women convicted of adultery were drowned during the modern age, up to the early 18th century.

Farther north, at parking lot P2, extends to a path leading to the **Öxarárfoss** waterfall, which is more than 39 feet (12 m) high. In the field in front of the canyon stands the **Thingvallakirkja** church, built in 1859, next to which is a building designed by architect Guðjón Samúelsson, inspired by old peat houses and built in 1930 to serve as a rectory. Today, it is the summer residence for the prime minister and houses the headquarters of the National Park Steering Committee. Opposite it is a small cemetery, **Thjóðargrafreiturinn** (National Cemetery), which was the burial place for important Icelandic figures. The remains of the Romantic poet Jónas Hallgrímsson were moved there in 1946, but no one has been buried there since.

Geysir

Located in the Haukadalur valley, the Geysir site is named after an eruptive hot spring, and is in fact where the word "geyser," as it's called in many other languages, comes from. The Icelandic term for geyser is *goshver*, literally "eruptive hot spring," whereas Geysir is the proper name for one of the springs in this area, and it means "gusher."

Geysers occur due to the interaction between water and underground magma. Water seeping into the ground reaches water tables deep underground, where they collect in chambers. The heat there brings the water to a boil, causing the pressure to rise until it escapes in an explosion of liquid and steam we can see on the surface.

Geysers are not permanent phenomena, because mineral deposits, underground landslides, and other geological events can alter the subsoil conditions and interrupt the occurence of geysers. Historically, in fact, geyser activity has fluctuated: earthquakes usually seem to awaken eruptive springs for some time, then they might wane until the next earthquake. Today, the Geysir geyser is dormant; only a pool of hot spring water remains. In the 1980s, the vent was cleared and eruptions resumed, but only if stimulated with soap. Occasionally, the jet reached heights of more than 328 feet (100 m). This practice was discontinued for environmental reasons in the 1990s.

About a two-minute walk from Geysir is the **Strokkur** ("Churning") geyser, which erupts with jets up to 98 feet (30 m) high and more frequently (every 5–10 min). The area is freely

Strokkur geyser.

accessible and has convenient trails for exploring. In addition to the Strokkur geyser, there are other springs and several fumaroles in the area. The visitor center is located on the opposite side of the road from the geothermal site..

Gullfoss

One of Iceland's most famous waterfalls is Gullfoss (Golden Waterfall), which plummets 104 feet (32 m) over two drops into a canyon with walls 230 feet (70 m) tall. The canyon is carved by the Hvítá River, which springs from Langjökull glacier. Popular legend has it that the waterfall was saved due to the tenacity of a local woman, Sigríður Tómasdóttir, whose activism allegedly dissuaded a foreign company from building a dam on the river to generate electricity. In reality, the project had already been abandoned for lack of funds, and the woman, who at the time owned the land on which the waterfall stands, had sold her share to a relative, who in turn sold it to the state in 1940. The woman feared that the state had decided to exploit the river's energy, so she tried to have her sale recognized as invalid, which would obstruct any work, but her attempt failed. The state, in any case, did not proceed with the work, and the waterfall was declared protected in 1979. Today, a plaque depicting Sigríður stands beside the lower path, which leads to the waterfall. It is also possible to see it from the overlook above, which can be reached from the tourist center

Gullfoss – Information Center Open June–Aug. 9 a.m.–9 p.m., Sept.–May 9 a.m.–6:30 p.m. • **Skálholt** 486 8801 Church open daily 9–6 p.m. **www.skalholt.is**

on the upper path, connected to the lower one by a staircase.

Skálholt

For the first few years following the conversion to Christianity in the year 1000, Iceland's bishops were foreigners. In 1056, Ísleifur Gissurarson, who had studied in Germany and been appointed bishop by the archbishop of Bremen, founded the country's first bishopric on his family estate in Skálholt. The seat of the diocese quickly became one of the most important centers of power in the country and remained so for more than seven centuries, becoming a kind of de facto capital (the official one was Copenhagen). Throughout its history, the Skálholt diocese was associated with a Latin school, which, along with its counterpart in the diocese of Hólar in the north, was the country's leading educational and cultural institution. Skálholt lost its prominence in 1784, when its buildings, except the church, were destroyed by a major earthquake and the institutions were moved to the Reykjavík area, where they would later remain.

Some of Skálholt's bishops were among the most prominent figures of their respective eras, such as Thorlákur Thórhallsson (1133–1193), an important reformer and founder of the Kirkjubær women's convent. He would later become the country's patron saint. Here, around the middle of the 16th century, the first chapters of the Protestant Reformation were enacted, forcibly introduced by emissaries of the Danish crown, which had acquired Iceland in

Gullfoss, the golden waterfall.

1380. It was here that the cleric Oddur Gottskálksson translated the New Testament into Icelandic while hiding in a stable. It was published in 1540, providing the basis for the full translation of the Bible that would be published a few decades later, with the approval of the crown.

At Skálholt, Bishop Klængur Thorsteinsson erected a cathedral made of wood (imported from mainland Scandinavia) after its consecration in 1152. This was the largest building in the country (even larger than the present cathedral) until it burned down in a fire in 1309 after being struck by lightning. Other smaller cathedrals were built in later centuries; the last was the one built in 1650 by Bishop Brynjólfur Sveinsson (depicted on the 1,000 kroner bill), which was preserved until 1802, when it was demolished and replaced with a small parish church. An archaeological excavation carried out between 1954 and 1958 reconstructed its appearance. A model of it can be seen at the National Museum of Iceland in Reykjavík.

The present church was consecrated in 1963. The cornerstone was laid on July 1, 1956, to mark the 900th anniversary of Bishop Ísleifur Gissurarson's consecration. The crypt contains several tombstones of Icelandic bishops from different eras, as well as the sarcophagus of Bishop Páll Jónsson (1155–1211), found during excavations. Numerous furnishings and church vestments that belonged to the bishopric are now on display at the National Museum of Iceland. The church is now used by both the Protestant and Catholic communities, for whom Skálholt is a pilgrimage site. Not far from the church is a monument erected in memory of Iceland's last Catholic bishop, Jón Arason, who was beheaded there on November 7, 1550.

The archaeological reconstruction of a wood and peat building, Thorláksbúð, located next to the cathedral was completed in 2012. There are records of it as far back as the 13th century but it was rebuilt and reused several times. Its appearance survives in sketches and watercolors by foreign travelers from the second half of the 18th century. Before it was finally destroyed, it apparently served as a chapel and storehouse. Today, Thorláksbúð preserves an ancient wooden altar from the Snæfellsnes Peninsula. In addition, the site is both a historic building connected to the place's past and a space for smaller ceremonies for which the cathedral isn't necessary.

Kerið

Kerið is located about 9 miles (15 km) north of Selfoss, on Route 35. It is a crater formed about 3,000 years ago and characterized by distinct deep red streaks due to the prominent presence of iron deposits. The most widely accepted theory of its formation says it was created from a cone-shaped volcano that, once emptied of the magma inside, would have collapsed, creating the present basin. Within it is a small lake with turquoise-colored waters, the depth of which varies depending on precipitation,

Kerið 116 C2 **kerid.is**

Thjóðveldisbærinn, a faithful reconstruction of the medieval Stöng farm, is located in the valley of Thjórsárdalur.

ranging from 23 to 45 feet (7 to 14 m). The crater is about 180 feet (55 m) deep and 557 feet (170 m) across.

Stöng

Stöng, in the Thjórsárdalur valley, is home to an archaeological site where a house from the medieval period was found buried following an eruption of the Hekla volcano in 1104. Behind the site is a path leading to **Gjáin**, a small valley with interesting lava formations and several waterfalls tumbling down the walls.

About 6 miles (10 km) northeast of Stöng, on a road off Route 322, is the parking lot for **Háifoss**, a waterfall that plummets 400 feet (122 m) into a canyon. Icelandic folklore considers it to be the home of an ogress.

Thjóðveldisbærinn (Commonwealth Farm), just south of Stöng on Route 32, is a reconstruction of the hypothetical appearance of the Stöng farm, completed in 1977. The peat building consists of a central unit, the hall, attached to three additional units with as many rooms. The adjacent church, a small chapel that was initially erected inside the National Museum of Iceland for an exhibition in 1997, was moved to its current location in 2000 to mark the millennium of the country's Catholic conversion. The current building is itself an archaeological hypothesis of what medieval churches must have looked like and is occasionally used for church services. It is open to the public in the summer. The site was used as a backdrop in the TV series *Game of Thrones*.

Another place of interest near Thjóðveldisbærinn is **Hjálparfoss** waterfall. This is a double waterfall that marks the point where the Fossá and Thjórsá rivers meet and cascade into a pool, before continuing on its course. ■

Thjóðveldisbærinn ☎ 423 8723 🕒 Open June–Aug. daily 10 a.m.–5 p.m. $ $ **www.thjodveldisbaer.is**

DRIVING ROUTE: THE GOLDEN CIRCLE

The Golden Circle is probably Iceland's most famous itinerary because of its proximity to the capital, Reykjavík, and the high concentration of destinations of great historical and natural value. Despite the large number of points of interest, the Golden Circle is often pared back to three main destinations: the UNESCO site of Thingvellir, the Geysir area, and the Gullfoss waterfall. However, it is possible to add many other destinations to the list.

From Reykjavík, take Route 1 toward Vík until you reach the town of **Selfoss** ❶. Here, you can stop to explore the old town with its reconstructions of period buildings, a true open-air museum. Continue on Route 1 for 9.3 miles (15 km) and take Route 30 toward Flúðir for 10.5 miles (17 km) until you reach the intersection with Route 31. Take it and, after 8 miles (13 km), you will reach the site of **Skálholt** ❷, where you can visit the cathedral, a reconstruction of a medieval wooden church, and the archaeological site of the former bishop's seat. Next to the cathedral, a footpath leads to the memorial dedicated to Jón Arason, the country's last Catholic bishop before the beginning of the Contemporary Age.

Return to Route 31 and follow it

Thingvellir's church, Thingvallakirkja, overlooks the Öxará River.

for 1.5 miles (2.5 km) to the intersection with Route 35. From here continue north for about 4.3 miles (7 km) until you reach the town of Reykholt, where you can freely visit the hydroponic greenhouses of **Friðheimar** ❸.

Drive another 11.8 miles (19 km) north on Route 35 to reach **Geysir** ❹, where you can admire the famous Strokkur ("Churning") geyser. From here you can continue on the same road, heading east, to reach **Gullfoss** ❺ waterfall. Park in the lower area, which arrives more quickly at the waterfall via a convenient path, or in the upper area, where you will find the tourist center and a path leading to the viewing balcony. The two levels are connected by a staircase. On sunny days, sprays of steam break up the sunlight, creating picturesque rainbows.

NOT TO BE MISSED:

Selfoss • Skálholt • Geysir • Gullfoss • Thingvellir National Park

Take Route 35 back to the junction with Route 37, which you will follow to the village of Laugarvatn, a total of 23.6 miles (38 km). Drive through the town and, at the roundabout, take the first exit onto Route 365 for about 3.7 miles (6 km) until you reach the turnoff onto the dirt road that leads to **Laugarvatnshellir cave** ❻, where The Cave People immersive museum is located. In ancient times, if we exclude the unconfirmed hypothesis of an occupation by Irish hermits, the caves were used as stables or shelter by shepherds, but, in the early 20th, they were permanently inhabited for a few years.

Back on Route 365, continue west until you merge onto Route 36, head north and continue 11 miles (18 km) until you reach the visitor center at **Thingvellir National Park** ❼. Here you can park (for a fee) and visit an exhibit about the history of the area inside. Then continue to the viewing balcony outside, overlooking the rim of the North American tectonic plate, and see the edge of the Eurasian plate across the valley, about 3 miles (5 km) away. You can also descend into the rift on the edge of the North American plate, the famous Almannagjá fissure. Follow the trail to Lögberg, or "rock of the law", marked by a flag, where the *lögsögumaður*, the highest legal authority of the medieval period, is believed to have recited laws by heart and promulgated decrees and rulings during the sessions of the general assembly, the Althingi, founded in 930 AD. Farther down the path, you will reach a small waterfall and Drekkingarhylur ("pool of drownings"), where adulterous women were drowned up to the 18th century. Continuing on past the parking lots, you can climb the path up the slope and reach the gap on the opposite side, where you can admire Öxarárfoss waterfall. On the way back, past Lögberg, you can deviate from the path to reach the Thingvallakirkja church. The rectory next to it, designed by architect Guðjón Samúelsson, is now a summer residence for the prime minister and houses the headquarters of the National Park Steering Committee. Back at the visitor center parking lot, turn back onto Route 36 and head west for 28 miles (45 km) to return to Reykjavík.

See also map p. 116
Selfoss
1–2 days
95 miles (153 km)
Thingvellir

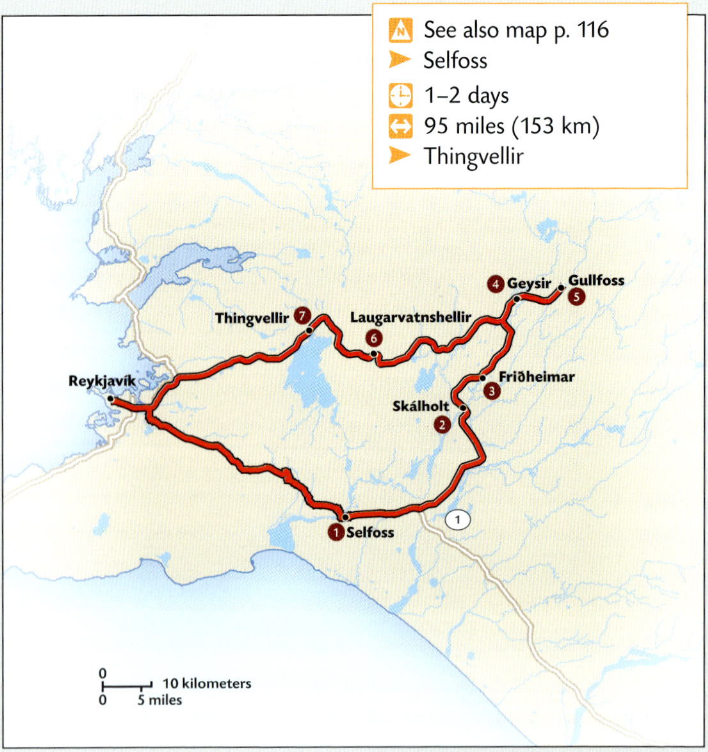

THE *NJÁLS SAGA*

Medieval Icelandic literary production was vast and varied; the *Njáls saga* is perhaps the most dazzling example of literary mastery from the period.

The *Njáls saga* is unquestionably the most beloved and appreciated saga among Icelanders. Due to its complexity and depth in depicting universal themes of human experience, it is a masterpiece of world literature. It is believed to have been composed in the late 13th century but is set between the mid-10th and early 11th. Although scholars agree on the possibility that characters or episodes in the saga are derived from oral tradition, there is no general agreement on how much of the material is literary invention.

The *Njáls saga* addresses themes of honor, revenge, and forgiveness, while also portraying the moral transformation that occurred in the Icelandic population with the conversion to Christianity in the year 1000. The saga has been handed down in some 60 manuscripts, about 20 of them dating to the medieval period. This is a large number compared to that of other sagas and testifies to the value placed on this text by Icelanders throughout the centuries.

The story is set mainly in the southern region, but it also touches on places located in all corners of the country. It starts with the marriages of a beautiful, frustrated, and vengeful woman, Hallgerður, whose first two husbands are murdered by her uncle on her request. Enter then the hero, Gunnar of Hlíðarendi, a valiant and noble-minded warrior who cultivates a deep and steadfast friendship with a man named Njáll who, although described as bearded and unmanly, commands great respect as a jurist of considerable renown.

Gunnar returns from a trip abroad laden with honors and riches and, at the summer assembly in Thingvellir, meets Hallgerður and falls in love with her, deciding to marry her despite being advised not to. The friendship between him and Njáll is put to the test when Hallgerður takes a disliking to Bergthóra, Njáll's wife, and incites her servants to kill members of Njáll's household. Thus begins a feud, which the two friends settle from time to time by paying each other the statutory weregild.

Hallgerður's fury, however, does not subside. She sends a servant to plunder and burn Kirkjubær's farm while the inhabitants are away. The servant is identified, however, and Gunnar, with the help of Njáll, manages to obtain an honorable plea bargain at the local court. On discovering his wife's responsibility,

"Hallgerður's Slap," a scene from the *Njáls saga*, painted by August Malmström, is housed in the Nationalmuseum in Stockholm, Sweden.

Gunnar slaps her, which she promises to remind him of in due time. Njáll manages to get his friend Gunnar off the hook on a couple of occasions, after some disagreements escalate into murder, but he prophesies that Gunnar will die if he ever kills two members of the same family. At this point, Mörður, an envious rival, works to make the prophecy come true: he compels the relatives of a man killed by Gunnar to take revenge. Thus, Gunnar must defend himself by killing a second member of the same family. This time, despite his influence, all Njáll can do is get Gunnar exiled for three years. The latter sets out on horseback to reach the coast and set sail, but on the way he falls off his steed and turns to look at the mountains of his homeland. The beauty thrills him and, in one of the most poignant scenes in Icelandic literature, the hero decides not to set out lest he leave his native land. His enemies then attack him, encircling his home. He defends himself from a distance with a bow, but the string breaks. Gunnar then asks his wife for a lock of hair to restring it; Hallgerður refuses, reminding him of the slap he gave her long ago. Thus, his enemies are able to catch Gunnar and kill him. One of Njáll's sons, Skarphéðinn, will later assist Gunnar's son in his revenge.

The scene then shifts to Njáll's family. His sons clash with Thráinn, a man who made them look bad in the court of Norway during an expedition. Since Thráinn refuses to repay them, Njáll's sons, together with their brother-in-law Kári, attack him. Skarphéðinn runs and slides down a frozen river to catch Thráinn. He kills him by slashing his skull with an axe. As part of the settlements following the murders, Njáll adopts Höskuldur, Thráinn's son, who then becomes his favorite. Njáll then attempts to marry him to Hildigunnur, who agrees on the condition that Höskuldur become a powerful lord. Once the demand is met, Höskuldur succeeds in marrying Hildigunnur.

At that time, the general assembly (Althingi) established Christianity as the national religion. Höskuldur's reputation and power grow to the point that he overshadows a neighbor, who urges Njáll's sons to kill their half-brother by appealing to their jealousy of him. Once Höskuldur is dead, Flosi, Hildigunnur's uncle, files a lawsuit that results in a colossal weregild ruling. Njáll's sons agree to settle what is owed but add to it a dress with a feminine cut, considered an insult to Flosi's manhood. The latter then refuses the payment and decides to go ahead with a personal revenge, setting fire to Njáll's house with the whole family inside. This is the most famous scene in the saga: Njáll refuses an offer to escape safely with the women and children, claiming that he is too old to stay alive and is obligated to avenge his children.

At that point, Njáll instills courage in the other people in the house by telling them that God will not let them burn in this world or the next. His body, his wife's body, and his grandson's body are found intact under a carpet among the remains of the house. However, his son-in-law Kári had managed to escape, disguised as a woman and veiled by the smoke. He initially seeks revenge, hunting down those responsible for the fire as far away as Orkney and Wales.

Later, Flosi makes a pilgrimage to southern Europe. Upon his return, Kári tries to join him, but is shipwrecked on the coast near his residence. At that point, Kári tests Flosi's nobility by asking him for help. As evidence of the change in morals that occurred with conversion to Christianity, Flosi reconciles with Kári by marrying him off to his niece, the widow of Höskuldur.

FROM THE CITY TO THE VOLCANOES

Primarily flat, the Southern region includes the land surrounding the Eyjafjöll mountain range.

Once you cross the Hellisheiði Plateau, which separates the Capital region from the south, you enter the southern region. Following Route 1 southeast, you will pass through several towns, such as Selfoss, the most important town in southern Iceland, and rural areas, including the municipalities of Rangárthing ytra, whose main town is Hella, and Rangárthing eystra, whose main town is Hvolsvöllur. In the easternmost part, you can see the imposing Eyjafjöll range, which is blanketed by the Eyjafjallajökull ice cap, also the name of the volcano below it, the one that blocked European air traffic in 2010.

Hveragerði

About 28 miles (45 km) south of the capital, beyond the mountains, lies Hveragerði, the first town you

Hveragerði – Information Center Sunnumörk 2-4 483 4601
Open June–Aug. Mon.–Thur. 8:30 a.m.–4:30 p.m., Fri. 8:30 a.m.–4 p.m., Sat. 9 a.m.–1 p.m. **www.east.is**

The white peaks of the glacial Eyjafjallajökull mountains.

encounter as you enter the southern region. With a population of 3,000, Hveragerði is famous for its geothermal activity. The town is home to **Hveragarðurinn** (Geothermal Park), which also has a geyser. To the north of town is the Reykjadalur valley, a popular hiking destination, where a hot-water stream flows.

Selfoss

The largest town in southern Iceland, with a population of more than 9,000, is Selfoss, which has long held little regard among locals and tourists alike. Its name means "Seal Falls" for the rapids that lie below the bluff where the church stands, where seals would sometimes be spotted. Selfoss was a rather unimportant farm until construction of the old bridge across the Ölfusá River, completed in 1891, which sparked the formation of a settlement. The bridge collapsed in 1944, and the present one was built and opened in 1945.

Like other towns that popped up without any coherent urban planning at crossroads, Selfoss for a long time had a reputation for being rather unattractive. This radically changed, however, in 2020, when the new town center was built in an abandoned area just across the bridge. Citizens voted on the project from a variety of possibilities in 2018. It was favored because it would redevelop a large central area of the town and attract tourists. It is an open-air museum of faithful reconstructions of historic buildings dating back to the 19th and 20th centuries that were destroyed or demolished. On the facade of each of these is a plaque with the history of the original building. This is an architectural choice that stands in sharp contrast to the rest of the country, where modernist and international architecture has been favored at the expense of traditional Icelandic architecture. Nevertheless, the renovation has been a huge success among both locals and tourists, who enjoy the picturesque corners and distinct atmosphere evoked by the traditional architecture.

In addition to the town center, Selfoss is home to the **Fischersetur** (Bobby Fischer Center), dedicated to the U.S. chess player who first claimed the title of world champion after defeating the Soviet Boris Spassky in a tournament in Reykjavík in 1972. The clash was particularly significant as it mirrored the tension between the two superpowers, Soviet and American, at the height of the Cold War. In 1992, Fischer defied a U.N. embargo by traveling to a tournament in Yugoslavia. U.S. authorities had him arrested for

Hveragarðurinn ✉ Hveramörk 13 ☎ 483 5062 🕒 Closed Oct.–March $ $ • **Selfoss – Information Center** ✉ Austurvegi 2 ☎ 480 1900 🕒 Open Mon.–Tues. 9 a.m.–4 p.m., Fri. 9 a.m.–2 p.m. **www.arborg.is** • **Fischersetur** ✉ Austurvegur 21 ☎ 894 1275 🕒 Open June–Aug. daily 1 p.m.–5 p.m. $ $ **www.fischersetur.is**

Located on the banks of the Ölfusá River, Selfoss is the most populous town in southern Iceland.

using a revoked passport in 2004. Iceland granted him citizenship and he retired there, until his death in 2008. He was buried in the cemetery at Laugardælakirkja church, just outside the city.

Íslenski bærinn

Íslenski bærinn is a peat house built on the grounds of the Austur-Meðalholt farm. The structure, dating back to the 19th century, underwent multiple alterations and improvements in 1895. Today, the building constitutes a private property that is still active and can be visited. Beds were placed in the main room of the house, the *baðstofa*. Those who lived there would eat and work while seated on the beds. A space in the farm complex visitor center houses a photo exhibition on the architecture and construction techniques of peat buildings. Courses on cutting and laying peat are also held every summer.

Hella

The most interesting attraction of Hella, a small town located 23 miles (37 km) east of Selfoss just off Route 1, is the man-made cave system located nearby. Scholars have not been able to date them with certainty, but some believe they were inhabited by Irish monks present on the island before the arrival of Norse settlers. The caves were carved out of porous rock, and the walls are engraved with crosses, writing, and other symbols. Of the 12 caves discovered, four are open to the public but can only be visited by guided tours through **Hellarnir við Hellu** (The Caves of Hella), located next to the main road just before entering the village. South of the town, along the Ytri-Rangá River, is the Ægissíðufoss waterfall, characterized by a series of small cascades and popular for salmon fishing.

Oddi

Located in the Rangárvellir valley, just a few miles from Hella, Oddi is a farm that was one of the most important centers of power in medieval Iceland, and it remained a parish seat of significance for several centuries. Sæmundur Sigfússon the Wise, one of the earliest chroniclers of Icelandic history (1056–1133), resided there. His grandson, Jón Loftsson (1124–1197), was one of the most influential and powerful lords of his time, and he was foster father and tutor to the famous Snorri Sturluson, author of the *Prose Edda*. Six pastors of the Oddi church became bishops of Iceland.

It is likely that a church has been present in Oddi since the conversion to Christianity in the year 1000, but the present building, designed by architect Guðjón Samúelsson in 1924, is made of wood clad in sheet metal. Some of the most valuable items belonging to the church are a 14th century silver chalice, an altarpiece depicting Christ in Gethsemane from 1895, and a baptismal font carved and painted by Ámundi Jónsson, an artist who lived in the area between 1738 and 1805.

Keldur

Keldur, located on Route 264, 6.8 miles (11 km) from the intersection with Route 1, is a peat farm of great historical value. It is mentioned in three sagas: the *Njáls saga* (see pp. 129–131), the *Sturlunga saga* (focusing on political struggles in the 11th and 12th centuries) and the *Thorláks saga helga* (*The Life of St. Thorlákur*). It belonged to one of Iceland's most important clans during the Free State period (930–1264), the Oddaverjar. One of the chiefs, Jón Loftsson (1124–1197), founded a monastery there, but it was dissolved as early as 30 years later. The building has been remodeled repeatedly over the centuries, but a stone part of it is thought to date from the 13th century, which would make it the oldest surviving section of a peat house in Iceland.

An additional item of interest is a secret underground tunnel, accessible by trapdoor, that peeks out onto the side of the knoll where the house stands. These tunnels are mentioned in the sagas, where they are referred to as escape routes in the case of siege. Keldur's, however, is the only one

Hellarnir við Hellu Ægissíða 4 620 6100 During winter season Tour in English daily noon & 2 p.m. in winter $$$ **www.cavesofhella.is** • **Keldur** Open June–Aug. daily 10 a.m.–5 p.m.

Everyday life on a sunny day near Keldur.

to have been found. The building consists of several rooms, namely storehouses, a pantry, stable and workshop. Next to it stands a church, Keldnakirkja, built in 1875. Inside is an altarpiece depicting the Last Supper, created by Icelandic artist Ámundi Jónsson in 1792. Affixed to the wall next to the altarpiece are two painted wooden statuettes from the medieval period, one depicting the Virgin and Child and the other St. Paul the Apostle.

The last owner of the farm was Skúli Guðmundsson, who lived there until his death in 1946. Later, the property passed to the National Museum of Iceland, which allows guided tours in the summertime.

Hvolsvöllur

The small town of Hvolsvöllur, 8 miles (13 km) southeast of Hella following Route 1, is home to one of the country's most famous and popular attractions, the **LAVA Centre,** an interactive museum about geology, volcanoes, earthquakes, and tectonic plates, where visitors are guided through the country's geological history and the geological phenomena that shape it. The museum uses high-tech equipment to educate visitors in an immersive way through direct observation and interactive tools. The facility has won numerous awards locally and internationally for its innovative design. Although it is the museum that captures the attention of visitors, Hvolsvöllur itself is a pretty town set in the heart of a region of unquestionable

LAVA Centre Austurvegur 14 415 5200 Open daily 9 a.m.–5 p.m. $$ **www.lavacentre.is**

natural beauty, with the outlines of numerous volcanoes looming on the horizon. The local church, at the edge of the village on the eastern side, is called Stórólfshvolskirkja, and dates to 1930. It contains an altarpiece painted in 1914 by Thórarinn B. Thorláksson and depicting Jesus blessing children.

Fljótshlíð

Fljótshlíð is the rural area east of Hvolsvöllur, bordered by the Markarfljót River to the south. It was one of the areas evacuated in 2010 following the Eyjafjallajökull eruption. Here you can find the **Breiðabólstaður** farm, where the **Breiðabólstaðakirkja** church stands. It was designed by Rögnvaldur Ólafsson and built in 1912. The church has a peculiar structure, despite having a classical cross layout, due to its side entrance at the foot of the bell tower, which is located in a corner of the building, filling the space between two arms of the cross.

A little to the east is the **Hlíðarendi** farm, which was the home of Gunnar Hámundarson, one of the main characters in the *Njáls saga* (*see pp. 129–131*. Thorlákur Thórhallsson, who would become the patron saint of Iceland, was born there in 1133. The building was the residence of local lords and administrators for a long time. The local church, **Hlíðarendakirkja**, was suppressed in 1802 and moved elsewhere but, in 1898, was erected again. Unlike most Lutheran churches, Hlíðarendakirkja is particularly rich in paintings, created by Icelandic artist Ólaf Túbals. One of the relics preserved in the building is a silver chalice from the medieval period.

Slightly east of the farm is the **Gluggafoss** waterfall, which falls 32

The interactive LAVA Centre in the southern town of Hvolsvöllur.

feet (52 m). The upper part of the cliff it falls from is composed of soft palagonite eroded by water, which creates holes and passages in the rock called *gluggar* (windows).

Vestur-Eyjafjöll

Some of the country's most visited attractions are nestled on the slopes of the Eyjafjöll mountain range, which reaches a maximum height of 5,465 feet (1,666 m) and lies under the Eyjafjallajökull ice cap. Along the foot of the mountains runs a steep ridge that once formed tall cliffs on the edge of the sea, now several miles to the south due to the rise in elevation of the ground from post-glacial rebound.

Heading toward the Eyjafjöll mountain range from the west, the first iconic sight one encounters is the **Seljalandsfoss** waterfall. It plummets 196 feet (60 m) from a ledge over a cave that you can access, getting a view of the falls from behind. North of Seljalandsfoss, along the cliffs, is **Gljúfrabúi**, a waterfall with a 131-foot (40 m) drop partially hidden inside a gorge carved out by the running water. The waterfall is accessible (water level permitting) through an opening in the rock face, so you can get a close-up view of the open cave and the Gljúfrabúi falling into it.

Next is **Írafoss**, close to Route 246, a picturesque waterfall framed by a narrow basalt gorge. Its name means "waterfall of the Irish." According to local legend, a Christian Irishman lived at the waterfall after being driven away on several occasions by pagan settlers. Slightly to the east of Írafoss stands the farm of **Ásólfsskáli.** The story passed down in *Landnámabók* (*Book of Colonizations*) is that the stream that flowed by the farm was full of fish, so the pagan Norsemen would drive out the Christian man, Ásólfur, who lived next to it. He moved a little farther west to the Miðskálaá River, where the fish increased disproportionately, deserting the stream by the old settlement. Ásólfur was driven out again, and this time settled at the Írá River, on which Írafoss is located. Again, the amount of fish in that river began to increase, so he was driven out of the region for good and moved to Akranes, in the west of the country, where he lived as a hermit.

Ásólfsskáli is a private farm that offers guided tours to the public to see the workings of traditional Icelandic farming and ranching firsthand. Its church, **Ásólfsskálakirkja**, was built in 1955 on the site of earlier churches. It contains an altarpiece painted by Matthías Sigfússon (1904–1984).

Austur-Eyjafjöll

The eastern part of the region at the foot of the Eyjafjöll range begins at Holtsós Lagoon. The road skirts steep cliffs for about 1.8 miles (3 km), after which three long, narrow valleys penetrate the mountains on the northern

Ásólfsskáli ☎ 861 7489 **www.asolfsskali.is**

The *Réttir*

Every year, in late August, Iceland's farmers begin crossing the highlands and mountains on horseback and quad bikes to retrieve sheep, which spend the summer roaming free in the highlands. Once rounded up, the sheep are sorted manually into special pens. Each family retrieves theirs, recognizing them by their tags, and transports them in person to their section of the pen. This practice is called *réttir*, and it is a sort of rural ceremony. Even city dwellers will take part, traveling to the countryside to help relatives and friends, turning the event into an opportunity to gather. The *réttir* takes place in early September and is publicized in newspapers and on local government websites. Visitors can take part by offering to help the farmers.

side. In the central valley is the town of Seljavellir, which can be reached by taking Route 242 for half a mile (1 km) and continuing north until the parking lot. At the end of the valley are hot springs, where you can find the **Seljavallalaug** pool, which was built in 1923 to teach children in the region to swim. The walk from the parking lot takes about half an hour, and it can be difficult to reach when it rains because of the high level of the stream visitors must cross. Access to the pool is free.

A couple of miles to the east, on Route 1, is the turn-off south to **Eyvindarhólar**. This is a complex of two farms in the heart of the plains a short distance from the sea. According to *Landnámabók* (*Book of Colonizations*), Eyvindur, son of Baugur, who had settled in Hlíðarendi, was banished from the Fljótshlíð region for murder and settled in Eyvindarhólar. The main attraction of this place lies in the unparalleled view of the Eyjafjöll mountain range and nearby Eyjafjallajökull glacier. The view also extends eastward to include a portion of Mýrdalsjökull glacier. The present church, **Eyvindarhólakirkja**, was consecrated in 1961, but there are records of a church on this site as far back as the 1200s. It would formerly have been located in the middle of today's cemetery. The altar and pulpit visible today come from the earlier churches, and the altarpiece consists of an oil painting of the Resurrection.

Just half a mile (1 km) east of the intersection for Eyvindarhólar, next to Route 1, stands **Rútshellir**, a stable carved out of a cave in a rocky outcrop. Icelandic writer and explorer Eggert Ólafsson's account from the mid-1800s reports that the stable had been used as a dwelling, whereas archaeological investigations revealed that a side chamber must have been used as a workshop. Engraved crosses were found inside, leading to the suspicion that Rútshellir was inhabited by some Irish monks who settled in Iceland before the arrival of Norse settlers (in the late ninth century), but their dating is problematic and therefore this theory is unconfirmed.

Just half a mile (1 km) farther east is **Drangshlíð**, a farm that houses a family-run hotel. In the land between the farm and Route 1 is **Drangurinn**, a rock that used to be sea stacks before the waters receded with the post-glacial rebound. Beneath it is a cave where a stable was carved out with buildings attached to the gap in the rock. Several folktales claim this place is inhabited by elves.

Past Mount Skóganúpur, which half encircles the valley, you will encounter the town of **Skógar**, where the **Skógafoss** waterfall is, an imposing wall of water 196 feet (60 m) high and 82 feet (25 m) wide. A folktale has it that a chest full of gold was hidden behind the waterfall by the settler of the area, whose name was Thrasi. Skógar is also home to the **Skógasafn** museum, one of the most important and extensive in the country, that specializes in local culture and history. In addition to numerous objects, artifacts, and relics that depict the life and customs of the people, the museum also includes an open-air section with several historic buildings from the 19th and early 20th centuries, including a peat house that can be visited, a church (Skàogakirkja), and a school building. The museum also has a large shed used as a museum of transportation in Iceland. It houses numerous vintage cars and vehicles.

From the museum parking lot, you can follow a path into a gorge that leads to Kvernufoss falls, a 98-foot (30 m) waterfall that can be accessed from behind via a hollowed out part of the rock face. ■

Skógasafn ✉ Skogasafn 1 ☎ 487 8845 🕒 Open June–Aug. 9 a.m.–6 p.m., Sept.–May 10 a.m.–5 p.m. $ $$ **www.skogasafn.is**

The annual réttir is one of the most important social rituals in the country.

THE COAST

The coast of the Southern region is low and sandy, characterized by black beaches and estuaries. The area is home to some small picturesque towns. Offshore lies the volcanic archipelago of Vestmannaeyjar.

Due to its formation, the southern coast of Iceland is unsuitable for maritime activities. The region's economy therefore doesn't take much advantage from its closeness to the sea, except for the town of Thorlákshöfn and the Vestmannaeyjar archipelago. These small communities have achieved enviable prosperity from the abundant fishing opportunities of the southern waters.

Thorlákshöfn

The small town of Thorlákshöfn, named after Iceland's patron saint, is the last viable port until Höfn in the far southeast of the country and is home to the tourist information center for the Ölfus area, **Upplýsingamiðstöð Thorlákshafnar.**

Just 9 miles (15 km) west of the village is the **Strandarkirkja** church. The present building was erected in 1888, but the history of the place is much older. In fact, there are several legends about its founding; one of them tells of a miracle that occurred in the bay in front of it, Engilsvík (Angel's Bay), where sailors returning from Norway were allegedly guided, apparently by an angelic light, after praying and vowing to build a church if they reached a safe harbor during a terrible storm. In 1950 a monument was erected in memory of the miracle. It depicts a woman holding a cross and is called Landsýn (Land in Sight). Many miracles have been attributed to the beneficent influence of the church.

About 6 miles (10 km) north of the town, following first Route 38 and then Route 39, you can reach the site of the **Raufarhólshellir** lava tunnel. It reaches a length of 4,593 feet (1,400 m), and was formed when lava cooled around a still flowing lava river. Once the space was emptied of the flowing lava, a long tunnel remained, now accessible only by guided tours.

Eyrarbakki

A small, picturesque village located between Route 34 and the sea, about 8 miles (13 km) off the beaten path south of Selfoss, Eyrarbakki is a particularly pretty town because of its traditional, colorful houses. In modern times, it was an important trading

Upplýsingamiðstöð Thorlákshafnar ✉ Hafnarberg 1 ☎ 480 3830 🕒 Open Mon.–Fri. 12:30–5:30 p.m. **www.olfus.is • Raufarhólshellir** ☎ 760 1000 🕒 Open daily 10 a.m.–5 p.m. $ $$$ **thelavatunnel.is**

Knarrarósviti, near Stokkseyri.

port, losing its significance only in the early 20th century. Bjarni Herjólfsson, who is said to have been the first European to spot North America after running off course while traveling to Greenland, was born nearby in a place called Drepstokkur. The village is home to **Byggðasafn Árnesinga,** a local history museum located in several buildings scattered throughout the town, and **Sjóminjasafnið á Eyrarbakka,** a maritime culture museum dedicated to the history of local fishing activity.

The local church, **Eyrarbakkakirkja**, was built in 1890. The most valuable object inside is an altarpiece depicting Jesus and the Samaritan woman in front of Jacob's well, painted by Queen Louise of Denmark, wife of Christian IX, in 1891.

Stokkseyri

Stokkseyri, 3.7 miles (6 km) southeast of Eyrarbakki, is another small coastal village with a serene atmosphere. The local church, **Stokkseyrarkirkja**, was built in 1886. It is made of wood covered with corrugated sheet metal.

A couple of miles east of the town is the Knarrarósviti (Knarrarós lighthouse), built in 1939, whose design exhibits a combination of art nouveau and functionalism.

Thykkvibær

Thykkvibær, 11 miles (18 km) south of Hella following Route 25, was the first

Byggðasafn Árnesinga & Sjóminjasafnið á Eyrarbakka ☎ 483 1504/483 1082 🕒 Open May–Sept. daily 10 a.m.–5 p.m., Oct.–Apr. by reservation $ $ **www.byggdasafn.is • Stokkseyri – Information Center** ✉ Gimli Kaffihús, Hafnargötu 1 ☎ 468 1486 🕒 Open noon–5 p.m. **www.stokkseyri.is**

village in Iceland in the Middle Ages. In fact, sources mention it as early as the 13th century, at a time when the country's settlements generally consisted of isolated farms. Here, the district's first school was founded in 1892. Today, the town is particularly famous for potato production. From the town, there are sweeping views of the mountains and volcanoes of southern Iceland. To the south lies Rangársandur, a vast black beach about 1 mile (2 km) wide.

Vestmannaeyjar

Vestmannaeyjar is a volcanic archipelago arranged along an arc-shaped system of about 80 volcanoes that poke out from the sea. The islands largely emerged about 10,000 years ago as a result of underwater eruptions, but volcanic activity has continued over the centuries. The last island to emerge from the depths, Surtsey, was formed in the 1960s. The easiest way to reach them is with the ferry service from the Landeyjahöfn pier (at the end of Route 254). It runs daily and takes about 35 minutes.

Only the main island is inhabited, and the population is concentrated in the small town of Vestmannaeyjarbær. The local economy is mainly centered around the thriving fishing industry and tourism, which have brought considerable wealth and prosperity to the local population of almost 5,000.

The name of the archipelago means "Islands of the Westerners," and its story is explained in the *Landnámabók* (*Book of Colonizations*): Hjörleifur, the sworn brother of the first Norwegian settler, Ingólfur Arnarson, is said to have landed at the headland of Hjörleifshöfði, now located farther inland. Here his servants, who were Irish, allegedly killed him then fled to an archipelago off the coast. After reaching the headland, Ingólfur caught sight of the islands and decided to go after them. He then avenged his brother, tracking down the Irish and slaying them. From then on, the islands would take the name Vestmannaeyjar, "Islands of the Westerners," which is what Norwegians called the Irish since Ireland lies west of Norway.

INSIDER TIP:

Take the ferry to the Vestmannaeyjar Islands from late April to mid-August to spot puffins.

—ROBERTO LUIGI PAGANI
Author of the guidebook

An archaeological excavation carried out in the 1970s and 1980s in the Herjólfsdalur valley unearthed finds that carbon dating places one or two centuries before the official

Vestmannaeyjar – Information Center ✉ Strandvegur 🕒 Open summer Mon.– Fri. 9 a.m.–6 p.m., Sat. 10 a.m.–4 p.m., Sun. 1 p.m.–4 p.m. **www.vestmannaeyjar.is**

An Icelandic lamb looks at the ocean from the island of Heimaey, Vestmannaeyjar archipelago.

colonization of the country, which took place between 870 and 930 AD. However, this data has been contested, and therefore, this theory of an earlier colonization cannot be confirmed. At any rate, in the Herjólfsdalur valley, where the famous Thjóðhátíð music festival is held each year, there is a reconstruction of a building found in the excavation located across the road from the archaeological site.

Over the centuries, the islands have been at the center of major events in the country's history. In 1627, half the population of the island of Heimaey, about 250 people, were kidnapped and enslaved by raiding Saracen pirates, mainly North Africans but also Europeans. The invasion is known in Icelandic as Tyrkjaránið, "the raid of the Turks," since, at that time, much of the Muslim world was under the control of the Ottoman Empire. One of the kidnapped Icelanders, Reverend Ólafur Egilsson, was chosen as a messenger to present a ransom demand to the Danish king. Ólafur reached Denmark, but his petition was rejected for lack of funds; once back in Iceland, he composed a memoir of the events, published only in 1852 and later translated into numerous languages. To learn more about local history, there is the **Sagnheimar byggðasafn** museum in the town center.

On **Heimaey** there are two volcanic cones formed by eruptions. The oldest, Helgafell, is about 6,000 years old and reaches 754 feet (230 m) in height, whereas Eldfell was formed in 1973 and is 656 feet (200 m) high. The lava flow destroyed some houses, but it was stopped with powerful pumps that cool the lava with seawater. The population had been fortuitously evacuated: due to unseasonably bad weather the previous day, all the fishing boats were moored in port and ready for use. The flow also caused a significant expansion of the island's surface area. The story of this event is told in the **Eldheimar,** built around the remains of one of the houses destroyed by the eruption. It is a very modern and interactive museum. Near the harbor, the **Sea Life Trust Beluga Whale Sanctuary** cares for animals that cannot be released back into the wild for various reasons, particularly belugas and puffins. Here you can visit animal exhibits and participate in guided tours of the facility's aquarium.

Also of interest is the local church, **Landakirkja**, completed in 1778. It is the third oldest church in Iceland, preceded only by the church in Viðey and the cathedral in Hólar. Major alterations were made over the next two centuries. At the entrance to the harbor, in a green area called Skansinn, named after a fort built in 1586 and drastically transformed by the 1973 eruption, is the medieval-style wooden church **Stafkirkjan**, donated by Norwegians to Iceland in 2000 to mark a millennium since the adoption of Christianity.

North of the town are some small peaks, which can be climbed via rather steep and sometimes dangerous inclines. These include the iconic **Heimaklettur** and the cliffs surrounding the Herjólfsdalur valley. South of the island, the Stórhöfði headland is a prime spot for observing puffin colonies in summer. From here you can enjoy a beautiful view of the islands to the south: Suðurey, Álsey, Brandur, Hellisey, and the reefs of Súlnasker and Geldungur (which can also be seen up close by boat tours that depart from town), as well as the inaccessible island of Surtsey, where only scientists studying its ecosystem are allowed to visit. ■

Sagnheimar byggðasafn ✉ Safnahúsinu við Ráðhúströð ☎ 488 2050 🕒 Open May–Oct. daily 10 a.m.–5 p.m., Nov.–Apr. Sat. 1 p.m.–4 p.m. $ $ **www.sagnheimar.is** • **Eldheimar** ✉ Suðurvegur/Gerðisbraut 10 ☎ 488 2700 🕒 Open daily 1:30 p.m.–4:30 p.m. $ $$ **www.eldheimar.is** • **Sea Life Trust, Beluga Whale Sanctuary** ✉ Heimaey 🕒 Open Jan.–Feb. & Nov.–Dec. Fri.–Sat. noon–4 p.m., March–Apr. & Oct. Thur.–Sat. 10 a.m.–4 p.m. & Sun. noon–4 p.m., May–Sept. daily 10 a.m.–4 p.m. $ $$ **belugasanctuary.sealifetrust.org**

Black sand deserts, soaring peaks, glacial tongues, and farms nestled at the foot of volcanoes

THE SOUTHEAST

The columnar basalt at Reynisfjara beach.

THE SOUTHEAST

The Southeast is a wild region of extremes, but while it includes some of the country's most popular destinations, most visitors pass through it quickly and leave behind a treasure trove of unexplored destinations where you can truly experience the soul of this country. So many of the landscapes that have made Iceland famous are concentrated here, from alluvial deserts to black sand beaches to the most majestic glaciers.

NOT TO BE MISSED:

Vík and its black beach **151–154**

Sólheimajökull glacier **152**

Kirkjubæjarklaustur and its surroundings **158–159**

Skaftafell National Park **162–163**

Hof peat church **164**

Jökulsárlón lagoon **165–166**

Höfn **167**

Langoustine in Höfn restaurants **164**

The part of Iceland stretching from the small town of Vík in Mýrdalur to Höfn in Hornafjörður is called Suðausturland, "Southeast region." This region differs in some ways from the rest of the country. It encompasses some of the most distinctive landscapes Iceland has to offer: glaciers and black deserts, called *sandar* (sing. *sandur*), formed as a result of *jökulhlaup*, the catastrophic floods

that occurred following subglacial volcanic eruptions.

The Southeast is a wild land, which, according to medieval sources, was the last in the country to be settled by the Norsemen because of the absence of natural harbors due to its shallow and sandy seabed. Over the centuries, numerous vessels, having come too close to shore, have wrecked here. Tradition has it that in some areas such as present-day Kirkjubæjarklaustur, Christian anchorites of Irish descent were already living there but left when the new settlers arrived. In addition to the rich history of this area, often mixed with legend, the unique natural landscapes make it one of the most traveled destinations in the entire country.

The western part of the region, stretching from the Jökulsá á Sólheimasandi River to the heart of the Skeiðarársandur floodplain, is mostly flat terrain that spans 12–18 miles (20–30 km) between the ocean and the ridges that used to be sea cliffs. Lined up at the foot of the hills are numerous farms and small villages.

The local economy is primarily agricultural, but over time tourism has gained prominence. In contrast, the eastern part, which extends to the edge of the Hornafjörður area, is situated among mountain peaks. Hvannadalshnjúkur towers above them all. The highest peak in the country, it rises out of the glacier and reaches an elevation of 6,922 feet (2,110 m). Everywhere along this stretch of land, the ice from Europe's largest ice cap can be seen creeping into the crevices between the mountains and sliding down into the valley.

Höfn, the capital of Hornafjörður municipality and the main hub of the area, is the first significant natural harbor you come across on your way from the Reykjanes Peninsula in the southwest. A large portion of this region is contained within the boundaries of Vatnajökull National Park. The largest park in the country and one of the largest in Europe, it is an important hiking destination for tourists and locals alike.

This region has been the scene of important events in the country's history. This is where, according to historical sources, the island's first settler landed.

A colossal eruption that occurred under Öræfajökull glacier in 1362 altered the region's landscape in a way that is still visible today. In 1783, another eruption that happened where there are now volcanic craters, named Lakagígar, changed the course of the country's history and impacted the climate of much of the Northern Hemisphere. It is a region of contrasts, where rugged natural expanses are speckled with pleasant bucolic scenes wherever it is possible to cultivate the land. ■

The peat church in the village of Hof, near Vatnajökull National Park.

BLACK DESERTS & GLACIERS

In this region, you can experience the striking contrast of the stark white glacial tongues and the pitch black basalt sand. Some of the most famous and impressive sights are found here: glaciers, black beaches, immense lava fields, the settings of exciting historical events, and the backdrop of numerous legends.

The white church and basalt stacks stand out in the background of Vík.

The western part, colloquially referred to by the ancient name of Vestur-Skaftafellssýsla, is confined to the east and west by vast alluvial deserts crisscrossed by treacherous glacial rivers and bordered to the north and south by inland plateaus and the sandy coastline respectively. The 18th century explorer Eggert Ólafsson, in his account of Iceland, indicates that geographical isolation left the language here more archaic compared to the rest of the country. The vast plain that characterizes this region used to be the seafloor, which emerged as a result of the melting of the ice cap that covered the entire island of Iceland during the last ice age. As the pressure of the ice decreased, the land swelled in a process called post-glacial rebound or isostasy. The once sheer sea cliffs are now several miles inland, forming an unbroken chain of steep ridges at the foot of which small settlements have sprung up.

Two large alluvial deserts occupy a conspicuous portion of this territory: the Mýrdalssandur, between Vík and Kirkjubæjarklaustur, and the Skeiðarársandur, farther east. These

The Northern Lights in Vík.

deserts formed as a result of the periodic floods caused by volcanic eruptions that still occur below the ice caps: the ice melts and water accumulates under the ice sheet and then gushes violently into the valley, sometimes sweeping away roads and bridges.

The first point of interest you will encounter on the north side of the road as you enter the region is the glacial tongue known as Sólheimajökull, which branches off the Mýrdalsjökull ice cap. You can take glacier hikes here with a glaciologist (*Icelandic Mountain Guides, 587 999, info@mountainguides.is, $$$, closed Sat.-Sun.*).

Vík

At the time of colonization, between the ninth and tenth centuries, the area where the village of Vík stands today must have been a vast bay, but the constant work of streams carrying sediment from the mountains has gradually extended the coastline and created a plain. It is the setting of *Katla,* a successful TV series named after the dangerous subglacial volcano. Because of the constant threat of flooding, Vík has an evacuation plan in the event of an eruption; the gathering point considered safest is the clearing where the town's church stands, **Víkurkirkja,** a popular vantage point overlooking the town, with the famous Reynisdrangar basaltic stacks in the background. Legend has it they are two trolls who became petrified as they attempted to drag their ship ashore.

Much of the Southeast was devoid of commercial establishments until the late 19th century. This meant

Víkurkirkja ✉ Víkurbraut 2 ☎ 846 6026 🕒 Visit on request only

INSIDER TIP:
Vík has one of the country's largest shopping centers, with souvenir stores, technical clothing stores and grocery stores.
—ROBERTO LUIGI PAGANI
Author of the guidebook

that local people, in order to sell their products or buy others not locally available, had to travel to other parts of the country. It was only when some farmers in Vík started economic activities, such as the opening of a slaughterhouse and a store, that the present village began to grow. Today Vík is one of the most important destinations in the region, not only because of its proximity to points of interest such as the black beach of Reynisfjara or the promontory of Dyrhólaey, but also because of the services it offers: in fact, one of the country's largest shopping centers is located there, with souvenir stores, technical clothing stores, grocery stores, and bars and restaurants (*Austurvegur 20, $$$, Mon.–Sun. 9 a.m.–9 p.m.*).

In the old part of the town is **Kötlusetur,** a tourist information center. There is no shortage of attractions, such as the **Skaftfellingur Museum,** dedicated to local history and culture, and the **Icelandic Lava Show,** where you can watch and listen to real molten lava flow and glow. **Thakgil** (accessible only in the summer), a gorge that serves as a starting point for popular hiking trails, is located just east of the town.

Reynisfjara

Beyond Reynisfjall mountain, which hugs Vík on the west side, lies Reynisfjara, the country's most famous black sand beach, where some of the most stunning columnar basalt formations can be seen. In the summer, a colony of puffins takes up residence there.

Kötlusetur ✉ Víkurbraut 28 ☎ 487 1395 🕒 Mon.–Sun. **www.kotlusetur.is** • **Skaftfellingur Museum** ✉ Víkurbraut 17 ☎ 487 1395 $ $ • **Icelandic Lava Show** ✉ Víkurbraut 5 ☎ 553 0005 $ $$ **icelandiclavashow.com**

The Icelandic Sweater

The Icelandic sweater is a quality assurance label. In order to qualify as such, it must be made exclusively from new wool from Icelandic sheep and must be worked entirely by hand on Icelandic soil, as well as follow the traditional design with a geometric pattern on the chest. It can be distinguished from imitations by the tag. Typically it also bears the name of the person who made it.

View of Reynisfjara Black Sand Beach.

Great caution must be exercised when visiting this beach: sudden waves crash over the shoreline without warning and rapidly expand over the beach, dragging passersby into the ocean, where the icy water and the strong undertow of the steep shoreline can prove fatal to even the most experienced swimmers. Particular attention should be paid to the part of the beach that pushes eastward, past the basalt formations and toward the stacks. The tide here rises suddenly and engulfs the entire beach, leaving anyone trapped there in danger.

On the other side of the beach, the promontory of Dyrhólaey, with its famous arch, is another prime spot for observing nature, including colonies of birds, such as gannets, puffins, and eider ducks, as well as the cliffs and stacks just offshore. At the highest part of the headland, near the lighthouse, you can contemplate the vastness of the sandy plains of Sólheimasandur, bordered to the north by the rugged slopes of the mountains.

Hjörleifshöfði

At the foot of Mýrdalsjökull glacier, 9 miles (15 km) east of the town, on the south side of Route 1, is a steep headland called Hjörleifshöfði, named after Hjörleifur, sworn brother of the first settler Ingólfur Arnarson. Hjörleifur is said to have landed here first, around 870 AD, and settled before being killed by his Irish servants. This promontory is not easily reached by some cars because of the rough and sometimes sandy road, but it is a prime destination for hiking and for observing the blooming lupines.

Álftaver, Meðalland & Landbrot

On the other side of the desert, you can turn off on Route 211 to reach the small town of **Thykkvabæjarklaustur** in Álftaver. An Augustinian monastery was founded here in 1168 but dissolved in the wake of the Protestant Reformation in the country. Participating in the founding of this important institution was Thorlákur Thórhallsson, who would go on to become a bishop and eventually the country's patron saint. One of the monastery's abbots, Brandur Jónsson, who lived during the 13th century, was a distinguished theologian and is credited with the *Alexanders saga*, a prose translation of the Latin poem *Alexandreis*, on Alexander the Great. A monk who lived in the monastery during the 14th century, Eysteinn Ásgrímsson, composed a 100-stanza devotional poem called *Lilja*, "Lily," considered one of the most important pieces of poetry from the Icelandic Middle Ages. Still today the saying *Öll skáld vildu Lilju kveðið hafa*, "All poets wish they had composed Lilja," is used when one regrets not having had the same brilliant idea as someone else. Located in the same spot today is a picturesque church, **Thykkvabæjarklausturskirkja**.

Near the town is an important group of pseudocraters, **Álftaversgígar**, formed from steam explosions caused by lava flowing over marshy soils. Considered a natural heritage site, these protected formations. They are part of the Katla Geopark, an area of geological interest that covers much of the western part of southeastern Iceland and belongs to the UNESCO World Geoparks group. Returning to Route 1 and continuing about 3.7 miles (6 km) north, there is a rest stop at the intersection for Hrífunes. From here, trails branch off and lead to the lava formations. Just north of the stopping point are several stone cairns in an area called Laufskálavarða. It was a tradition in centuries past that those crossing the desert for the first time should build one for good fortune.

EXPERIENCE: Ice Caves

In the winter, it is possible to visit the caves of Vatnajökull's largest glacial tongue, Breiðamerkurjökull. In summer, the high amount of water flowing through them makes them inaccessible. They can only be visited with experienced guides, and special vehicles are necessary to reach them because of the rough terrain. They change constantly as water carves new openings on its way to the Jökulsárlón glacial lagoon. Inside them, you can admire the deep blue glow of the ceiling. The layer of ice separating you from the surface can exceed 32 feet (10 m) at its thickest points (*troll.is/ice-caves-in-iceland*).

Continuing on the main road, you can reach the intersection with Route 204, which merges with Route 1 about 31 miles (50 km) east at the town of Kirkjubæjarklaustur. The road partially skirts the edge of the colossal Eldhraun lava field, passing through the town of Meðalholt, where there is the lovely Langholtskirkja church, completed in 1862.

Continuing north, you enter the village of Landbrot. Near the Seglbúðir fishing club guesthouse, you can park and walk to Tröllshylur, a series of turquoise and emerald green pools and ponds set in oddly shaped lava formations. Once you reach the town of Kirkjubæjarklaustur, you can walk back down from the gas station by following the 5.5-mile (9 km) circular hiking trail that skirts Hæðargarðsvatn lake and passes through several pseudocraters called Landbrotshólar, some of which are massive, like Gluggasker. These are also protected as part of the Katla Geopark. The area where they can be found encompasses about 19 square miles (50 sq km) and is the largest area in the country affected by this geological phenomenon.

Grafarkirkja in Skaftártunga

At the intersection with Route 208, 2.5 miles (4 km) north of the one with Route 204, you can reach the beautiful Grafarkirkja, a church rebuilt on the site of an older one in 1931. Inside it contains two valuable bells dating to the first half of the 18th century, but it is particularly famous for the beauty of its surroundings and the cemetery in which it stands.

Skaftáreldahraun

With an area of more than 216 square miles (560 sq km), Skaftáreldahraun is the second-largest lava field in the world, formed as a result of a catastrophic erup-

The *Langspil*

In the autobiography of Reverend Jón Steingrímsson (see p. 157) there is an early account of the *langspil*, the most important instrument in Icelandic folk music. It is similar to several other instruments typical of the northern European folk tradition. It is an elongated wooden zither consisting of a sound box with the widest end at the bridge and the neck ending in a carved scroll like a violin, to which pegs are attached to adjust the tension of the four strings. The instrument is placed horizontally on one's legs or some sort of stand and then played by plucking the strings or with a bow. Usually, pressing the first string along the soundboard with the thumb modulates the tone by producing a drone that accompanies the harmonic virtuosity of the vibration of the other strings. Although it almost disappeared from use around the beginning of the 20th century, the langspil is currently experiencing a revival.

Eldhraun, the moss-covered lava fields.

tion that occurred in 1783 and 1784 in the Laki area along a 15-mile (25 km) fracture.

The eruption released toxic substances into the atmosphere that eventually poisoned the land, air and water, leading to the deaths of livestock and wildlife and causing famine, known as the "mist hardships," one of the darkest episodes in Icelandic history. The Danish monarchy, whose sovereignty would last until 1944, even contemplated evacuating the entire island and relocating the inhabitants to central Jutland.

One noteworthy story from this event involves the area's priest, Jón Steingrímsson, who did his best to help his parishioners. Steingrímsson wrote an account of the events of those two difficult years that contains important geological and natural observations regarding the phenomena. In one of the most difficult and discouraging moments, as the lava advanced inexorably toward the town of Kirkjubæjarklaustur, he summoned his parishioners to attend their last Mass, given in a black fog, knowing they were nearing the end. During the dramatic sermon, he urged the participants to repent and trust in divine providence. The Mass would later go down in history as the Eldmessa, "fire Mass". When it ended, it was clear that the lava had come to a halt just outside the town.

The lava front, called Eldmessutangi, is still visible in the riverbed where it ended, just west and within walking distance of Kirkjubæjarklaustur. Beneath the ground, lava that solidified around pockets that were still liquid created more than 200 long tunnels and caves.

Fjaðrárgljúfur

Carved out over millennia by the incessant flow of the river, this 328-foot (100 m) deep and 1.2-mile (2 km) long canyon is one of the most photographed attractions in the country. Following an increase in its popularity, platforms have been laid along marked paths to prevent visitors from damaging the area by trampling the fragile local flora.

Kirkjubæjarklaustur

The region of Síða is characterized by pleasant farms that spring up like small oases between the rugged highlands to the north and vast sandy marshes to the south. The main town is Kirkjubæjarklaustur.

According to medieval sources, the first Norse settler in this area was Ketill the Stupid, grandson of Ketill Nasoplat, a Norwegian nobleman who lived in the ninth century, ancestor of some of Iceland's most important settlers, and thus progenitor of some of the most powerful clans in medieval Iceland. Ketill the Stupid was Christian and settled in a place where, as the story goes, only Christians could dwell and where hermit monks of Irish descent had lived. Here he built the Kirkjubær, ("church farm"), estate. Upon his death, according to medieval sources, a pagan named Hildir intended to take possession of the property but died instantly after crossing the border. A women's convent (*klaustur*) of the Benedictine order was founded here in 1186. Numerous legends have arisen around the convent and the presence of the nuns.

During the 20th century, a forest was planted on the slopes behind the village that is now home to Iceland's tallest tree, a Sitka spruce that stands almost 100 feet (30 m) tall. From the foot of the striking Systrafoss waterfall, which resembles a nun's veil, you can follow a path of medium difficulty to Sönghellir, a cave in the rock face where it is said that nuns used to sing their hymns to welcome the monks of Thykkvabæjarklaustur when they visited. On the plateau at the top of the ridges is Systravatn lake, where, legend has it, a monster dragged a nun by luring her with a golden object. From here, you have an incredible view of the landscape below and, on a clear day, you can distinctly see Öræfajökull glacier farther east.

West of the parking lot in front of the waterfall, following the road on foot, you can also reach the Rauðárfoss waterfall, which flows over a wall of metallic red color. Continue on to a steep promontory that is detached from the rest of the rock face: this is Systrastapi, where legend says that two nuns from the ancient convent who burned at the stake are buried. One of them allegedly joined the devil and desecrated the holy host, whereas the other allegedly blasphemed the pope. Following the Reformation, flowers sprouted on the second nun's grave, indicating that her sin had been redeemed.

Kirkjubæjarklaustur ✉ Skaftárstofa Infopoint ☎ 487 4620
🕒 Mon.–Sun.; Jan.–Apr. closed Sat. & Sun.

In the village itself is the site of the old church where Jón Steingrímsson recited the "fire Mass," at the heart of the village cemetery. Next to it is the chapel erected in memory of the priest and the archaeological excavation of the Benedictine monastery.

At the traffic circle on the way out of the village, on the left side of Route 204, you can reach the curious natural formation known as Kirkjugólf, "church floor." Long considered the tiled floor of the old convent church, it is instead the polished top of a columnar basalt formation that emerges at ground level. On the parking lot path, one passes a rocky mound rising from the ground; this is Hildishaugur, or the mound of Hildir, the pagan who had attempted to take over the Kirkjubær estate upon the death of Ketill the Stupid. Just beyond Route 204 is the graceful waterfall Stjórnarfoss. The natural amphitheater beside the waterfall was formerly the seat of the local assembly.

INSIDER TIP:
From Lake Systravatn, you can catch superb views of the landscape below, and on a clear day you can see the Öræfajökull glacier.

—ROBERTO LUIGI PAGANI
Author of the guidebook

Stjórnarfoss waterfall, not far from the town of Kirkjubæjarklaustur.

Prestbakki

Leaving Kirkjubæjarklaustur heading east, the edge of the mountains recedes, creating a wide, flat valley dotted with woodlands and farms. Prestbakki is worth visiting and can be reached by turning on Route 202. This was the former residence of Jón Steingrímsson (see p. 157), and it is now the site of the most important church in the local parish, **Prestbakkakirkja á Síðu,** famous for its particularly ornate and well-maintained interior.

The mountain that runs all the way to the road farther east is the famous Keldunúpur, named after the protagonist of a medieval saga set in these parts: *Saga of Gunnar, the Idiot of Keldunúpur*. There is a passage in the rock face, clearly visible from the road, and through the opening there seems to be an engraved white cross. According to local folklore, it was an engraving made by the hermits who lived here before the arrival of the Norsemen, whereas the cave is the place where the hero of the saga, Gunnar, supposedly buried his treasure.

Foss á Síðu

Foss á Síðu is a small town at the foot of a steep ridge where a pencil-thin waterfall plummets to the ground. On the opposite side of the road, farther down to the east, is a very famous natural formation, Dverghamrar, consisting of two huge columnar basalt formations resembling the ramparts of a castle and, according to local lore, serving as the residence of dwarves. A short distance beyond the headland are the rapids of Fossálar. The bucolic atmospheres of Síða give way to a wilder landscape dominated by rock and moss.

Fljótshverfi

The first natural formation of interest you will come across in this region is Orrustuhóll, a moss-covered craggy mountain shaped like a mushroom cap. The site of a historic battle, this ancient rocky outcrop, surrounded by remnants of lava from the 1783–84 eruption, can be climbed for excellent views of the surrounding region. About 6 miles (10 km) farther east is Kálfafell, a prominent mountain where the Kálfafellskirkja Church, rebuilt in the mid-20th century on the site of an earlier one, is located. At the edge of the vast floodplain of Skeiðarársandur, you will pass below Iceland's highest rock face, Lómagnúpur (2506 ft, 764 m).

At the foot of the mountain stands the Núpsstaður farm and, next to it, the Núpsstaðakirkja, one of only five peat churches to have been preserved. The small building, with its peat-covered roof and pitch-painted wooden facade, is from the 17th century.

The site is private property and inaccessible but can be observed from the road. ■

Prestbakkakirkja á Síðu ✉ Prestbakki ☎ 6968707 🕒 On request only

AROUND VATNAJÖKULL

The eastern part of the Southeast region runs along the foothills of mountains over which looms the imposing Vatnajökull ice cap, giving its name to Iceland's largest national park. Ice dominates the landscape, with numerous tongues snaking down through the mountains.

Svartifoss waterfall, surrounded by the well-known basalt columns.

The eastern part of southeastern Iceland sits within the administrative limits of Höfn in Hornafjörður, the region's only substantial population center with more than 2,000 inhabitants. Here are the main access points to Vatnajökulsthjóðgarður, which, with an area of more than 5,405 square miles (14,000 sq km), is Iceland's largest national park. Within its boundaries are impressive, extremely varied landscapes with plenty of destinations, hiking trails, and outdoor activities of all kinds.

As you approach the park from the west, you will encounter vast expanses of black sand. These were created from the debris the glaciers carried for thousands of years along with the endless flowing of rivers, which are sometimes calm, sometimes treacherous, and other times ruinous and destructive. These expanses stretch for about 24 miles (40 km), between the edge of Fljótshverfi and Skaftafell National Park, and are called Skeiðarársandur, Iceland's largest floodplain, with an area of about 386 square miles (1,000 sq km).

Eruptions of volcanic systems in the area can melt the lower layer of the ice sheet resulting in floods, like the catastrophic one in 1996 when a debris

The Hidden Volcano

Öræfajökull is a volcano covered by the southernmost branch of the Vatnajökull ice cap. The first expedition there was led by Icelandic naturalist Sveinn Pálsson in 1794. During his ascent, Pálsson noticed how the glaciers were affected by a downward sliding motion due to gravity. He also observed the presence of ash deposits from ancient eruptions.

avalanche swept away Hringvegur and three bridges.

Despite the moonscape appearance of the area, the easternmost part of Sandur, near Skaftafell, has been undergoing a steady process of greening for some years: large numbers of native birch trees have colonized large tracts of desert.

Skaftafell

The district that runs along the slopes of the mountains below Öræfajökull glacier, the southernmost part of Vatnajökull glacier, is called Öræfi, "wasteland." Despite the name, this area is rich with incredible vistas of the thriving nature, like Skaftafell for example, which became a protected area in 1967 and later was absorbed by the larger **Vatnajökull National Park,** established in 2008. The beauty of its landscapes has made it a favorite destination of Icelanders. From here, you can admire Iceland's highest peak, Hvannadalshnjúkur, a 6,922-foot-tall (2,110 m) tall stubby hump that emerges from the ice cap.

Skaftafell is not only a nature destination, but also a region packed with rich history. During the Middle Ages, numerous wood and peat farms dotted the plains, but a devastating eruption in 1362 turned the pleasant, agricultural region into a deserted and depopulated district. For a lesson in the area's history, you can join an excursion from the park's **Visitor Center** to visit Selið, a faithful reproduction of the farms in the area.

The park is home to the famous Svartifoss (Black Waterfall), one of the most popular destinations for visitors. The waterfall is about 3 miles (5 km) away. It falls over an amphitheater-shaped rock face formed by symmetrical basalt columns. The water drenches the surrounding rocks with its spray and turns them black. On the same trail, you can also climb to the Sjónarsker observation point, which offers unparalleled views of the entire region. More challenging hikes are also possible, to reach destinations like the Sjónarnípa

Vatnajökull National Park ✉ Urridaholtsstraeti 6-8 ☎ 575 8400 🕒 Reduced hours for facilities in winter $ $$ **www.vatnajokulsthjodgardur.is** • **Visitor Center** ✉ Skaftafellsstofa ☎ 470 8300 🕒 Open Jun.–Sept. 8 a.m.–7 p.m., Feb.–May. & Oct. 9 a.m.–6 p.m., Nov.–Jan. 10 a.m.–6 p.m. **www.vatnajokulsthjodgardur.is** **Jökulsárlón** •

ridge or the peaks of Kristínartindar. One particularly beautiful spot is Morsárdalur valley, west of the visitor center. It is home to a portion of the glacier that lies on the valley floor, fractured from the ice cap above. Iceland's highest waterfall, Morsárfoss, flows from the foot of the cap all the way to the valley below.

On the western side of the valley lies what remains of one of Iceland's original forests, Bæjarstaðarskógur, where a small thermal pool, Heitu Lækir, carved out by the coursing of hot streams, can be found. From the pool, which is located on the hillside in a clearing surrounded by trees, there are sweeping views of the entire valley and the peaks of the national park. The entire trail covers about 12.5 miles (20 km). For those who are looking for a less strenuous option, there is an easy, flat path that starts from the east side of the Visitor Center and leads to the mighty glacial tongue of Skaftafellsjökull.

INSIDER TIP:
A small thermal pool is hidden in what remains of one of Iceland's original forests on the west side of the Morsárdalur valley.

—ROBERTO LUIGI PAGANI
Author of the guidebook

Freysnes

Freysnes is a village located at the foot of Svínafellsjökull glacial tongue,

The Jökulsárlón glacial lagoon.

EXPERIENCE: Höfn Langoustine

Höfn is considered Iceland's langoustine capital. Here Humarhátíð (Langoustine Festival) is held every summer with cultural events and entertainment. The star of the *Nephrops norvegicus*, which is the key ingredient in the famous *humarsúpa*, "langoustine soup." Many different versions are available, but one constant is that they always include spices and fresh cream. Langoustines are also grilled, pan-fried, or served in rich salads. Pay attention to English translations: "langoustine" is sometimes incorrectly translated as lobster on English-language menus.

which served as the backdrop for some scenes in the film *Interstellar* (2014). It is possible to reach the glacier via a dirt road about 1.5 miles (2 km) long that reaches a parking lot near the tongue. Svínafell Farm, a short distance away, was an important center of power in the medieval period, as the seat of the Svínfellingar clan, one of the most important families on the island. It also figures in the *Njáls saga* (see pp. 129–131), the most famous of the Icelandic sagas, in which it is the home of Flosi Thórðarson, who is responsible for the burning of the protagonist's family, Njáll. A descendant of Flosi's brother Sigmundur Thorgilsson, he was one of the most powerful lords of his time, and the progenitor of the Svínfellingar clan. He died in 1118 on a pilgrimage to Rome. Today the farm, which is located on the opposite side of the road from the gas station, offers accommodation and space for camping.

Hof

Moving south from Skaftafell along the slopes of the mountains below the great Öræfajökull glacier, this small town has five old peat churches, as well as a new one, Hofskirkja. The small town has only a few buildings, including a hotel, guesthouse, and elementary school. The only notable attraction is the church, consecrated in 1885. It stands on land that must have housed a church as early as 1343. Peat buildings were regularly rebuilt as the peat decomposed and fell apart. Most of Iceland's old churches were replaced during the 19th and 20th centuries by wooden or concrete structures. Hofskirkja is not open to the public, but it is possible to get a glimpse inside through the windows.

Ingólfshöfði

It is difficult to overstate the significance of this place, where natural and historical value meet. A promontory located between the mountains and the sea on the edge of vast flooded beaches known as Leirur, Ingólfshöfði is believed to be the site of Ingólfur Arnarson's first Icelandic landing. Atop the headland, a column with an engraved phrase commemorates the event. The destination can only be reached by guided tours organized by the owners of the surrounding land who have resided here for generations.

Mýrdalsjökull

Moving past the southern part of the Öræfajökull massif, you will enter a region called Suðursveit, which runs along the coast, between the mountains and the sea heading northeast. The most important attraction in this region is without a doubt **Jökulsárlón,** a glacial lagoon where small icebergs can be seen floating placidly toward the Atlantic, a natural setting for famous films such as *Die Another Day* (2002) and *Batman Begins* (2005).

The lagoon formed as the glacial tongue called Breiðamerkurjökull receded after reaching its maximum extent in the late 19th century, when it had almost reached the coast. At the time of Iceland's colonization and throughout the Middle Ages, the glacier was several miles farther inland, as evidenced by records indicating the presence of farms in the valleys now engulfed by ice. With the onset of the Little Ice Age, beginning in the 14th century, Iceland's glaciers advanced considerably, often destroying farms and farmland. Then, as the glacial tongues melted and receded, which began in the late 19th and early 20th centuries, lakes were created in the furrows previously carved by ice. The depth of these furrows can be considerable; Jökulsárlón is 931 feet (284 m) deep. The proximity of the ocean means that salt water enters the lagoon through a small waterway at high tide. The salt water in the lagoon accelerates the melting of the glacier due to climate change, causing it to recede at about 3 feet (1 m) per day. Since the early 20th century, when the glacial tongue was at its maximum extent, it has receded more than 5 miles (8 km), creating the lagoon, which covers an area of 7 square miles (18 sq km). At this rate, within a few decades, a deep fjord is likely to form.

The lagoon ecosystem is home to various animals, including herring, capelan, trout, salmon and small crus-

Glacier Lagoon ✉ Jökulsárlón ☎ 478 2222 🕒 Mon.–Sun. **icelagoon.is**

A resident of the Jökulsárlón glacial lagoon.

The port city of Höfn, capital of the region.

taceans, which provide an important food supply for seals found in the lagoon, sheltering from predators. You can catch them popping up among the blocks of ice. Also worth noting is the presence of birds such as skuas and arctic terns, especially in the summer.

There is a small dining area at the site with kiosks selling street food, and you can also take excursions on an amphibious vehicle or Zodiac tender.

Fjallsárlón

One of the most popular glacial lakes can be reached a short distance (about half a mile, 1 km) off Route 1. This one is much smaller and much less frequented than Jökulsárlón. Surrounded by rugged mountains and a much closer glacial tongue, it offers an impressive backdrop despite its much smaller size. From the visitor center, where there is a restaurant (*Frost restaurant, 666 8006, info@fjallsarlon.is*), you can participate in excursions aboard Zodiac tenders and stay overnight on floating structures.

Kvíárjökull

In the southeastern part of Öræfajökull, Europe's second largest active volcano, lies a glacial tongue bor-

Fjallsárlón ☎ 666 8006 **fjallsarlon.is • Kvíárjökull visitvatnajokull.is**

dered by moraine hills that form a giant amphitheater. This is Kvíárjökull. You can park at the end of the very short road off Route 1 just before the bridge and walk to the lagoon at the foot of the glacier. Largely untouched by mass tourism, it remains a wild and remote area due to the uneven and sometimes rough terrain. On the west side, you can see a rock arch that resembles the shape of two trolls kissing. In the fall, starting in August, abundant quantities of black crowberries are found here.

Thórbergssetur

From the road, down the slope that dips toward the sea, there is a curious building whose outer wall is painted to resemble a bookshelf lined with giant books. This is a museum dedicated to one of the most important Icelandic writers of the 20th century: Thorbergur Thórðarson (1888–1974), who was born and raised in this area. He was an unconventional intellectual with penchant for sharp satire and a keen observer and critic of the society of his time. He was sentenced to pay a fine by the Icelandic Supreme Court for "offending a foreign nation" in vitriolic articles against the German Nazi party published in 1934. He is highly regarded in his homeland for his rich vocabulary and mastery of language, despite being self-educated and from a humble background. Some of his novels, such as *Bréf til Láru* (*Letters to Lára*) or the trilogy set in his native district, Suðursveit, are considered some of the most important classics of Icelandic literature.

Höfn

Höfn is the region's capital and the most important city in the Southeast. It is located on a tongue of land in a wide bay dotted with islets, reefs, and shoals. Founded in 1897 by a merchant who established his business here, Höfn means "harbor" in Icelandic. The local economy is heavily focused on langoustine fishing and fish processing. The town's harbor, as well as its economy, could be jeopardized by post-glacial rebound, a phenomenon that causes the seafloor to rise as a result of the slowly shrinking Vatnajökull glacier and subsequent release of pressure from the ice. It could make the waters unnavigable.

Near the harbor is a building called Gamlabúð, which houses the Vatnajökull National Park information center. Here there is an exhibition on the nature in the park, local avifauna, and the impact of climate change on local life. In the undeveloped area south of town, at the tip of the peninsula, is a monument to seafarers. From here, a path leads to the coast. Renowned for its lan-

Thórbergssetur Hala 867 2900 Mon.–Sun. 10 a.m.–6 p.m **thorbergur.is** • **Höfn** Gamlabúð Höfn Visitor Centre 470 8330 **visitvatnajokull.is**

goustine dishes, local restaurants never fail to include them on their menus.

Hoffell

North of Höfn, driving along Route 984 for about 2.5 miles (4 km), you will reach the Hoffell thermal baths, which are very basic but set in stunning natural surroundings. Continuing for another 2.5 miles (4 km), you can reach the glacial tongue of Hoffellsjökull. The road is extremely bumpy, therefore having a suitable vehicle for these conditions is strongly recommended.

Stokksnes

Ten and a half miles (17 km) from Höfn is Stokksnes, on the extreme tip of the peninsula of the same name. From here, it is possible to view the famous Vestrahorn Mountain, a coveted photographic destination. You must park at the **Viking Café** and pay the toll. They will give you a barcode to pass through the barrier on the road leading to the peninsula. In addition to the many hiking trails, there is an abandoned film set that re-creates a Nordic Iron Age village. The site is dilapidated and the buildings unsafe, so caution is advised when exploring it. ■

Hoffell ✉ Hoffell 2 B, Hornafjörður ☎ 478 1514 **info@glacierworld.is** • **Viking Café** ✉ Horn ☎ 478 2577 🕒 Mon.–Sun. **vikingcafe.is**

The picturesque thermal baths of Hoffell.

WALKING & DRIVING ROUTE: THE DISTRICTS OF FIRE

Skaftárhreppur is home to the so-called Districts of Fire, Eldsveitir, a name adopted after the eruption in 1783–84. The area offers numerous opportunities to enjoy nature in total solitude.

The area around Svínafellsjökull glacier, which is part of the larger Vatnajökull glacier, is ideal for those who enjoy hiking.

This itinerary, which traverses the region between the two great deserts of Mýrdalssandur and Skeiðarársandur, is extremely scenic and provides deeper exploration of a region rich in remote natural destinations, where peace and silence reign. It's the experience one might expect from a trip to Iceland. Numerous deviations and trails can be taken off Route 1 to reach hidden valleys, canyons, waterfalls, and lakes. The arctic char in Kirkjubæjarklaustur is a typical product appreciated throughout the country and worth tasting.

Coming from the west, begin by leaving Hringvegur and taking Route 209. This was once Route 1 and is partially unpaved but extremely scenic because of its elevation, snaking along the sides of the hills. From here, turn north on Route 208 to reach the Gröf-wood church, **Grafarkirkja** ❶. Once back on Route 1, continue by car 8.5 miles (14 km) eastward. On the north side you will find a dirt parking lot opposite a small valley in the **Eldhraun** lava field ❷, where some larch trees grow. From this small oasis you can follow walking trails through the rocks.

Driving another 6.2 miles (10 km) on Route 1, you will reach the town of Kirkjubæjarklaustur. Stop at the Vatnajökull National Park visitor center then explore the forest trails that start at the foot of the **Systrafoss** waterfall ❸, which can be reached by car, parking just below the falls at the edge of the forest. In 1945, residents planted 60,000 dwarf birch trees here, and later firs, pines, and larches were added. When you finish your walk, you can enjoy lunch at Kjarr Restaurant (*Klausturvegur 2, 546 1400, kjarrrestaurant.is, open Jun.–Sept.*)

See also map p. 148
Grafarkirkja
44 miles (70 km)
2 days
Fossdalsá

and sample Klaustur arctic char (Klausturbleikja), a kind of salmon renowned throughout the country. From here you can drive out of the town and take the north exit at the roundabout, following Route 203 to **Geirland** 4. Park on the dirt road next to the river and follow the path through the fields to the foot of the mountains where you will find a hut housing an old electric turbine and information panels on the history of electricity and its use in the area (always open).

Back on Route 1, continue 4.3 miles (7 km) eastward until you reach the Hörgsland campground. Descending from the north side of the road, you can follow a path that winds up the side of the narrow, wild valley of **Rauðardalur** 5, on the western side. It then crosses the river and continues on the eastern side. Along the stream that crosses it are several waterfalls. As you head to the next stop, you can take a break at the Hamrafoss Café (*Hamrafoss, 894 1576*), about 2.5 miles (4 km) east of Hörgsland (*487 6655, postur @horgsland.is*). The café, with its cozy, family atmosphere, overlooks the **Foss** waterfall. On the opposite side of the road, weather permitting, you can ask permission from the landowner to climb up a steep path that leads to a gap in the cliff face and comes out on the plateau that is home to **Lake Thórutjörn** 6. A folk legend claims it was inhabited by a mythical animal, the nykur, a horse with a bright gray coat that drags anyone who attempts to ride it into the abyss. The hike on the plateau is about half a mile (1 km). However, the climb is challenging and the terrain slippery; take extreme caution. Alternatively, you can continue 12.5 miles (20 km) eastward along Route 1 and stop at the viewpoint overlooking **Lómagnúpur Mountain** 7. If you have an off-road vehicle, you can take the mule track north and reach the impressive **Fossdalsá River** 8 waterfall, about 2.5 miles (4 km) away.

NOT TO BE MISSED:

The Skaftáreldahraun lava field • Systrafoss waterfall • Foss á Síðu • Lómagnúpur Mountain

Skaftafell & Vatnajökull National Park

In 2008, the national parks of Skaftafell and Jökulsárgljúfur, along with the Vatnajökull glacier area, were combined into what is now Vatnajökull National Park, which covers almost 14 percent of the entire area of the country, an impressive 5,460 square miles (14,141 sq km), the second largest national park in Europe. Encompassing an extremely large area that stretches from the south of Iceland to the east and north, it has five visitor centers. These centers have rangers available to offer information on hiking routes, road conditions and geographical or natural features of interest. These visitor centers are called Skaftárstofa, near Kirkjubæjarklaustur; Skaftafellsstofa, in Skaftafell; Gamlabúð in the town of Höfn; Gljúfrastofa, in the north of the country, near Ásbyrgi Canyon; and Snæfellsstofa, in the east, just north of Skriðuklaustur.

The best access point is undoubtedly the Skaftafell area and, in particular, the Skaftafellstofa Visitor Center, where there is parking (for a fee), a campground, toilets, and a refreshment stand. A number of hiking trails of varying difficulty start from here, winding along mountains and valleys etched by glacial tongues. The mild climate favors the development of relatively lush flora, with birch, willow, and rowan woodlands and bluebells, saxifrages, angelica, and chamerium flowers. The fauna is also quite rich compared to other areas of the country. In addition to the native arctic fox, there are also mink and numerous bird species, such as the thrush, the common redpoll, the common wren, the raven, the merlin, the snow bunting, the meadow pipit, and the ptarmigan, once the hunting spoils of members of the less affluent classes who were prohibited regular consumption of meat from the farms.

Vatnajökull glacier has an area of 3,050 square miles (7,900 sq km), an average thickness of 1,246 feet (380 m) and maximum thickness of 3,116 feet (950 m), and it's located at the tectonic fault that runs through the island. Grímsvötn is the most active volcano in the entire country, whereas Bárðarbunga is the largest. Subglacial eruptions are particularly dangerous for two reasons: on the one hand, the interaction between lava and water produces explosive eruptions that launch debris (tephra) a great distance; on the other hand, melting ice causes *jökulhlaup*, or floods, which are sometimes catastrophic. Since the weight of the glacier crushes the rock of the mountains below, the water bursting downstream carries a large amount of black sand and debris, which are deposited on the floodplain, becoming a black sand desert. The presence of the glacier, however, seems to somewhat mitigate the volcanism below it, and with the current thinning of the ice sheet, scientists expect an increase in activity.

In past centuries the glacier was called Klofajökull, "Divided Glacier," and it appears that until the 16th century it could be crossed to reach the North. Some speculate that two smaller ice caps existed in the past, and they were united by the growth in the late medieval and later periods, coinciding with an era of cooler climate known as the Little Ice Age. The name comes from the fact that the glacier had two bulges, separated by a depression, which has nonetheless been covered with ice since the time of the island's colonization, although the edge of the

Systrafoss waterfall along the Fossá River, near the small village of Kirkjubæjarklaustur.

ice cap was about 6–9 miles (10–15 km) farther back than it is today.

After several centuries of growth, the glacier began to lose mass. Since 1989, about 47 cubic miles (200 cu km) of ice has melted, with a surface loss of more than 154 square miles (400 sq km). Post-glacial isostasy, or the swelling of the land as the glacier melts, is slowly causing the seabed at the island's coastline to rise. This threatens to make the port of Höfn inaccessible. This will have catastrophic consequences for the town's economy, which is heavily dependent on the fishing industry. The melting of the glaciers also poses a risk to water resources, since they are a massive reserve of water released gradually and steadily. Without glaciers, extreme episodes of alternating floods and droughts are likely to increase. In light of current developments, the changes triggered by the disappearance of glaciers will be one of the greatest challenges for the next generations.

Majestic valleys, the bucolic atmosphere of the countryside, and the grandeur of two great fjords

THE WEST

Mount Kirkjufell, near the town of Grundarfjördur.

THE WEST

Home to the powerful medieval Sturlungar clan, the West has been the scene of important events in the country's history and is the backdrop for some of the most popular sagas, such as the *Egils saga*, the *Eiríks saga*, and the *Laxdæla saga*. The Snæfellsnes Peninsula, due to the presence of a small glacier, black beaches, cliffs, lava fields, and picturesque villages, is sometimes referred to as "Iceland in miniature."

The town of Borgarnes.

The Western region (Vesturland) is an area of vast spaces, where undulating fields are trodden by large herds of Icelandic horses, where the silhouette of the Snæfell volcano towers over diverse landscapes, such as islands, cliffs, fishing villages, lava fields, and pleasant farms. In the southernmost part there are two large fjords.

The first one you encounter on your way from the capital is Hvalfjörður, usually skipped over by taking the 3.5-mile (6 km) tunnel under it. The area isn't traveled much but it has many scenic corners with hidden gems like the Glymur waterfall, the second highest in the country, at 650 feet (198 m).

The second fjord is the shallow and turquoise-colored Borgarfjörður. On its northern shore is the small town of Borgarnes (population about 2,000), the main town of the region. Reykholt, on the other hand, which is more inland, was home to the medieval lord and poet Snorri Sturluson, considered the most important Icelandic author of the period. Today, Reykholt is home to a museum and research center. Just beyond it flow the springs of Hraunfossar, one of the most photographed spots on the entire island.

Snæfellsnes is a good sample of all the best Iceland has to offer. Mount Snæfell (4,744 ft, 1,446 m), an active volcano, looms at the far end of the peninsula and is covered by an ice cap.

On the northern side, the small town of Stykkishólmur, with its traditional cottages, is one of the most photogenic villages in Iceland. It is a port for ferries that go to the fjords across the Breiðafjörður Gulf. The ferry stops at the famous Flatey Island, a sort of time capsule with no paved roads or cars, where numerous traditional dwellings stand against a backdrop of the gulf and its surrounding

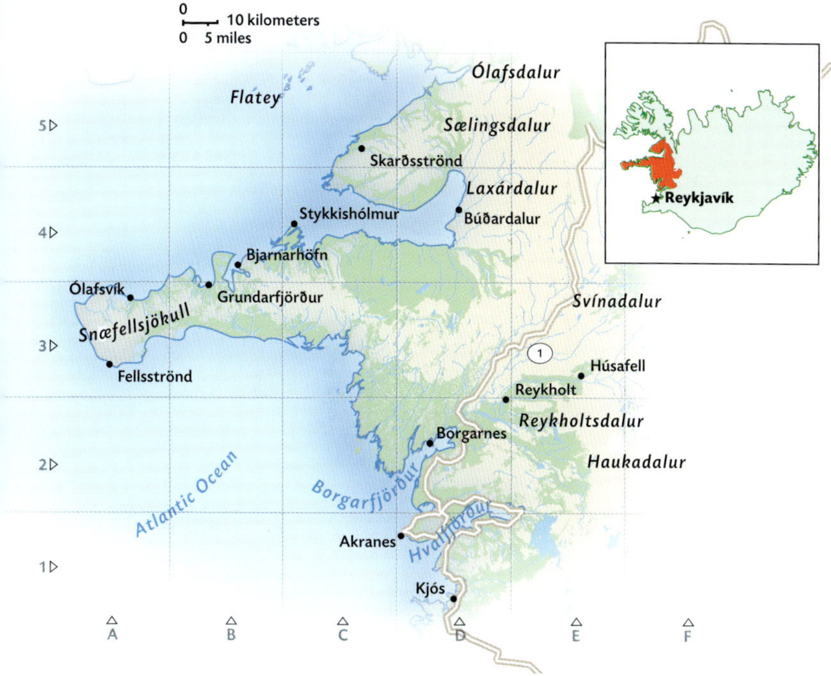

mountains. The smallest library in Iceland is located here.

The peninsula's perimeter offers an endless string of surprises, such as the small museum dedicated to fermented shark production (an Icelandic culinary specialty with an unpleasant ammonia scent that is for the most adventurous of eaters) at Bjarnarhöfn, the Djúpalónssandur black beach, the cliffs at Arnarstapi, and the beach at Ytri Tunga, a prime viewing spot for seals.

The region of valleys (Dalir) in the northernmost part holds great historical importance. It was the home of important families and prominent figures, such as the Skarðverjar clan; the colonizer Auður Menteprofonda, a character in the *Laxdæla saga*; Erik the Red from the *Eiríks saga*; as well as the birthplace of Árni Magnússon (1663–1730), the most important collector of Icelandic manuscripts. ■

NOT TO BE MISSED:

Hvalfjörður fjord 178–179

The settlement museum in Borgarnes 181

Eiríksstaðir peat farm 194–195

Djúpalónssandur beach 191–192

The town of Stykkishólmur 186–187

Flatey island 187–188

The cliffs of Arnarstapi 193

The shark museum in Bjarnarhöfn 188-189

THE GREAT FJORDS

The southernmost part of western Iceland includes the regions around the Hvalfjörður and Borgarfjörður fjords. The former is distinct for its wild and less-traveled settings, far from the traffic found in the Hvalfjarðargöng underground tunnel, whereas the latter has mostly flat and hilly landscapes in the north and is characterized by rural agricultural villages. It is here that one of the most important sagas in Icelandic literature was set: the *Egils saga*.

The coast opposite the town of Akranes offers a striking view of Akrafjall.

Visitors to these fjords and the surrounding areas often rush through this region, which is common in many parts of the West. Tourists tend to prefer to move quickly through on their way north. Nevertheless, these destinations offer a myriad of delightful vistas and less-crowded points of interest well worth visiting.

Hvalfjörður

At about 18.5 miles (30 km) long and 3 miles (5 km) wide, Hvalfjörður occupies a vast area full of sights. Its name means "whale fjord," although there are no resident whales in the fjord. The name is believed to come from Hvalfjall (Whale Mountain), which resembles the back of a whale. An alternative explanation comes from local folklore, which attributes the origin of the name to a red-headed whale that allegedly haunted the waters of the fjord, causing shipwrecks and deaths. It was allegedly a man transformed into a sea monster by an elven woman after he refused to recognize their daughter.

On the southern shore of the fjord is the farm of Saurbær, off the main road where the small Saurbæjarkirkja church stands. Continuing along Route 47, you can follow the edge of the fjord until you reach the start of the peninsula halfway along the southern shore of the fjord. Here you will find the **Hvammsvík** thermal baths, where you can alternate between diving into the fjord's icy waters and relaxing in warm pools. At the end of the fjord is the Botnsdalur valley, where one of the country's highest waterfalls, Glymur (650 ft, 198 m) is hidden.

On the northern shore, on the other hand, you can find the **War and Peace Museum,** which is dedicated to occupation of the island by Allied forces between 1940 and 1945, as well as the Hallgrímskirkja í Saurbæ church, consecrated in 1957 and dedicated to the Baroque poet and psalmist Hallgrímur Pétursson, pastor of the church between 1651 and 1669.

Glymur waterfall, not far from Hvalfjörður.

Kjós

On the southern coast of the fjord, turning off Route 47 onto Route 461, you can find the Kjós area, and more specifically Lake Meðalfellsvatn, located in a pleasant and popular resort area. Several little-known valleys cut through the slopes of the Esja mountain range and offer scenic vistas far removed from tourist traffic.

Akranes

At the foot of Akrafjall mountain, which rises to 1,876 feet (572 m), is the town of Akranes, an important industrial center, especially for cement production, and one of the country's largest fishing ports. It has never been affected by the flow of tourists, but it is home to

Hvammsvík ☎ 510 5900 🕒 Open daily 11 a.m.–10 p.m. $ $$$ (online reservation required) **hvammsvik.com** • **War and Peace Museum** ✉ Hlaðir, Hvalfjarðarsveit ☎ 660 8585 🕒 Open June–Aug. Fri.–Sun. 11 a.m.–5 p.m.; in the remaining months by appointment for groups $ $ **warandpeace.is**

an important museum of local history and culture, **Byggðasafnið í Görðum,** where temporary exhibitions are also held. At the far end of town, you can get to the old lighthouse (Akranesviti) built on the rocks. Just outside the urban center to the north is the promontory and viewpoint Elínarhöfði.

Borgarfjörður

The fjord's name is derived from a farm called Borg, the first settlement in the area, founded by the Norwegian Skalla-Grímur Kveld-Úlfsson, father of Egill, a warrior and poet and the protagonist of the *Egils saga Skalla-Grímssonar* (*Saga of Egill Skalla-Grímsson;* see p. 182), one of the greatest literary masterpieces of the European Middle Ages. The southern part of the fjord is bordered by a mountain range. In the middle stands the pyramidal peak of Skessuhorn (3,172 ft, 967 m). On the northern shore lies the town of Borgarnes, the main town for the Western region.

North of the fjord are more flat landscapes that alternate with vast swampy areas and cultivated fields. Farther to the northeast, you will encounter the Holtavörðuheiði hills, which mark the border between the West, the central highlands, and the

Byggðasafnið í Görðum Garðaholti 3 433 1150 Open May 15–Sept. 14 daily 10 a.m.–5 p.m.; Sept. 15–May 14 by appointment $ **www.museum.is**

Panoramic view of the Borgarfjörður fjord.

North. Deep valleys penetrate the highlands: in the southernmost part, the Skorradalur valley is furrowed by a long, narrow lake surrounded by forests like Stálpastaðaskógur on the northern shore, which has walking trails. In the middle is the large Reykholtsdalur valley, which is a mecca of cultural and scenic landscapes. Finally, the Norðurárdalur valley extends toward the northern coast of the island.

INSIDER TIP:
Don't miss Landnámssetur Íslands, a museum dedicated to the oldest period in Icelandic history.
–ROBERTO LUIGI PAGANÍ
Author of the guidebook

Borgarnes

Tho slopes of Hafnarfjall might look smooth and polished but they are made up of dark rubble, and it is one of the places where Iceland's fiercest winds blow. These highlands are the gateway to the Borgarfjörður region. On the other side, you have access to the Western region and the town of Borgarnes on the northern shore of the fjord. This town has the best services in the region, with stores, bars, and restaurants. The **Landnámssetur Íslands** (Iceland's Settlement Center) is a museum dedicated to the earliest period of Icelandic history and contains an exhibit on the *Egils saga*, which allows visitors to better understand the story of this fundamental text in the Icelandic literary tradition. **Safnahús Borgarfjarðar,** the local museum, has various exhibits on different topics, such as Icelandic birdlife, peat houses, and traditional sewing and embroidery. The local church, Borgarneskirkja, is worth a visit if only to admire the view from the top of the hill on which it stands.

Just outside the town, on Route 54 to Snæfellsnes, you can find the farm of Borg á Mýrum. Next door is the local church, Borgarkirkja, from 1889, which contains an altarpiece by English painter William Gershom Collingwood. Also located here is a monument to Egill Skalla-Grímsson, whose location offers a view of the mountains south of the fjord.

Reykholtsdalur

At the mouth of the valley is the town of Deildartunguhver, home to thermal baths. Just beyond,

Borgarnes – Information Center ✉ Brúartorg 4 ☎ 437 1400 ⌚ 10 a.m.–6 p.m. **www.west.is • Landnámssetur Íslands** ✉ Brákarbraut 13-15 ☎ 437 1600 ⌚ 10 a.m.–9 p.m. $ $$ **www.landnam.is • Safnahús Borgarfjarðar** ✉ Bjarnarbraut 4-6, Borgarnes Center ☎ 433 7200 ⌚ Open May–Aug. Mon.–Fri. 1 p.m.–6 p.m., Sat. 11 a.m.–3 p.m.; Sept.–Apr. Mon.–Fri. 1 p.m.–6 p.m. $ Free admission **safnahus.is**

THE *EGILS SAGA*

A masterpiece in its genre, this saga follows the life of a warrior, Egill, who combines physical ugliness and a harsh temperament with a poetic sensibility and literary talent so refined that it manages to save his life on more than one occasion, somewhat like Iceland itself: a wild and difficult land home to great authors and poets.

The *Egils saga Skalla-Grímssonar* is a monument of literature and one of the most significant works in Icelandic culture. The sagas are indispensable reading for anyone who wishes to better appreciate and understand the local culture because they are inextricably woven into the identity of the Icelandic people. The oldest written record of the *Egils saga* is a fragment from 1240.

The story begins in Norway with a clash between Egill's grandfather, Kveld-Úlfur, and King Haraldur Fairhair. The story begins in Norway with a clash between Egill's grandfather, Kveld-Úlfur, and King Haraldur Fairhair. He kills Thórólfur, Kveld-Úlfur's son, and forces the latter's father and brother, Skalla-Grímur, to flee to Iceland. The two attempt to obtain some compensation from the king, but their request is in vain, and the Kveld-Úlfur dies on the journey. The coffin with his corpse is thrown into the sea, and Skalla-Grímur decides to settle in the place where the coffin lands: the future town of Borg. Here, he leads a peaceful existence raising his sons Thórólfur and Egill. Egill turns out to be a difficult and troublesome child: at the age of three, he rides a horse to a party he is forbidden to attend, and when he is seven he kills a boy who had wronged him in a ball game with an axe.

As an adult, Egill travels to Norway with his brother to the home of Bárður, a member of King Eiríkur's entourage Axeblood. When Bárður offends Egill by offering him curdled milk instead of beer, thus he uses his gifts as a fierce warrior and refined poet to compose offensive verses against his host, who serves him a poisoned horn in revenge. Aware of the poison, Egill kills Bárður and flees, thus making an enemy of the king. He is captured sometime later, but a friend of his, Arinbjörn, persuades the king to accept compensation in exchange for Egil's life. Egill then composes the laudatory poem *Höfuðlausn*, "Head-Ransom," written in the saga, a literary text of such beauty that the king decides to spare his life.

Egill lives a long life, spending his old age in Iceland. He dedicates another of the poetic masterpieces of the Nordic Middle Ages, *Sonatorrek* (*The Loss of Sons*), to two of his prematurely deceased sons, Gunnar and Böðvarr. It explores his feelings of grief and loss. Before his death, Egill allegedly hid his treasure in the Mosfell area near Reykjavík: some Icelanders are still looking for it today.

on Route 518, lies the town of Reykholt, the historic seat of the powerful medieval lord and poet Snorri Sturluson. He was the author of the *Prose Edda*, a manual of Nordic court poetry containing a wealth of information on the mythology of the pre-Christian period, and likely also the author of the *Heimskringla*, a collection of sagas about the Norwegian kings. The village is also home to **Snorrastofa,** an important research center for medieval studies that houses a library and an exhibition on Sturluson. The archaeological excavation behind the study center and church includes the hot pool where Sturluson himself apparently bathed. Today you can also visit an old, reconstructed church from the late 19th century that is part of the National Museum of Iceland.

Another 11 miles (18 km) down Route 518, you will come to Hraunfossar springs, which flow from an underground lava field that stops abruptly at the edge of a canyon carved out by the Hvítá River.

Húsafell

Continuing on Route 518 into the valley, you can reach the area of Húsafell, one of the starting points for exploring Langjökull glacier, which has a man-made tunnel and caves carved into the ice. Inside them, you can see black marks left by ash from ancient volcanic eruptions.

Snorrastofa Hálsasveltavegur 433 8000 Open May–Aug. daily 10 a.m.–5 p.m.; Sept.–Apr. Mon.–Fri. 10 a.m.–5 p.m. **www.snorrastofa.is**

Hraunfossar Falls, in Húsafell, in autumn.

On the road between the Snaefellsnes Peninsula and Reykjavík.

On the opposite side of the valley, north of Húsafell, still on Route 518, if you take the turnoff to **Víðgelmir,** you will find a lava tunnel formed around 900 AD. At just over a mile (2 km) long, it is one of the three largest lava caves in the world. Visits are possible only with a guide. Evidence of past human existence has been found inside, probably dating back to the late Iron Age, before Iceland's conversion to Christianity.

Just south of the turnoff to Víðgelmir is the intersection with F578, which leads to Súrtshellir Cave, about 5 miles (8 km) away. This cave is about 1 mile (1.5 km) long and steeped in local superstitions about the presence of ghosts. Archaeological studies have uncovered a site that must have had a sacred role in the pre-Christian period. Experts have found two structures, a dry-stone wall and an enclosure, as well as piles of domestic animal bones that they believe were sacrificed in propitiatory rites done out of a fear of coming natural disasters.

Heading North

Continuing north on Route 1, you will enter the narrow Norðurárdalur valley, which alternates between lava fields and more agrarian landscapes, with a few farms located at the foot of the mountains. Just before the village of Bifröst, home to a university campus, is Glanni waterfall, on the Norðurá River. The falls are not impressive, at only about 26 feet (8 m), but it is worth a stop for the basalt rocks over which the water flows.

Just half a mile (1 km) beyond Bifröst is the parking lot for Grábrók, a 557-foot (170 m) volcanic crater. The magma that now makes up the adjacent lava field known as Grábrókarhraun flowed from it 3,400 years ago. A convenient wooden staircase leads to the rim of the crater, so you can walk up along the edge of it. Looking to the north from there, you can see the conical mountain Baula, one of the most distinctive and celebrated features of the landscape of western Iceland. Its reddish-orange tint comes from the presence of rhyolite in the rock. ■

Víðgelmir ✉ Fljótstunga ☎ 783 3600 $ $$$ **thecave.is**

SNÆFELLSNES: ICELAND IN MINIATURE

The Snæfellsnes Peninsula is a popular and easily accessible destination for a day trip from Reykjavík. For this reason, it is often recommended to those who aren't staying long in Iceland and just in the capital, but who would also like a taste of those natural elements that make Iceland so special. The expression "Iceland in miniature" refers to the many sights Snæfellsnes holds that are characteristic of the entire country, but on a smaller scale, including glaciers, black beaches, lava fields, fjords, small villages, caves, and geological formations.

Snæfell volcano.

The Snæfellsnes Peninsula was made famous by French writer Jules Verne, who imagined the Snæfell volcano as a gateway for exploring the bowels of the Earth in his novel *Journey to the Center of the Earth*. Nobel laureate Halldór Laxness's novel, *Under the Glacier*, is also set right here on the slopes of the volcano. The volcano truly reigns over the region, towering above the other mountains, which form the backbone of the peninsula. Because it is crisscrossed by secondary roads that deviate from Route 1, this peninsula, like the

Westfjords Peninsula, is often ignored by tourists who travel the main circuit, but it is popular with those who opt for short tours that start from the capital or neighboring regions.

Stykkishólmur

On the northern coast, Stykkishólmur is one of the country's most picturesque villages, thanks to the prevalence of traditional-style buildings. The ferry to the Westfjords departs from the pier here, reaching Brjánslækur after a stop on Flatey Island. Inside **Norska húsið** (Norwegian House), a building constructed in 1832, is the museum of local history and culture and a space for temporary exhibitions. On the hill on the west side of the town is **Vatnasafn** (Library of Water). This art installation preserves water from Iceland's glaciers in glass columns, creating plays of light. The lower floor of the museum is used as a residence for writers.

Norska húsið ✉ Hafnargata 5 ☎ 433 8114 🕒 Open Aug. 15–Sept. 15 daily noon–4 p.m. (openings updated on social profiles) $ $ **www.norskahusid.is** • **Vatnasafn** ✉ Bókhlöðustígur 19 ☎ 865 4516 🕒 Open June–Aug. daily 11 a.m.–5 p.m.; Sept.–May. Tues.–Sat. 11 a.m.–5 p.m. $ $ (tickets sold at Norskahúsið)

The city of Stykkishólmur.

The Book of Flatey

The *Flateyjarbók* – *Book of Flatey*, was composed by two Icelandic priests between 1387 and 1393 in the monastery of Thingeyrar for a local lord, Jón Hákonarson. The codex then passed to the hands of a powerful northwestern family, and for the next two centuries it was kept in the family seat on the island of Flatey. In the mid-1600s, national consciousness began to awaken, and Nordic monarchs were looking for material they could use to reconstruct and extol the glorious national past. Iceland was the Nordic nation that had best preserved its history due to its fixation with genealogies and writing the heroic deeds of ancestors in prose. At that time, Denmark controlled Iceland, so the Danish king commissioned the Icelandic Bishop Brynjólfur Sveinsson to collect as much material on the past as possible. The last owner of the *Flateyjarbók*, one Jón Finnsson, despite initial reluctance, gave the volume to the bishop and it ended up in Denmark, where it remained until the 1970s, when it was returned to Iceland, which had by then been independent since 1944.

On the north side of the small harbor, connected to the south side by the pier, is the islet Súgandisey, which offers a superb view of the Gulf of Breiðafjörður and its countless islands. Slightly farther south, 3 miles (5 km) down the road leading out of the village, lies the 744-foot (227 m) high Helgafell Hill. In the *Eyrbyggja saga*, one of the oldest, the pagan priest and local lord Snorri Goði, converts to Christianity and builds a church on top of this hill. At the foot of it is a cemetery where, tradition has it, the beautiful and terrible Guðrún Ósvífursdóttir rests, a protagonist of the *Laxdœla saga* (see pp. 197–199). In 1184, an Augustinian monastery initially established on Flatey Island was moved here and remained active until the Protestant Reformation in 1550.

Flatey

You can reach Flatey Island on a ferry in 1.5 hours from Stykkishólmur. It stops there on its way to the fjords; you have two and a half hours before the ferry returns to Stykkishólmur. There are no paved roads on the island, and you cannot take your car there, but Flatey is so small that you can get around easily by foot.

Once a rich center of trade, with a population of as many as 400 individuals in the early 20th century, the island today is inhabited by not even ten people. The main point of interest, in addition to the beauty of the surrounding nature and the abundance of birds in summer, is the pretty village, now almost exclusively vacation homes used by the descendants of former owners. The village consists of brightly painted, traditional Icelandic-

The small library on Flatey Island.

style buildings, with the local church, **Flateyjarkirkja,** located just south of the village. Consecrated in 1926, it features interior frescoes painted by Catalan artist Baltasar Samper in the 1960s. Behind the church, a wooden house is home to **Bjarg,** Iceland's smallest library. Built in the 19th century and refurbished in the late 20th, it holds quite a few books that visitors can view, as well as a prized copy of the *Flateyjarbók*, the most treasured parchment codex of the Icelandic Middle Ages (see sidebar p. 187), which was long owned by a wealthy family living on the island. North of Flatey is a small cliff, Lundaberg, where you can spot puffins in the summer.

Bjarnarhöfn

As you leave the village and continue west along the coast, turning north off Route 54, you will reach the Bjarnarhöfn farm. This is the site of **Hákarlasafn** (Shark Museum). Iceland's famous fermented shark, *kæstur hákarl*, is produced in this area. Shark meat from Greenland is left to ferment in large containers for several weeks and then dried under special sheds. Inside the museum you can learn a great deal about the biology of the animal as well as the production of the local specialty. There's even a chance to try it for those with strong stomachs. The flavor is similar to that of

Flateyjarkirkja ✉ Flatey 2 **flatey.com • Bjarg (library)** $ Free admission **flatey.com • Hákarlasafn** ☎ 438 1581 🕒 Closed in winter months $ $ **bjarnarhofn.is**

certain pungent cheeses, and the scent is reminiscent of ammonia. Not far from the farm is a small wooden church, Bjarnarhafnarkirkja, from 1857, containing some valuable objects such as a 17th century pulpit, a late 13th century chalice, and a 17th century altarpiece.

Returning to Route 54, on its southern side, is a large lava field created 4,000 years ago, Berserkjahraun. The name, which means "lava field of the *berserkir*," comes from the *Eyrbyggja saga*. According to the story, a local lord named Styr had obtained two fierce Swedish warriors (*berserkir*) as gifts from his brother. One of them had fallen in love with Styr's daughter and asked for her hand in marriage. Styr didn't want to consent, but fearing repercussions, he sought advice from Snorri Goði. The latter suggested that he allow it on the condition that the warrior complete an impossible mission: open a road through the lava. To Styr's dismay, the warrior succeeded, but instead of honoring his word, Styr invited them into a sauna, under the pretext of letting them relax after their hard work, and had them killed. The road through the lava, still visible today, is called Berserkjagata. Scholars believe it is the work of early settlers, although a stone mound nearby is considered the burial place of the two warriors.

Grundarfjörður

Grundarfjörður is a small town built on a bay surrounded by striking mountains. For several centuries it was an important trading station. Inhabited since the age of colonization (870–930 AD), it also appears in the *Eyrbyggja saga*. The village houses the **Saga Centre** information center and museum, as well

The preparation of fermented shark meat, *kæstur hákarl*.

INSIDER TIP:
In the tiny town of Ólafsvík you can buy local handicrafts.

–ROBERTO LUIGI PAGANÍ
Author of the guidebook

as the Grundarfjarðarkirkja church, consecrated in 1966. East of the village, off Route 576, you reach the site of the old local church, which has been there since the 12th century. The present building, Setbergskirkja, dates from the late 19th century. A little more than a mile (2 km) west of the village, along Route 54, Kirkjufell mountain rises on the north side. It can be photographed behind the must-see Kirkjufellsfoss waterfall, reached from the parking lot on the south side.

Ólafsvík

Continuing west on Route 54 along the coast, you will merge onto Route 574, which leads to Ólafsvík. This very small town was the first in the country to receive trading post status from the Danish king, in 1687. Here, you can visit **Gallerí jökull,** a small store where you can buy local handicrafts. From the cliff face behind the village is Bæjarfoss waterfall, which can be reached from the parking lot of the modern church.

Continuing west toward Hellissandur, take the turnoff south for Ingjaldshólskirkja, the oldest concrete church in the world, built in 1903. Inside is a fresco depicting Christopher Columbus. A local legend, debunked by scholars, claimed that the explorer visited this place in 1477, along with the crew of a ship from Bristol, and learned of the existence of lands unknown to him to the west. Next to the church are two monuments by sculptor Páll Guðmundsson, depicting the 18th century explorer and writer Eggert Ólafsson and his wife, Ingibjörg Guðmundsdóttir, both of whom grew up here.

Snæfellsjökull National Park

The far end of the peninsula is dominated by the imposing conical silhouette of the Snæfell volcano, which can be seen as far away as Reykjavík. The crater reaches a height of 4,744 feet (1,446 m) and is perpetually covered by a small glacier, Snæfellsjökull. The park's **Visitor Center** is located in Hellissandur. The area was declared a park in 2001. The extreme tip of Öndverðarnes has a small lighthouse,

Saga Centre ✉ Grundargata 35 ☎ 438 1881 ⌚ Open 1 p.m.–5 p.m. $ Free admission **www.grundarfjordur.is** • **Ólafsvík – Information Center** ✉ Kirkjutún 2 ☎ 433 6929 **snb.is** • **Gallerí jökull** ✉ Norðurtangi 3 ☎ 862 1440/866 3282 ⌚ Open May 20–Sept. 15 daily noon–5 p.m.

A pebble beach in Snæfellsjökull National Park.

which can be reached on Route 579 after passing the charming golden beach of Skarðsvík.

Staying on Route 574 and veering south, you will encounter the crater of Saxhöll, which you can walk to the top of. On the southern part of the coast is the black beach of Djúpalónssandur, which can be easily reached and has convenient parking. In the narrow gorge leading to the beach, a series of five boulders weighing between 50 and 340 pounds (23 to 154 kg) were used by sailors to test their strength. Lifting the second lightest one, weighing 120 pounds (54 kg), was a requirement to be accepted as an oarsman. The beach is strewn with the rusting remains of a vessel, the British trawler *Epine GY7*, which was wrecked following a storm in March 1948. The fragments of the boat are protected, and it is prohibited to move them. At the end of the beach, between the rocks, are two ponds. The first, Djúpalón, is said to have been blessed by Bishop Guðmundur the Good, who lived between the 12th and 13th centuries.

Snæfellsjökull – Visitor Center ✉ Skriðuklaustur ☎ 470 0840 ⏲ Open Apr. Mon.–Fri. 10 a.m.–4 p.m.; May Mon.–Fri. 10 a.m.–4 p.m., Sat.–Sun. & holidays noon–5 p.m.; June–Aug. daily 10 a.m.–5 p.m.; Sept. Mon.–Fri. 10 a.m.–3 p.m., Sat.–Sun. & holidays noon–5 p.m.; Oct. Tues.–Wed. 10 a.m.–3 p.m. **www.vjp.is**

Vatnshellir cave, in Snæfellsjökull National Park, was formed by a volcanic eruption that occurred 8,000 years ago.

Following a footpath over the cliffs through the lava, you reach Dritvík Bay, where there are ruins of ancient fishermen's shelters in the area.

Next to the road, about 3 miles (5 km) from Djúpalónssandur, is **Vatnshellir** cave, which extends about 20 feet (32 m) below the surface. The site can be explored exclusively by guided tours. Just 1.2 miles (2 km) away is the parking lot for the two Lóndrangar stacks (200 and 246 feet, 61 and 75 m, respectively). They can be seen from an observation platform off a short walking path. They are the remains of a basalt volcanic neck, or hardened lava within a volcanic crater that later eroded and disappeared. A seer claimed that one of the two stacks was a church for elves and the other a library. An older legend claims that it was a pair of trolls petrified by sudden daylight.

The Southern Coast

The southern coast of the peninsula contains a score of interesting destinations within relatively short distances. Hellnar is the first small town you encounter, with a lovely little church, Hellnakirkja, from

Vatnshellir – Summit Tour Guides ☎ 787 0001 $ $$
www.summitguides.is

1945. Not far away, heading east, is Arnarstapi, a town known for its cliffs and their unique rock formations, such as the famous Gatklettur arch. Here stands a statue dedicated to Bárður Snæfellsás, protagonist of the *Bárðar saga Snæfellsáss*.

About a mile (2 km) away on the F570 dirt road, just outside Arnarstapi, are the Sönghellir caves, famous for their echoes and as the home, according to legend, of the family of the area's settler, the legendary Bárður Snæfellsás. Eleven miles (19 km) east of Arnarstapi lies Búðir and its famous Búðakirkja church. From it, a path through the lava field leads to the eruptive cone of Búðaklettur.

Continuing on Route 54 for another 12.5 miles (20 km), you will reach the town of Ytri Tunga, home to a large colony of seals. About 3 miles (5 km) eastward, you reach Staðarstaður, which was the residence of Ari Thorgilsson the Wise, author of the *Íslendingabók* or *Libellus islandorum*, the oldest known Icelandic text, a compendium of the country's history from its origins. The only surviving versions are 17th century copies of a lost manuscript that probably dated back to the 13th century. The local church was erected in the first half of the 1940s. About 22 miles (36 km) east is a turnoff leading to the site of Gerðuberg, where a row of basalt pillars stands. On the same road, you can find Rauðamelskirkja, a church built in 1886. ■

Bárðar saga Snæfellsás

Half human, half orc, Bárður was raised by the giant Dofri in the mountain of the same name in Norway. He traveled to Iceland, landing in Djúpalón, where he would build himself a homestead, Laugarbrekka. Bárður had several daughters who were very beautiful and quite tall. The eldest daughter was named Helga. Thorkell, Bárður's half-brother, lived in Arnarstapi and had two sons, Rauðfeldur and Sölvi, who played with Bárður's daughters.

One day, when the coast was freezing cold, Rauðfeldur pushed Helga onto a piece of ice causing her to end up in Greenland. Bárður became very angry, so he grabbed Rauðfeldur and hurled him into the Rauðfeldsgjá ravine and then threw Sölvi off Sölvahamar, a rock near Arnarstapi. He then fought with Thorkell, wounding him in the leg.

Having taken his revenge, Bárður disappeared onto the Snæfellsjökull glacier, where, according to legend, he hid his treasure on Mount Bárðarkista. He later became a kind of protective spirit, said to roam the region with a gray hood, a walrusskin rope around his body, and a staff that he used when walking on glaciers, helping people in distress who called upon him.

THE VALLEYS

The Dalir region consists of long, narrow valleys dotted with farms. Like the Westfjords to the north, it is sparsely visited by tourists who tend to stay close to Route 1. Despite this, it is a region full of fascinating spots to see.

Eiríksstaðir, a reproduction of Erik the Red's home.

The valleys that give this region its name are divided into those in the southeastern part, east of Route 60, and those in the northwestern part, on the peninsula stretching westward between the coasts of Fellsströnd and Skarðsströnd.

Haukadalur (Snæfellsnes)

If you turn off Route 60, which leads to the westfjords, and take Route 586, you enter Haukadalur valley. Here, to the east of the lake along the road, lies **Eiríksstaðir,** the site of an archaeological excavation where the remains of a farm-house from the ninth or tenth century were found. A reconstruction of the building has been completed using only tools and techniques from the period, and you can visit it on a guided tour. This farm is believed to have been the home of Eiríkur (or Erik) the Red, one

Eiríksstaðir ✉ Haukadal ☎ 899 7111 🕒 Open mid-May 1 p.m.–4 p.m.; Jun. 1 11 a.m.–4 p.m.; June 20–Sept. 10 a.m.–4 p.m. $ $$ **eiriksstadir.is**

of the main characters in the *Eiríks saga rauða*.

Laxárdalur

Although it doesn't show many traces of its ancient past, this valley intersected by the Laxá River was the epicenter of events that took place over several generations, beginning with settlement during the age of colonization. These events are narrated in a saga of the same name. A charming church, Hjarðarholtskirkja, built in 1904 and designed by Rögnvaldur Ólafsson, survives today. It stands on the grounds of Hjarðarholt, which was the residence of Ólafur the Peacock, father of Kjartan Ólafsson, one of the prominent characters in the *Laxdœla saga* (see pp. 197–199). The site can be reached by turning off Route 60 onto the 587 and continuing for 1.8 miles (3 km).

Búðardalur

The boot-shaped fjord that separates the northern part of the Snæfellsnes Peninsula in the south from the coast of the Fellsströnd Peninsula in the north is called Hvammsfjörður. On the inner coast lies the small town of Búðardalur. Here, you can find **Vínlandssetur,** a tourist information center that also houses an exhibition devoted to the Icelandic exploration of North America.

Sælingsdalur

If you turn off Route 60 and take Route 590, you will find the village of Laugar, the birthplace of Guðrún, the protagonist of the *Laxdœla saga*. A lovely hot-water pool located on the slopes behind the buildings is named after him. A peat house built in the

Vínlandssetur Búðarbraut 1 434 1441 10 a.m.–4 p.m. $$
vinlandssetur.is

The *Eiríks Saga* & and the New World

In this saga, Erik the Red is banished from the country following a murder and spends his years of exile exploring a land that had been accidentally sighted shortly before, to which he gives the name Greenland. He colonizes it, settling in the southwest. Soon the region is populated with numerous settlers from Iceland and Norway, and it is only a matter of time before someone is pushed off course on the crossing to the new land and spots the North American coastline. This occurs around the year 1000. One attempt to colonize the New World follows, but the ship sinks due to clashes with the Native peoples who greatly outnumber the settlers. A Norse settlement was found in the 1960s on the island of Newfoundland, Canada, and numerous Norse artifacts have been found at Inuit archaeological sites in the Canadian Arctic archipelago, testifying to contact and exchanges between the two ethnic groups.

View of Hvammsfjörður, north of the Snæfellsnes Peninsula.

Old Norse style serves as a changing room. The local history museum, **Byggðasafn Dalamanna,** was closed in 2021 due to an inadequate amount of space to house it, but there are plans to reopen it.

Svínadalur & Ólafsdalur

Crossing the Svínadalur valley, where Kjartan Ólafsson was murdered by his half-brother Bolli according to the *Laxdæla saga*, you reach a flat area at the mouth of the Westfjords Peninsula. Then, turning off Route 60 onto 590, you reach the wooden Staðarhólskirkja church, from the late 19th century. Continuing to the coast and deviating east on Route 690, you enter the hidden valley of **Ólafsdalur** near Gilsfjörður. Here the country's first agricultural college was founded in 1880. In summer, the school building (from 1896) is open to the public and hosts exhibitions. A number of hiking trails run through the valley, which is shaped like a spectacular amphitheater. On the eastern side, another valley opens between the mountains; at the far end are the Hvarfsdalsfossar waterfalls. If you walk south a short distance from the building of the agricultural institute, you can reach an archaeological excavation that uncovered a building from between the ninth and tenth centuries, probably a typical dwelling of that period. The remains of everyday objects such as a spindle whorl, a comb, and glass beads were found there.

Fellsströnd Peninsula & Skarðsströnd

The peninsula, which sits west of Dalir, is set back from the main road that runs through the region, Route 60. Instead, a single dirt road (the 590) runs around it and connects to Route 60 at two points, in the north and south. It is not one of the more popular places to travel in the country. The natural beauty of the surroundings and interesting local history, however, make it a perfect destination for those seeking the characteristic beauty of Iceland but in a more solitary location.

(continued on p. 199)

Byggðasafn Dalamanna Laugar í Sælingsdalur **dalir.is** • **Ólafsdalur – Cultural site** olafsdalur@gmail.com Open July & Aug. varies annually $ **olafsdalur.is**

THE *LAXDÆLA SAGA*

Set mainly in the Eastern region, this saga deals with universal themes like love, hatred, honor, and revenge, and is rightly considered one of the most artistically successful works in the Icelandic literary corpus.

The *Laxdæla saga–Saga of the Inhabitants of Laxádalur*, is one of the greatest works in the saga literary genre and one of the most highly regarded. The oldest manuscript containing the complete work is the famous *Möðruvallabók*, from the mid-14th century, but fragments of another from a century earlier have also survived.

The saga spans several generations, beginning with that of the colonizer of the Dalir area, Auður the Deep-Minded. The main plot of the saga revolves around the tragic loves of Guðrún Ósvífursdóttir, who marries four times. Not being in love with her first husband, she divorces him under the pretext of having seen him wearing a woman's garment (a low-cut shirt she had made herself). Her second husband, whom she did love, dies by drowning. Guðrún begins courting a very promising young man, a descendant of Auður the Deep-Minded, Kjartan Ólafsson. However, the latter must leave for a trip to Norway, where he is held hostage by King Ólafur Tryggvason, who wants to force the Icelanders to be baptized. With him is his adopted brother, Bolli, with whom he is very close. Bolli manages to return to Iceland and tells Guðrún that Kjartan will not return because he is having an intimate relationship with the king's sister. Bolli then asks for her hand in marriage, and she accepts.

When Kjartan returns, with a wedding gift for Guðrún, he finds her married. This opens an irreparable rift in their relationship: Bolli tries to make peace, but a series of thefts, provocations and mutual insults, usually triggered by Guðrún, who cannot forget the pain, brings things to a head. Kjartan takes revenge for some of the thefts, humiliating his half-brother Bolli by besieging his farm for three days and then preventing the couple from buying land. Guðrún seeks revenge by provoking his brothers and urging them to kill Kjartan. She insists that her husband Bolli join them, despite his reluctance. He is still very fond of his half-brother. The brothers and Bolli ambush Kjartan along the Svínadalur. Kjartan defends himself heroically, and the brothers demand that Bolli kill him. When Kjartan sees his half-brother advancing, he drops his weapon and allows himself to be stabbed. Bolli takes his half-brother's lifeless body in his arms as he dies. The murder is then prosecuted and the brothers exiled; Kjartan's father, Ólafur, who was also Bolli's foster father, spares the latter from

A depiction of the death of Kjartan, one of the main characters in the *Laxdæla saga*.

exile, demanding only compensation (a weregild). Kjartan's other brothers, however, cannot forgive his murder. Upon Ólafur's death, his widow Thorgerður incites her sons to avenge Kjartan by appealing to the honor of her ancestor, Egill Skalla-Grímsson. When Bolli is killed, Guðrún is pregnant. Years later, the son, now grown, avenges his father's death, incited by his mother. Guðrún finally remarries but her last husband also dies prematurely. She spends the last years of her life as a nun.

At the end of the saga, the son asks his now elderly mother which man she had loved the most. She answers tersely, citing the merits of each of them, but the son is not satisfied and presses her, demanding a clear answer. She responds with a phrase that has become famous in Icelandic culture, "*Theim var ég verst er ég unni mest*– I acted most cruelly with the one I loved most." An enigmatic phrase that still puzzles today, although most interpret it as a reference not so much to one of her husbands but to Kjartan.

One and a half miles (2.5 km) west of the intersection with Route 60 is a rocky hill with a large cross on top, Kroshólaborg. According to legend, this is where the settler Auður the Deep-Minded erected a cross and went to pray. Just beyond, in the first valley you come across, on the north side of the road, is Hvammur í Dölum, which was Auður's residence. Sturla Thórðarson, father of the poet Snorri Sturluson and, according to ancient sources, a descendant of Auður, also lived in Hvammur. In the second half of the 17th century, the young Árni Magnússon, who would become a professor in Copenhagen and the most important collector of Icelandic manuscripts, grew up there. The Hvammskirkja Church, consecrated in 1884, and a monument erected in memory of Snorri Sturluson, are also located here.

Proceed south on Route 590 along the coast of Fellsströnd. When you reach the tip of the peninsula, where the coast deviates sharply to the northwest at the tip of Langeyjarnes and takes the name Skarðsströnd, the road crosses a narrow gap in the rock, Klofningsskarð, named after the mountain along which the road runs, Klofningur. If you leave your car at the parking lot, you can climb the hill to get a view of the Breiðafjörður Gulf with its 3,000 islands and islets.

Continuing on the road, you will come across the site of Skarð, which was the seat of one of Iceland's most powerful families for centuries. Some of the most valuable manuscripts are connected to this town. A powerful local lord, Governor Björn Thorleifsson, was killed by a group of Englishmen in 1467, but his wife, Ólöf Loftsdóttir, gathered men and avenged his death without shedding a single tear. The local church, Skarðskirkja, was rebuilt in the early 20th century but contains older artifacts, such as a 17th century pulpit. ■

The cross was erected where Auður the Deep-Minded used to retire in prayer.

Remote and untamed with a rich history, the fjords are one of the less explored regions. Silence and isolation are part of the allure

THE WESTFJORDS

■ Bolungarvík, the starting point for exploring the Hornstrandir Nature Reserve.

THE WESTFJORDS

The Westfjords include the triangular-shaped peninsula bordered on the south by the Gulf of Breiðafjörður, to the north and east by the long inlet of Ísafjarðardjúp, and to the west by the Denmark Strait. This is where most of the inhabited areas are concentrated. Surrounded by spectacular nature, these small villages are usually located on strips of land that jut toward the heart of the fjords, and are separated by long stretches of scenic roads that wind in and out of deep inlets.

Eider ducks inhabit the area around Reykhólar.

The coast facing the Gulf of Breiðafjörður is depopulated and untamed, while the western coast has several historically fascinating villages. Visitors can alternate a stopover in these villages and an exploration of the surrounding wilderness. The sea at the shores of this peninsula is shallow and is an ideal habitat for numerous bird species. The northeastern part includes the region's capital, Ísafjörður, and Bolungarvík, the second largest and most important center.

Historically, communication between the settlements and the outside world was primarily by sea. The valleys and sparse flat areas suitable for human settlement are encircled by steep mountain ranges, which sometimes overlook the sea and have always posed a significant obstacle to overland connections. The fjords are excellent natural harbors, though, and despite the isolation created by the mountains, they have always been connected through maritime traffic and frequent visits by sailors, fishermen, and whalers from all over Europe. It may seem paradoxical but the isolation of the coastal communities, which often attracts those seeking destinations off the beaten track, has not always characterized this region When travel was primarily by sea rather than overland, the Westfjords were the focal point of an intense network of international trade.

NOT TO BE MISSED:

Rauðisandur beach **206–207**

The cliffs of Látrabjarg **208**

The Hnjótur local history museum **207**

The Flateyri Bookstore, the oldest in Iceland **210–211**

The botanical garden at Skrúður **210**

The Ósvör Maritime Museum **214**

The small town of Ísafjörður **212–213**

The waterfall Dynjandi **209–210**

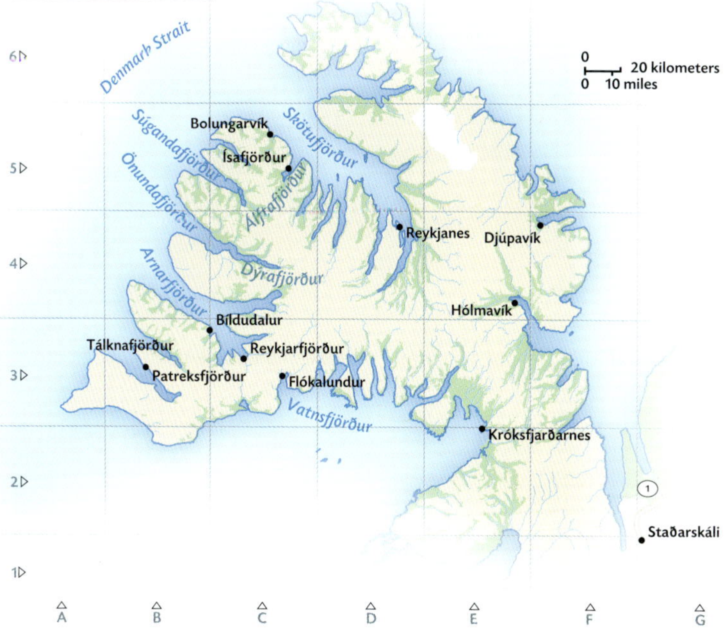

Króksfjarðarnes

Iceland's first settlers landed on the Króksfjarðarnes Peninsula–one of the settings of the Gullthóris saga–as early as the Middle Ages. This scenic spot at the mouth of the fjords is home to the headquarters of the local craft association, Handverksfélagið ASSA, and its shop.

Reykjanes

For centuries, the village of Reykhólar was the seat of a very powerful family who controlled large territories in the west. The family also had access to the abundant resources provided by the Gulf of Breiðafjörður and its islands, where eiders nest. Björn Thorleifsson, a local lord who lived in the early 16th century, is regarded as the author of the *Reykjahólabók*, a monumental collection of hagiographies and one of the most voluminous and valuable manuscripts produced in Iceland.

It is preserved today in the Royal Library in Stockholm. In Reykhólar, the **"Báta-og hlunnindasýningin"** or "Boat and Gift of Nature" exhibition illustrates the use of the area's resources in past centuries. The local church, Reykhólakirkja, dates from 1963. South of the settlement is **Norður & Co,** a sea salt production plant that uses geothermal heat. Guided tours are available.

Báta-og hlunnindasýningin ✉ Maríutröð 5a ☎ 434 7830 🕒 Open June–Aug. daily 11 a.m.–6 p.m. $ $ **www.reykholar.is** • **Norður & Co.** ✉ Hafnarslóð 1 ☎ 537 9095 **www.nordursalt.com**

Statue of the Viking navigator Flóki of the Ravens, near Flókalundur.

History of Iceland's Colonization

The history of the colonization of Iceland has been handed down in a text that is unique in European literature: the *Landnámabók*, or *Book of Settlements*, is essentially a catalog that covers all of Iceland starting from Reykjavík and moving along the perimeter in a clockwise direction. The *Landnámabók* lists the names of the settlers of each area and sometimes includes additional genealogical information and biographical details. Scholars largely agree that political and economic interests heavily influenced the text, which presumably was used to support historical claims to territorial control and genealogical prestige.

According to the *Landnámabók*, a Norwegian named Naddodd landed in the eastern part of the island in the ninth century and gave it the name Snæland, "Land of Snow," because of the snow that began to fall as he was returning to his boat. A second explorer, Garðar Svavarsson, a Swede, was the first to circumnavigate Iceland and named it Garðarshólm, "Garðar's Islet."

Finally, Flóki Vilgerðarson reached the island after releasing ravens on the high seas and following them ashore. He landed on the south coast of the fjord peninsula and stayed there for the winter, which was particularly harsh. He had no hay for his animals and after his cattle died, he was forced to return home but before he left, he climbed the highest mountain near his base camp and saw drifting ice in the fjord on the other side. Thus, he named the island the "land of ice," *Ísland*. A number of scholars believe that this account is at least partly fanciful. It is more likely that Iceland's name derives from the fact that the Vatnajökull ice sheet is the first thing visible when approaching the island from the southeast.

Flókalundur

The settlement of Flókalundur consists essentially of the hotel-restaurant of the same name. According to medieval sources, it is said to have been the place where the explorer Flóki of the Ravens landed, giving the island its name.

A monument honoring him can be seen in front of the hotel. Hellulaug, a free thermal pool, is located about 600 feet (200 m) east of the building. Driving up on Road 60 from Flókalundur, visitors will see a curious concrete statue: a bust erected over a shelter large enough to hold a person. The laborers who constructed the bridge over the nearby river in 1948 built it in their spare time. It is a well-loved example of folk art.

Hotel Flókalundur ✉ Vatnsfirði ☎ 456 2011 $ $$$ **www.flokalundur.is**

View of the Rauðisandur beach, etched with waterways.

The Southwestern Peninsula

The peninsula is characterized by landscapes with a strong, intense character. Towering cliffs plunge hundreds of feet into the ocean, and immense unspoiled beaches and deep coves are surrounded by untamed mountains. The peninsula can be reached only by taking Road 62 to the turnoff for 612.

The first point of interest is the shipwreck of the Garðar BA 64, stranded on the beach. The vessel was completed in Norway in 1912 and acquired by an Icelander after World War II, when it was used first for whaling and then for herring fishing. In 1981, it ran aground in the Skápadalur Valley, where time is slowly wearing it down.

The Scandal of the Breiðavík Reformatory

The main hotel building on Breiðavík Bay was once a reformatory, run by the government between 1903 and 1979. In a 2007 episode of the popular investigative television program *Kastljós*, a man who had been housed at the facility as a boy revealed that he had been routinely abused, physically and sexually. Following his revelations, several other people who had been at the facility as youths came forward, and the case exploded into one of the most serious scandals in contemporary Iceland, a situation aggravated by the fact that the authorities had long ignored the complaints and even covered up the facts. The scandal inspired a successful television series, *Brot* (*The Valhalla Murders*).

Rauðisandur is a beach isolated from the hinterland by a steep, rugged elevation. Its present isolation contradicts the fact that it was once a relatively populated center and the seat of the district governors. The reddish color of the sand is caused by shell fragments of the bivalve mollusk *Chlamys islandica*, the Icelandic sea scallop. The lagoon area that surrounds the beach is often invaded by water, so the easiest way to reach the beach is to take the turnoff to the left at the foot of the mountain as far as the campsite and then continue on foot. If you turn right, it will take you to the village of Saurbær and its black church, Saurbæjarkirkja. Originally built in the mid-19th century in Reykhólar, the church was diassembled and moved to its present location in 1982 and is currently administered by the National Museum.

Several valleys with white beaches and turquoise waters line the shore of the fjord, including the tropical looking Örlygsson beach. At the end of the valley, in a town called Hnjótur, is the **Minjasafn Egils Ólafssonar,** a museum of local history with a very rich collection of everyday objects and artifacts that testify to the ancient customs and ways of life there in centuries past. Dirt road 612 goes up the plateau, skirting Breiðavík Bay, where a golden-white beach is surrounded by steep

Minjasafn Egils Ólafssonar ☎ 456 1511 🕒 Open May–Sept. daily $ $

The Garðar BA 64 shipwreck.

The little fishing village of Patreksfjörður.

cliffs. Beyond Breiðavík is the island's westernmost point, Bjargtangar and its lighthouse., which overlooks the Látrabjarg cliffs, among the highest in Iceland (1,445 feet/441 m–at their highest point) and among the largest in Europe (about 9 miles, 14 km). Home to millions of birds including puffins, razor-billed auks, boobies, and guillemots, Bjargtangar is the nesting site for large portions of the entire population of some species. For example, 40 percent of the razor-billed auk population in Iceland nests here. The best time for bird-watching is in the evening, when the birds return to their nests.

Patreksfjörður

The largest town in the area offers a fair number of amenities along with the natural beauty of the fjord where it is located. According to the *Kjalnesinga saga* (see pp. 100-101), the name of the fjord and its village was chosen by an Irish settler named Örlygur. Allegedly commissioned by a bishop named Patrick to erect the first Christian church in Iceland, Örlygur built the church in the foothills of the Esja Mountains, in the southern part of the country. Consecrated in 1907, Patreksfjarðarkirkja is one of the oldest concrete churches in the country. On the pulpit inside it is a painting by Icelandic artist Erró, dating from 1957.

Tálknafjörður

The economy of this small town is based primarily on the fishing industry. The local geothermal pool is considered the best in the region. About 2.5 miles (4 km) west of town is Pollurinn, a series of small shallow pools of geothermal water that overlook the fjord. There are a number of hiking trails in the side valleys, and the ruins of a Norwegian whaling station on the southern shore of the fjord, at Suðureyri, on the dirt road that runs along the fjord.

Bíldudalur

This small town is located in an inlet of the Arnarfjörður. The local church, consecrated in 1906, was designed by architect Rögnvaldur Ólafsson. It contains two altarpieces, one dating from 1737 depicting the Last Supper and one painted in 1916 by Thórarinn B. Thorláksson, depicting the Virgin weeping at the tomb. The pulpit, decorated with images of Christ and the Apostles, dates from 1699. Behind the church is the **Skrímslasetur,** (Sea Monster Museum), which features fun, elaborate exhibits about the monstrous sea creatures of Icelandic folklore.

Arnarfjörður

The colossal Dynjandi waterfall is located in one of the longest coves of the fjord. The fall cascades over the rocks for seven jumps of a total height of 328 feet (100 m). Its base is almost 200 feet (60 m) wide. Dynjandi became a protected natural monument in 1981. From the paved parking lot, visitors can take a walking path for about half an hour to reach the base of the waterfall located farther up the elevation. Along it are other smaller waterfalls.

Skrímslasetur ☎ 456 6666 🕒 Open mid-May–mid-Sept. daily 10 a.m.–6 p.m. $ $ **skrimsli.is**

Dynjandi, near Arnarfjörður, is the most famous waterfall in the Westfjords region.

Dýrafjörður

Thingeyri is the largest town on the fjord. Its neo-Gothic local church, Thingeyrarkirkja, built in 1911, was designed by the architect Rögnvaldur Ólafsson, who demanded that its entrance face north so it would be visible to those approaching Thingeyri from the sea. Inside the church are two 17th-century candelabra and an altarpiece by the famous painter Thórarinn B. Thorláksson that depicts Christ blessing children against the background of an Icelandic landscape.

In the heart of the settlement stands **Simbahöllin,** which operates as It is used as a cafeteria but also as a museum of sorts, since the interior has been preserved as it was in the early 20th century. Locals who congregate there often provide visitors with tourist information. It also hosts music events and live performances. The village was the setting for the 2022 film *Sumarljós og svo kemur nóttin* (*Summer Light, and Then Comes the Night*), based on the novel of the same name by writer Jón Kalman Stefánsson.

On the northern side of the fjord, take Road 624 to reach the Skrúður, Iceland's oldest Botanical Garden (*admission by donation*). Founded in 1909 by a local priest, it was intended to serve as a hands-on laboratory for school students in Núpur. It was restored in 1992, after being left in a state of disrepair, and now belongs to the municipality of Ísafjörður. It constitutes a kind of monument to the history of forestry and horticulture at high latitudes.

Önundarfjörður

The village of Flateyri is located on the northern shore of the fjord. The main attraction is most likely the **Gamla Bókabúðin á Flateyri** (Old Flateyri Bookshop), Iceland's oldest business still in operation. It opened in 1914, and is currently run by a descendant of one of the founders. Inside the historic building, original furnishings have been maintained, and the rooms that were once inhabited by the owners' family are now a museum. The rooms look just as they did in 1950, when the founder of the bookstore died, making it the only dwelling of the era preserved entirely in its original appearance. The wooden building on the opposite side of the street, the Svarta pakkhúsið, is home to an exhibition on local maritime culture.

Thingeyri – Information office ✉ Hafnarstræti 5 ☎ 623 8258 **www.westfjords.is • Simbahöllin** ✉ Fjarðargötu 5 ☎ 899 6659/869 5654 🕒 Open June–Aug. daily 10 a.m.–6 p.m. except for the first two weeks of June and the last two weeks of Aug., noon–6 p.m. $ $ **www.simbahollin.is • Gamla Bókabúðin á Flateyri** ✉ Hafnarstræti 3, 425 Flateyri ☎ 840 0600/866 5954 🕒 Open May daily 11 a.m.–4 p.m., June–Sept. daily 10 a.m.–5 p.m., Oct–Apr Sat. noon–4 p.m. $ Admission by donation to visit the bookshop's historical rooms **flateyribookstore.com**

Iceland's oldest bookshop, Gamla Bókabúðin á Flateyr.

In 1995, a major avalanche hit the village, killing 20 people. A memorial to the victims was placed next to the church, Flateyrarkirkja, consecrated in 1936.

Súgandafjörður

Suðureyri, a tiny village on the fjord, was long isolated from the rest of the region by the surrounding mountains. A few mule tracks that were passable solely in summer provided the only overland connection between the village and the surrounding areas. Today, access is through the tunnels that opened in 1996, the longest in the country (29,921 ft, 9,120 m). At the time they were built, they were Iceland's largest road project. The local church, Suðureyrarkirkja, was consecrated in 1937.

Leave the village and go around the mountain to reach the village of Staður and its church, the Staðarkirkja, erected in 1855. Vigdís Finnbogadóttir, the country's first female president, promoted the restoration of the church, which was completed in 1990. The church has two bells, one dating from the 17th century and the other from the 18th century, an 18th-century altarpiece, and a brass baptismal tray dating from 1487.

Ísafjörður

The capital of the Westfjords region combines the extreme charm of a frontier village with the comfortable atmosphere of a small town that offers modern conveniences. Its name does not refer to the fjord where it is located, which is called Skutulsfjörður. Most of the town is situated on a strip of land that juts into the middle of the fjord but some neighborhoods lie along the banks. The **Byggðasafn Vestfjarða**

(Museum of Local History) is located in a wooden building dating from 1784 which was built as a warehouse by the Danish authorities. Its focus is on the maritime life and culture of the region. It is also home to some special exhibitions, such as a display of accordions, whose collection consists of more than 220 specimens, the oldest of which dates back to 1830. Across from the building's entrance is the regional Tourist Information Center.

Also located in the city center is the small, curious **Hversdagssafn**

The *Sólarkaffi*

This tradition that originated in Ísafjörður and spread to other towns celebrates the day that the sun becomes visible from town again, with coffee and sweets. The winter sun sits very low on the horizon, and though it lights up the sky, it cannot be seen from the town from late November until January 25, the day when locals celebrate Sólarkaffi (Sun Coffee).

Ísafjörður – Information center Aðalstræti 7 450 8060 Open June–Aug. Mon.–Fri. 8 a.m.–6 p.m., Sat.–Sun. 8 a.m.–3 p.m.; Sept.–May Mon.–Fri. 8 a.m.–6 p.m.; Sat.–Sun. 8 a.m.–3 p.m.; Sept.–May Mon.–Fri. 8 a.m.–4 p.m. **www.isafjordur.is • Byggðasafn Vestfjarða** 456 3291/ 862 9908 Open June–Aug. daily 10 a.m.–5 p.m., Sept. 1–15 daily 11 a.m.–3 p.m. or by appointment $ **www.nedsti.is**

Boats and ships enter the port of Ísafjörður, the capital of the Westfjords region.

Ósvör Maritime Museum near Bolungarvík.

(Museum of Everyday Life), where displays explore the mundane in an attempt to highlight its inherent beauty. The objects on display offer a glimpse of contemporary, everyday life in the fjords. Some of the installations are interactive. **Safnahús Vestfjarða** is situated on the roundabout that leads to the center of the town. It houses an art museum and photo exhibition, as well as the local community library. There is a ski resort south of the town, on the hills that overlook the valley leading to the tunnel along Road 60.

On the southeast side of the fjord, opposite the airstrip, you can park and take the steep but short trail that leads to Naustahvilft. The massive depression on the top of the mountains was carved out by ice from the last glaciation. According to local folklore, it is a mark left by the backside of a female troll who sat down to rest on the mountain. It offers one of the best panoramic views in the area. Ferries leave from Ísafjörður for the Hornstrandir Nature Reserve (see pp. 222-223).

Bolungarvík

On the right, just beyond the tunnel that connects Ísafjörður to Bolungarvík, is a detour leading to the **Ósvör Sjóminjasafn.** At this open-air maritime museum, you can immerse

Hversdagssafn ✉ Hafnarstræti 5 ☎ 694 4266/770 5503 🕒 Open Mon.–Fri. 11 a.m.–5 p.m., Sat.–Sun. 11 a.m.–2 p.m.; closed Sept.–May $ $$ **everydaylife.is • Safnahús Vestfjarða** ✉ Túngata ☎ 450 8220 🕒 Open Mon.–Fri. noon–6 p.m., Sat. 1 p.m.–4 p.m. **www.safnis.is**

Snow blankets the village of Bolungarvík in winter.

yourself in the atmosphere of Iceland's past as you explore the wood and turf buildings of a typical fishing post from the late 19th and early 20th centuries. An unnamed but very similar place is the setting for Jón Kalman Stefánsson's novel *Himnaríki og helvíti* (*Heaven and Hell*), one of his most celebrated masterpieces. A guided tour illustrates the development and changes in Iceland's fishing industry through the ages. The **Náttúrugripasafn Bolungarvíkur** (Bolungarvík Natural History Museum) is located across the bay from Ósvör. It offers exhibits about numerous species of birds and mammals.

As you leave the village and move toward the far end of the peninsula, you will find Bolafjall mountain, which towers 2,093 feet (638 m) between a narrow valley and the sea. In 2022, an observation platform was opened on its peak. Occasionally, the fata

Ósvör Sjóminjasafn Við Óshlíðarveg 892 5744 Open mid-June–mid-Aug. daily 10 a.m.–4 p.m. or by appointment $ **www.bolungarvik.is** • **Náttúrugripasafn Bolungarvíkur** Vitastíg 3 456 7005 Open June–mid-Aug. daily 10 a.m.–5 p.m. or by appointment $ **www.bolungarvik.is**

morgana phenomenon occurs here. It creates a mirage that seems like a glimpse of the Greenland coastline, which is actually not visible from Iceland because of the curvature of the Earth's surface. At the end of the 630 dirt road is Skálavík, a bay between two steep mountain walls. On sunny days, families with children often populate its sandy beach.

Álftafjörður

The village of Súðavík, situated on the western shore of the fjord, is a small community that is home to the **Melrakkasetur** (Arctic Fox Center). The center is open in summer with a fascinating museum and a research center that studies the island's only native mammal. Behind the center's renovated historic building, visitors

Melrakkasetur Eyrardalur 4 Open Sept.–May 9 a.m.–3 p.m., June–Aug. 9 a.m.–6 p.m. $ **www.melrakki.is**

The Melrakkasetur is dedicated to studying the arctic fox, Iceland's only native mammal.

can often catch a glimpse of this rare animal.

Skötufjörður

The largely uninhabited Skötufjörður offers a prime spot for seal-watching. On the western side of its mouth, near the Hvítanes Peninsula, visitors can observe one of Iceland's largest colonies of seals as they lounge on a series of flat rocks called Langasker. To avoid crowds that would disturb the animals, no parking is available in the immediate vicinity. Visitors must park farther down the road and then walk back. Less than 0.6 mile (1 km) farther south is the small farm of **Litlibær.** The building, which is protected by the National Museum, was constructed in 1985 from wood, stone, and turf. The primary source of revenue for its inhabitants was fishing. It was inhabited until 1969 and is now used as a museum.

Vatnsfjörður

The small fjord is home to a farm that was a center of power in the district in centuries past. Nearby is the charming Vatnsfjarðarkirkja church. The present building was designed by architect Rögnvaldur Ólafsson and consecrated in 1912, but there was likely a church on the site as early as the 13th century. Inside the church is a crucifix carved by a local cleric, Hjalti Thórarinsson, who lived between the 17th and 18th centuries. He also made a pulpit and a cabinet

Litlibær ☎ 695 5377 🕒 Open 10 a.m.–5 p.m. **litlibaer.is**

The family of Gísli, protagonist of the *Gísla saga*, is said to have lived on the coasts of Westfjords.

Black lava salt produced by Saltverk.

with a carving depicting the Norwegian king Ólafur the Saint. These are now in the National Museum. The altarpiece depicting the risen Christ is by the 19th century Danish artist J.F. Møller.

Reykjarfjörður

From Road 61, take detour 634 to reach Reykjanes. The building on the right side was formerly the district school but is now used as a hotel. On the left, opposite the hotel, you can see steam rising as thermal waters reach a small beach and mix with the cold waters of the fjord. Behind the hotel is the **Saltverk** plant. Guided tours illustrate how sea salt is produced using geothermal energy.

On the eastern shore of the fjord, 1.2 miles (2 km) before the curve that leads inland, is the town of Arngerðareyri. It has an abandoned pier and a curious half-collapsed building called Kastalinn. In the last century, Arngerðareyri was a relatively important center where the ferry that connected it to Ísafjörður landed. Then, it had a hotel and a store, but today the only building still standing is the Kastalinn. Dating from the first half of the 20th century, the building is quite luxurious considering the area and offers a curious contrast to the surrounding landscape. It consists of two blocks of different heights with flat roofs that are surrounded by decorative battlements. It was abandoned in 1966, after the construction of modern roads made the ferry less essential. ■

Saltverk 519 6510 Open by appointment $$ **saltverk.com**

THE COAST OF STRANDIR

The eastern coast of the Westfjords Peninsula is called the Strandir region. It runs from the western shore of Hrútafjörður to the edge of the Hornstrandir Peninsula, which, despite the similarity of its name, does not belong to the region. Here, a long series of bays and inlets are squeezed between steep mountain walls and the ocean.

Hólmavík is the largest town in the Strandir region.

The road that crosses this area is a dead end and you will have to retrace it in order to continue, a fact that discourages many from visiting the region, in spite of its natural charm and its interesting, turbulent local history. Indeed, the area became the epicenter of witch hunts in the 17th century. At the northern edge of the region is Drangajökull glacier, which, with an area of about 75 square miles (200 sq km), is the fifth largest in the country. None of the glacier exceeds an altitude of 3,280 feet (1,000 m), unlike other glaciers. It is also the only one that has not lost mass in recent years; this is due to a localized increase in snowfall on its surface that compensates for summer melting.

Staðarskáli

A stop at the busy local gas station is a must for anyone traveling to or from the north of the country. It was the site of one of the first fuel pumps in Iceland in 1929. In his poem *Staðarskáli Is Iceland* Thorarinn Eldjárn called it "a cultural and psychological phenomenon and, in a sense, a miniature of Iceland that mirrors its society," a focal point where travelers, townspeople, and country people meet. On the opposite side of the valley from the gas station is the local church, Staðarkirkja, along Road 701, which turns off from the main road. The wooden church dates from 1884 and has an antique altarpiece painted on wood that depicts the Last Supper and inlaid decorations above the altar.

Hólmavík

Overlooking sheltered Steingrímsfjörður, this village is the last outpost of the region, except for small clusters of houses and isolated farms. Aside from its small, charming port, the village's most curious attraction is undoubtedly the **Galdrasýning á Ströndum** (Museum of Sorcery and Witchcraft), a small museum devoted to the history of Icelandic magical practices, illustrated in manuscripts and folklore. On display are curious reproductions of objects and creatures from the local tradition that include the *tilberi*, a little milk-stealing monster spawned by witches and the *nábrók* (necropants), *pants made of human skin that are said to have magical powers.*. Reproductions of traditional magical seals are also preserved here, together with a wealth of historical information. The Tourist Information Center is also located here.

About 7.5 miles (12 km) south of Hólmavík, next to Road 68, is the **Sauðfjársetur** (Sheep Farming Museum), where you can get a close-up view of current breeding techniques and tools. During the summer, it hosts a national ram competition.

Vegvísir

This magical symbol, which is very popular in local merchandising, is often described as a "Viking compass," but it did not actually appear until the second half of the 19th century, in the manuscript known as the *Huld*, currently preserved at the National and University Library of Iceland, Reykjavík. Carrying the compass is said to keep you from getting lost in bad weather.

Vegvísir, the so-called Viking compass.

(continued on p. 221)

Galdrasýning á Ströndum Höfðagata 8-10 897 6525 Open May 15–Sept. daily 10 a.m.–6 p.m., Oct.–May 14 Mon.–Fri. noon–6 p.m., Sat.–Sun. 1 p.m.–6 p.m. $ **galdrasyning.is** • **Sauðfjársetur** 693 3474 Open in summer 10 a.m.–6 p.m., by appointment in winter $ **saudfjarsetur.is**

ICELANDIC MAGIC

In the modern age, with the vacuum left by the abolition of saint worship and other Catholic customs, Icelanders developed a unique magical tradition inspired by European esotericism.

The Icelandic magic preserved in local folklore has no ancient roots. It developed in the modern age as a form of popular superstition, influenced by the population's Christian cultural background. During the Renaissance, new forms of Judeo-Christian esotericism developed in Europe and were probably imported to Iceland by students and scholars returning from sojourns in cultural centers on the continent. One of the most widespread forms of magic involves the carving of magical staves. These were often inspired by the seals found on European treatises on *goetia*, or the art of commanding demons, but the properties attributed to these staves are said to be extremely diversified. Known as *galdrastafir*, literally "symbols of magics," they first appear in Icelandic grimoires (books of magic) around 1500, the first record of any forms of magic in Iceland.

Ancient book of magic spells.

The oldest manuscript with proto-*galdrastafirs* is the so-called "AM 434 a 12mo," known as *Lækningakver* or the *Doctor's Booklet*, dating from the early 1500s. It is preserved in Copenhagen. The booklet's mix of herbal remedies, cures for diseases, spells for avoiding misfortunes, and religious prayers or invocations suggests how magic, religion, and medicine were inextricably linked at that time. The simple symbols in this manuscript resemble crosses and asterisks, but in later centuries, they developed into extremely complex geometric seals. They have nothing to do with runes, the writing system first used during the Nordic Iron Age, but they have often been associated with them in retrospect since their complexity and interweaving of lines often resemble the simple figures of some runic letters. Since there is no trace of these symbols before the beginning of the 16th century, their origins cannot be attributed to the pagan religions of the pre-Christian period.

The Coast Leading to Djúpavík

On the opposite shore of the fjord from Hólmavík is Drangsnes, a small cluster of houses. On the side of the road, facing the sea, there are popular geothermal hot tubs where you can soak while you enjoy views of the fjord and the uninhabited islet of Grímsey. Changing rooms and showers are located on the opposite side of the road.

Among the least densely populated areas in the country, this is a succession of beaches, coves, and valleys along the extremely rugged coastline. In good weather, the drive through the area is one of the most spectacular in the country because of the impressive elevations that soar steeply above the dirt road, squeezed between the piles of rocks and debris, and the ocean. Numerous beaches below the road are covered with tree trunks that have been carried by currents all the way from Siberia. Having been in the salt water of the ocean for an average of five years, they are an excellent building material that does not rot. In the past, the trunks were used to construct buildings, and today farmers use them to build fences for their livestock. The view from the south side of Kaldbaksvík is remarkable, with Mount Lambatindur (2,800 ft, 854 m) towering over the coast.

The small village of Djúpavík became a wealthy and thriving center in the early 20th century, thanks to the herring fishing industry. The decline of the herring population led to the closure of the plant in 1956, and in 1984 the factory was bought by a local who converted part of it into the **Hótel Djúpavík.** An exhibition in the old factory hall illustrates the plant, with original machinery. You can reserve a guided tour at the hotel. Other rooms in the complex are used for art exhibits, concerts, and other cultural events.

Trékyllisvík Bay surrounds the islet of Árnesey. South of the bay, Árneskirkja church, consecrated in 1850, contains an 1859 altarpiece by German artist Carl Fries and an 18th-century chalice. Following the strange incidents that began to happen in 1652, the area became the scene of a sensational trial that ended with three men from the area convicted of witchcraft. All three were burned at the stake. One of them, probably afflicted with mental disorders, confessed to having talked to the devil, while the other two were convicted of using magic to kill the livestock of others. A short distance from the church is the **Minja og handverkshúsið Kört**, which provides tourist and historical information and offers a space for local crafts. ■

Hótel Djúpavík ✉ Djúpavík 524 Árneshreppur ☎ 451 4037 $ $$ djupavik.is • **Minja og handverkshúsið Kört** ✉ Árnes II, Trékyllisvík ☎ 451 4025 🕒 Open 10 a.m.–6 p.m. in summer, by appointment in winter

HORNSTRANDIR NATURE RESERVE

In this remote area, trails of varying difficulty lead through an untamed landscape that is home to a large population of arctic foxes, which are protected in this area. The whales you might see from the cliffs and the silences you experience are added attractions at this nature reserve.

Over the centuries, humans established a considerable number of settlements on the Hornstrandir Peninsula. The population could rely on a fair amount of natural resources that included fishing, seal hunting, and collecting seabird eggs. The outlaws and fugitives that took refuge here often attempted to board foreign ships in order to escape the peninsula. The villages are usually located in the center of amphitheater-like valleys that have been carved into the peninsula's elevations by ice. The difficulty in connecting these settlements to one another and to the rest of the country gradually led to their aban-

The cliffs at the Hornstrandir Nature Reserve.

donment, around the middle of the 20th century. Constructing numerous long tunnels to connect a handful of families with one road was not economically viable.

Today, depopulation has left Hornstrandir as one of the last truly untamed areas in Europe, and in fact the area became a protected nature reserve in 1975. Since then, some of the descendants of the former inhabitants have reclaimed the dwellings of their ancestors. They usually use them as summer homes, but no one resides here permanently.

Located in the center of Ísafjörður is the tourist information center, **Hornstrandastofa.** Here you will find rangers who can help plan your excursions, as well as a small exhibit that illustrates what life was like in Hornstrandir in centuries past. The only way to reach the peninsula is by ferry (May-August only) from Ísafjörður, from Bolungarvík, or from Norðurfjörður, in the Strandir region. You can take half-day, round-trip excursions or stay for several days before taking a ferry back to civilization.

Hornstrandir is a popular destination for hikers that gives you a chance to experience the thrill of trekking through the wilderness with no services, in total solitude. The reserve covers an area of 330 square miles (580 sq km) and has a rich but delicate alpine ecosystem that includes 260 plant species. Exploring this area is not easy and only experienced travelers with the right equipment should attempt it. It is possible to camp for free at designated campsites or to rent space on private land where some amenities are available. Hesteyri, perhaps the most popular stopping point, is home to the old local doctor's house, which is now used as lodging for travelers. It is also the setting for a famous horror novel, *Ég man thig* (*I Remember You*) by the celebrated writer Yrsa Sigurðardóttir. The novel became a movie, directed by Óskar Thór Axelsson. The most famous point of interest is surely Hornbjarg, a colossal cliff whose highest point, Kálfatindur, soars 1,750 feet (534 m) above the sea. The inner part of the cliff slopes steeply inland, creating a basin surrounded by the elevations that separate it from the coast. ■

The Black Viking

According to the *Landnámabók*, the settler of Hornstrandir was Geirmundur the Dark, son of a Norwegian king ousted by Haraldur Fairhair in the late ninth century, who escaped to Iceland and became a powerful lord. In his book, *The Black Viking*, Bergsveinn Birgisson tells a partly fictionalized version of the story of Geirmundur.

Hornstrandastofa ✉ Silfurgata 1 ☎ 591 2000 ⏲ Open June–Aug. Mon.–Sat. 8 a.m.–4 p.m., all other months Mon.–Fri. 1 p.m.–3 p.m. **ust.is**

Ancient turf houses, geological marvels and charming small towns: the North is characterized by its diversity

THE NORTH

The small Skarðsviti lighthouse watches over the mouth of Miðfjörður.

THE NORTH

The Northern region is extremely diversified, characterized by the presence of deep fjords, massive mountains, and towns with fascinating history. Most of the country's surviving turf buildings are concentrated here, a window into the history of the Icelandic people. The area is the primary setting for the *Grettis saga*, one of the most highly regarded medieval epics.

The Northern region (Norðurland) encompasses a vast area that stretches from Hrútafjörður to the peninsula of Langanes, and is traditionally divided into two parts. The western part includes the area of Skagafjörður and the smaller fjords to the west, while the east includes the area of Eyjafjörður as far as the Langanes Peninsula.

The climate of this region tends to vary more extremely than that of southern Iceland since it benefits less from the influence of the Gulf Stream. Its winters are sometimes harsher and snowier, with more than 8 feet (2.5 m) of snow per year on average, compared with 3.2 feet (1 m) per year in Reykjavík, and its summers can be noticeably warmer than in the south.

Over the centuries, the west coast has been the landing place for the numerous polar bears that get stuck on chunks of ice that have broken away from the glacier near Greenland's shores. These bears have been a danger for the population and when they reach the shores of Iceland exhausted and starving, they are usually put down.

From a naturalistic point of view, the Northern region combines the beauty of its great fjords with that of the deep valleys that cut into its innermost areas. Here, there are numerous settlements of interest, including the seat of the diocese of Hólar, founded in 1106, as well

NOT TO BE MISSED:

The Glaumbær museum 230

The Grafarkirkja turf church 232

The Siglufjörður herring museum 233

The Akureyri botanic garden 238–239

Laufás heritage site 251

The Húsavík whale museum 246

The Lake Mývatn region 239–241

The Ásbyrgi canyon 243

The thermal baths in Akureyri 239

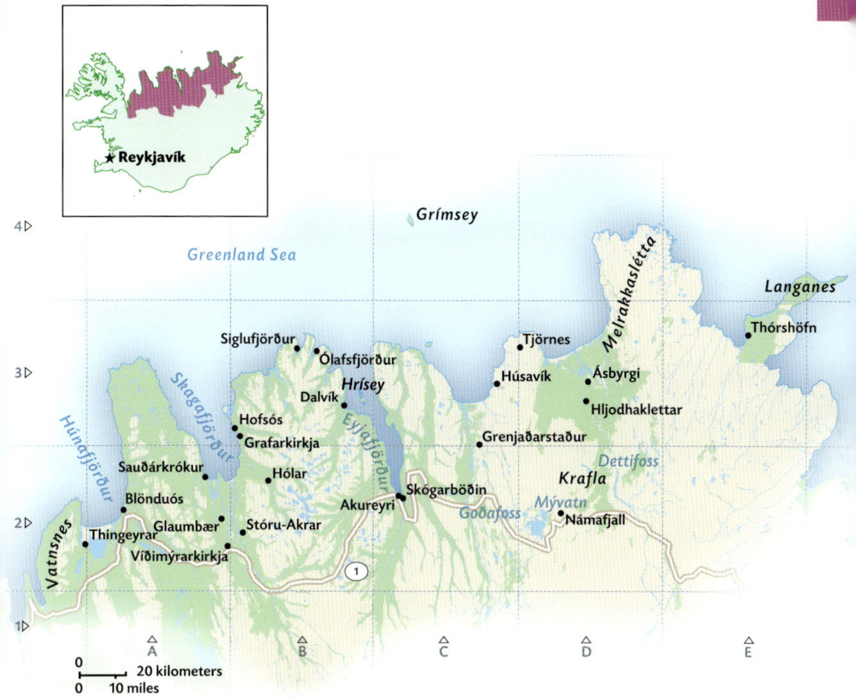

as a series of larger villages such as Blönduós, Sauðárkrókur, Siglufjörður, Dalvík, and Húsavík, most of which are located along the coast.

The North also boasts the country's only city outside of the Southwestern region and the third largest population center, Akureyri (approximately 20,000 inhabitants), Iceland's northern capital. The small town offers many amenities such as hotels, restaurants, shops, and museums, and is a very popular base for whale-watching tours. Its botanical garden, about 62 miles (100 km) from the Arctic Circle, is a masterpiece of the interaction between nature and human ingenuity.

Farther east, the territory surrounding Lake Mývatn offers geological wonders such as pseudocraters, fumaroles, and lava formations. It is one of the most visited and appreciated areas in the entire country, as are the Dettifoss waterfall, one of the most impressive in Europe, and the Ásbyrgi canyon. The Melrakkaslétta and Langanes Peninsulas make up the most remote part of the region. It is the farthest from the capital and perhaps the least visited of Iceland's coastal regions.

Most of the historic turf buildings that have survived the test of time are concentrated in the North: Glaumbær, Laufás, and Grafarkirkja, Iceland's oldest church. Visitors can explore the lives of Icelanders in centuries past by touching the reality of their daily lives. ■

SKAGAFJÖRÐUR & THE TROLL PENINSULA

This western area of northern Iceland is one of the lesser known: it is penalized by being on the route between the capital and the town of Akureyri. Nevertheless, it is as dense with points of interest as any other part of the country.

The Hvítserkur basalt sea stack towers in the waters of Húnafjörður.

The Northwest region includes the areas between Hrútafjörður and Skagafjörður. The first point of arrival, coming from the south, is the town of Staðarskáli, located at the end of Hrútafjörður. The landscape here is characterized by barren scenery, but nature becomes much more luxuriant toward Skagafjörður, where numerous farms and woodlands create pleasing panoramas when the weather conditions are right.

Vatnsnes

Coming to the north by car from western Iceland, the route descends from a barren plateau to the shores of desolate Hrútafjörður, the first fjord you'll reach.. The next is the smaller Miðfjörður, which borders the western part of the Vatnsnes Peninsula. On its eastern shore, on Road 72, 3.7 miles (6 km) north of the junction with Route 1, is the small village of Hvammstangi, home to the **Selasetur Íslands** (Iceland's Seal Center), a seal research hub with a museum dedicated to these animals. Farther north along Road 711 is the picturesque Skarðsviti lighthouse and the Illugastaðir campground, a prime spot for observing seal colonies. The conditions of the road around the Vatnsnes Peninsula have been poor for years, so it is a good idea to check its accessibility before getting behind the wheel. Húnaflói Bay is located beyond the northern point of the peninsula, descending southward. A short distance from the bay's southernmost beaches is Hvítserkur, rock formation that resembles an ancient helmet half sunk into the sea. The sea stack, which has been reinforced with concrete to protect it from erosion, can also be reached on foot at low tide. Ten and a half miles (17 km) farther south, a turnoff onto Road 717 leads to Borgarvirki, an ancient rudimentary fortress consisting of a rocky amphitheater on the top of a hill, encircled by an imposing drystone wall

Thingeyrar

A 3.7-mile (6 km) detour along road 721, leads to the village of Thingeyrar, where visitors will find **Thingeyrakirkja,** a 19th-century masonry church, and a small exhibit explaining the history of the area. The church was built between 1864 and 1867 by a prominent local lord who had oxen haul the stones across the frozen Hóp lagoon, nearby. Once the site of an ancient regional assembly, the building later housed a Benedictine monastery, founded in 1112, that would become one of the most important in the country. It is likely that the *Flateyjarbók* (see p. 187), Iceland's largest and most valuable medieval manuscript now housed at the University of Iceland, was composed here.

Blönduós

The rushing Blanda River runs through this pretty village that overlooks the Húnaflói Bay. A footbridge that crosses the river leads to Hrútey, an island in the middle of the river's rapids, covered in woodlands and crisscrossed by convenient walking paths. The **Heimilisiðnaðarsafnið** is an interesting museum located in the part of the village that lies on the river's northern bank. It offers information about wool production and the history of the textile industry in Iceland.

Sauðárkrókur

With a population of between 2,000 and 3,000, Sauðárkrókur is the most

Selasetur Íslands ✉ Strandgata 1 ☎ 541 2345 🕒 Open Oct.–Apr. Mon.–Fri. 11 a.m.–3 p.m., May–Sept. daily 10 a.m.–5 p.m. $ $ **selasetur.is** • **Thingeyrakirkja** ✉ Thingeyrakirkja 541 ☎ 895 4473 **thingeyraklausturskirkja.is** • **Heimilisiðnaðarsafnið** ✉ Árbraut 29 ☎ 452 4067 🕒 Open June–Aug. 10 a.m.–5 p.m. $ $ **textile.is**

INSIDER TIP:
Sauðárkrókskirkja is home to an immersive museum where virtual reality allows visitors to experience one of the most important battles in medieval Iceland.

—ROBERTO LUIGI PAGANI
Author of this guidebook

important town in the area. Located here is the 19th-century **Sauðárkrókskirkja** Church, which has an altarpiece dating from 1895 by Danish artist Anker Lund. The town is also home to the immersive museum **1238: The Battle of Iceland,** where virtual reality allows visitors to immerse themselves in the experience of Örlygsstaðir, one of the most decisive battles of the Icelandic Middle Ages. About 9.3 miles (15 km) north of Sauðárkrókur, along dirt road 748, is the town of Reykir, with its famous hot springs pool, **Grettislaug.** The pool was named after the protagonist of the *Grettis saga*, one of Iceland's most important medieval epics.

Glaumbær

This area is named after the estate that was based here for a millennium. It is home to **Byggðasafn Skagfirðinga,** an open-air anthropological museum that houses one of the best-preserved and most interesting turf buildings in the region, the Glaumbær farm. The site was home to the legendary explorer Guðríður Thorbjarnardóttir, who took part in the expedition that attempted the colonization of the New World from Greenland. She later made a pilgrimage to Rome and then finally returned to Iceland where she erected a church in Glaumbær and ended her days as a devout nun. The building is a good illustration of the lifestyle of Icelanders between the late Middle Ages and the 19th century. It preserves a classic example of a *baðstofa*, a multipurpose hall where people slept on beds arranged along the walls at night, and where they worked and ate using the beds as benches during the day. The museum also offers a dedicated virtual reality space that allows visitors to see the rooms of turf houses with actors at work, and a renovated 19th-century building that houses exhibitions and a café with period furnishings and staff in national costume.

Sauðárkrókskirkja ✉ Aðalgata 1 ☎ 453 5930 🕒 Open by appointment **www.saudarkrokskirkja.is • 1238: The Battle of Iceland** ✉ Aðalgata 21 ☎ 588 1238 🕒 Open Mon.–Sat. 10 a.m.–4 p.m. $ $$ **1238.is • Grettislaug** ☎ 841 7313 🕒 Open Mon.–Sun. 8 a.m.–10 p.m. $ $ **• Byggðasafn Skagfirðinga** ☎ 453 6173 🕒 Open May 20–Sept. 20 Mon.–Fri. 10 a.m.–6 p.m., Sept. 21–Oct. 20 Mon.–Fri. 10 a.m.–4 p.m., Oct. 21–Mar. 31 by appointment, Apr. 1–May 19 Mon.–Fri. 10 a.m.–4 p.m. $ $ **www.glaumbaer.is**

Víðimýrarkirkja

A very short detour from Route 1, just outside the town of Varmahlíð, leads to **Víðimýrarkirkja,** one of only five turf churches surviving to the present day in all of Iceland. It is a very graceful wood and turf building with a grass-covered roof. Its present form dates from the early 19th century, but its history begins in the Middle Ages, when the Chieftain of the Sturlungar clan, Snorri Sturluson, erected a fortress there. The event is narrated in the *Sturlunga saga,* a collection of accounts of 13th-century events in Iceland. Currently, it is the only turf church that can be visited.

Stóru-Akrar

Continuing on the opposite side of the valley along Road 1 is the Miklibær farm, home to the preserved turf house Stóru-Akrar, from the mid-18th century. For a time, it was the residence of Skúli Magnússon, the man considered the "father" of Reykjavík, who lived there when he was the region's *sýslumaður* (prefect). The house no longer holds any furnishings but it still provides an interesting example of Icelandic housing in the modern age, perhaps more accurate than the other large, more opulent turf farms that usually date from the 19th century.

Víðimýrarkirkja ☎ 453 6173 🕒 Open June–Aug. Tues.–Sun. noon–6 p.m. $ $ **www.glaumbaer.is**

Wild horses run free on the Vatnsnes Peninsula.

Hólar

The importance of this center, surrounded by lush valleys, in the context of Icelandic history is evident. In 1106, the northern diocese was founded here and, along with the southern diocese, was the most important cultural center on the island. Bishop Guðbrandur Thorláksson sent the first Icelandic translation of the Bible to print in 1584. The cathedral, **Hóladómkirkja,** the oldest masonry church in the country, was built here in 1763. In 1950, the bell tower was erected and dedicated to Jón Arason, the last Catholic bishop of the diocese.

The University of Hólar, founded in 2007, specializes in the subjects of tourism and animal husbandry.

Grafarkirkja

Between the junction for Hólar and the town of Hofsós is the turf church Grafarkirkja, the oldest church in Iceland, parts of which date back to the 17th century. The inside of the church is not accessible for conservation reasons, but visitors can park beyond the gate at the side of the road and walk

Hóladómkirkja ☎ 453 6300 🕒 Open Mon.–Sun. 10 a.m.–6 p.m.

Aerial view of Grafarkirkja, the oldest church in Iceland.

inside to observe its exterior and the beauty of the natural setting that surrounds it.

Hofsós

This small village is home to the very interesting **Vesturfarasetrið,** the Icelandic Emigration Center. The center is dedicated to the migration of Icelanders to North America during the 19th century due to population growth and a reduction in available resources, a situation that was exacerbated by the catastrophic eruption of the Askja volcano in 1875. Another famous attraction of this village is the local municipal swimming pool. Located on a sort of balcony at the top of the cliff, it offers a memorable view of the fjord.

Siglufjörður

This small town's natural setting would be enough to justify a visit, but there are many other points of interest that make it a must-see destination. In addition to its pretty local church, **Siglufjarðarkirkja,** consecrated in 1931, the town is also home to the immersive Síldarminjasafn (Herring Museum). Distributed throughout a series of facilities, it offers insight into one of the most decisive periods in Icelandic history, when the explosion of the fishing industry changed the nation's economy and life forever.

The **Thjóðlagasetur** (Folk Music Center) is a research and promotion center dedicated to Bjarni Thorsteinsson, who first collected and studied Icelandic folk music, cataloging it in a monumental collection published in 1909. In addition to preserving a number of traditional musical instruments, every year since 2000, the center has organized the Siglufjörður Folk Music Festival (Thjóðlagahátíð Siglufjarðar), a summer school, and a series of exchanges with folk musicians from around the world who visit the town to perform. From the town center, visitors can climb the mountainside along paths that offer panoramic views. In the winter, skiing facilities are available near the village.

Ólafsfjörður

Coming from Siglufjörður, before the small town of **Ólafsfjörður,** is uninhabited Héðinsfjörður, the scene

Vesturfarasetrið ☎ 453 7935 🕒 Open June–Sept . 11 a.m.–6 p.m. or by appointment **hofsos.is • Siglufjörður – Tourist information center** ✉ Gránugata 24 ☎ 467 1555 🕒 Open June–Aug. Mon.–Fri. 9 a.m.–5 p.m., Sat.–Sun. 11 a.m.–3 p.m., limited hours in all other months **www.visittrollaskagi.is • Síldarminjasafn** ✉ Snorragata 10 ☎ 467 1604 🕒 Open June–Aug. 10 a.m.–6 p.m., May & Sept. 1 p.m.–5 p.m., winter months by appointment $ $$ **www.sild.is • Thjóðlagasetur** ✉ Norðurgata 1 ☎ 467 2300 (in summer); 692 6030 (in winter) 🕒 Open June–Aug. noon–6 p.m., Sept.–May by appointment **siglofestival.com • Ólafsfjörður – Tourist information center** ✉ Ólafsvegur 4 ☎ 464 9215 🕒 Open Mon.–Fri. 1 p.m.–5 p.m. **www.visittrollaskagi.is**

of an air disaster in 1947, when a commercial aircraft crashed into the face of Hestfjall mountain. Twenty-five people lost their lives, and to this day, the accident remains the most serious in the country's history. Despite the tragic event, the fjord is an extremely serene place, ideal for hiking. A scenic parking lot with signs that give historical information about the area is located right next to the road, in the heart of the valley, near the shore of Lake Héðinsfjarðarvatn. Beyond the tunnel is the small village of Ólafsfjörður, set in amazing natural surroundings. The **Pálshús,** one of the oldest buildings in the village, now houses the local museum, with a particularly interesting exhibit on Icelandic bird life.

Dalvík

Dalvík is often used primarily as a starting point for visiting the islands of Hrísey and Grímsey, but it does have some points of interest of its own. At the local museum, the **Hvoll – Byggðasafn Dalvíkur,** visitors can enjoy three floors of exhibits dedicated to the area's cultural and natural history. Located on the western edge of town, the local church is modern, built in classical architectural style and consecrated in 1960.

Continuing north, the road opposite the church leads to an area called Upsir, where there is a small cemetery whose chapel has a curious history. The Upsakirkja, which served Dalvík, once stood here. In 1853, the old turf church was replaced by a wooden one, which was swept away by a storm in the early 1900s. Many of the relics it contained were heavily damaged, including the Upsir Christ, a wooden crucifix of Icelandic manufacture from the 13th century, and the 18th-century altarpiece by Hallgrímur Jónsson, one of the most important artists of the period. These artifacts were recovered and are now kept in the National Museum. A new wooden church was later erected, but when it was also damaged by bad weather, the decision was made to build the present Dalvík Church. The wooden form that served as the entrance for the old church was preserved and reused in the lovely chapel that stands today in the heart of the cemetery.

Hrísey

Accessible by ferry from Dalvík, the island of Hrísey was inhabited from the time of the colonization period (9th–10th centuries), when Narfi Thrándarson, a character from the *Víga-Glúms saga*, lived there. The village grew with the explosion of

Pálshús ✉ Strandgata 4 ☎ 466 2255/848 4071 🕒 Open May 15–Sept. 15 1 p.m.–5 p.m. $ $ **www.palshusmuseum.is • Dalvík – Tourist information center** ✉ Goðabraut ☎ 846 4928 🕒 Open Mon.–Fri. 9 a.m.–5 p.m., Sat. noon–5 p.m. **www.dalvikurbyggd.is • Hvoll – Byggðasafn Dalvíkur** ✉ Karls-Rauðatorg 7 ☎ 460 4928 🕒 Open June–Aug. 10 a.m.–5 p.m., by appointment in winter $ $

The décor of a locale in Siglufjörður testifies to the importance of the herring market to the town.

herring fishing in the 19th and 20th centuries, and until 2015, it was used for the mandatory quarantine of all farm and domestic animals imported from abroad. With an area of about 4.2 square miles (11 sq km), it is Iceland's second largest island. Located in the small town is the **Hús Hákarla-Jörundar** (House of Shark Jörundur, a famous local shark fisherman), which was built using timber salvaged from some Norwegian ships wrecked near the island in 1884. It includes an information point and an exhibit about local history as well as shark fishing. Three hiking trails run along the southern portion of the island, while the northern part is divided among private properties. Some sections of the southern cliffs are spectacular and are home to numerous species of seabirds.

Hús Hákarla-Jörundar Norðurvegur 3 695 0077 Open in summer 2 p.m.–5 p.m., in winter by appointment $ **www.hrisey.is**

The coast of Grímsey Island straddles the Arctic Circle.

Grímsey

Located about 25 miles (40 km) north of Iceland's northern coast, Grímsey can be reached by ferry from Dalvík, or by plane from Akureyri. The area of the island is about 2 square miles (5 sq km) and its population is limited to a few dozen inhabitants, whose main occupation is fishing. This island is the only part of Icelandic territory that straddles the Arctic Circle. The position of the circle is not fixed; it tends to migrate farther north or farther south over the centuries (currently it is moving northward at an average of about 45 ft/14 m year). For this reason, the monument that marks it is a large 8 metric tons stone sphere that can be moved to reflect the line's migration. At the time of this writing, the stone is about 325 feet (100 m) from the northern tip of the island, but by the mid-21st century, the circle will have moved beyond the northern edge of the island, which will no longer straddle it. Grímsey's local church, Miðgarðakirkja, dates back to the mid-19th century and was the northernmost church in the country. It was destroyed by fire in 2021, and construction work on a new building was undertaken the following year. ■

AKUREYRI & THE DIAMOND CIRCLE

This cosmopolitan center with its untamed atmospheres has interesting museums, restaurants, and a fair amount of cultural activity. Akureyri is an urban oasis surrounded by unparalleled natural wonders.

You can soak in the hot pools of Grettislaug, named for the protagonist of the *Grettir saga*.

The northeastern part of Iceland is one of the most desirable areas for visitors because of the high concentration of natural beauty and cultural points of interest in a relatively small area. Visitors can observe the whales that abound in the cold waters of the northern coast on one of the whale-watching tours that depart from the town of Akureyri and the village of Húsavík. The interior is home to historically significant towns and natural areas that offer unique views.

Akureyri – Tourist information center ✉ Geislagata 9 ☎ 460 1000
🕒 Open June–mid-Sept. Mon.–Fri. 8 a.m.–6.30 p.m., mid-Sept.–Apr. daily 8 a.m.–4 p.m., May daily 8 a.m.–4 p.m. **www.visitakureyri.is**

EXPERIENCE: Whale-watching

Humpback whales, minke whales, and some dolphins are among the most frequently sighted species but with a little luck, you might also spot orcas or blue whales. Tours of this type are available year-round, but the species you sight may vary. Whale-watching tours can take place on ships or smaller boats. On a ship, the price is lower and watching is from a distance so as not to disturb the animals, while on a smaller boat tour, you can get significantly closer, but the price is generally higher and you run the risk of disturbing the animals *(husavikadventures.is)*.

Akureyri

It appears that Akureyri was not a town in ancient times; in fact, the first document to mention it is a 1562 conviction against a woman accused of having relations with a man who was not her husband. In the 17th century, it became a trading base for Danish merchants, who occupied it only during the summer months. Permanent settlement did not begin until 1778. A few years later, Akureyri was elevated to the status of trading station by the Danish authorities, in the hopes that this would provide the impetus for the formation of a larger urban center at a time when there were no real towns let alone cities in Iceland. It was not until the second half of the 19th century that the town began to grow. Today it offers numerous services and recreational activities, and is even home to a university.

The town's primary museums include the **Minjasafnið á Akureyri** (Akureyri Museum), specializing in the local history of the Eyjafjörður region, and the nearby **Nonnahús,** dedicated to children's book writer and Jesuit priest Jón Sveinsson (1857–1944), who lived in the house. The **Listasafnið á Akureyri** (Akureyri Art Gallery) is a Bauhaus-style building that hosts art exhibits by Icelandic and foreign artists.

Prominent in the small town center is the modern church, Akureyrarkirkja, designed by architect Guðjón Samúelsson with stained-glass windows depicting key figures in Icelandic religious and cultural history. From the entrance of the church, visitors can follow the road that overlooks the fjord to reach the charming Péturskirkja, a Catholic parish church.

Minjasafnið á Akureyri & Nonnahús ✉ Aðalstræti 58 ☎ 462 4162 🕒 Open June–Sept. 11 a.m.–5 p.m., Oct.–May 1 p.m.–5 p.m. $ $ **www.minjasafnid.is** • **Listasafnið á Akureyri** ✉ Kaupvangsstræti 8 ☎ 461 2610 🕒 Open noon–5 p.m.; closed Dec. 24, 25, 31 & Jan. 1 $ $ **www.listak.is** • **Lystigarður Akureyrar** ☎ 462 7487 🕒 Open June–Sept. Mon.–Fri. 8 a.m.–10 p.m., Sat.–Sun. 9 a.m.–10 p.m. **lystigardur.akureyri.is**

The **Lystigarður Akureyrar** (Akureyri Botanical Garden) is located a little farther on. Founded in 1912, it is now home to more than 2,000 species of plants. During the summer months, it creates a sharp contrast from the subarctic views of the fjord it faces.

Just south of the town is Kjarnaskógur Forest, which was planted in 1947 and is now the town's most important recreational area. Its 1,975 acres (800 ha) have more than 1.5 million trees.

Skógarböðin

The **Skógarböðin** (Forest Baths), are a spa created by reusing thermal water from an aquifer that was discovered by accident during tunneling work in the area. Located on the eastern side of the fjord, the baths are surrounded by trees and overlook the waters. The parking lot is right next to Road 1, just across the fjord coming from Akureyri. The spa includes two infinity pools, two swim-up bars, and a sauna.

Goðafoss

Just off Route 1, 21 miles (34 km) east of Akureyri, is Goðafoss (Waterfall of the Gods). It was named for the legend that Thorgeir Ljósvetningagoði, who was responsible for converting the country to Christianity, threw his pagan idols into it. The waterfall plummets 39 feet (12 m) into a spectacular rocky amphitheater. It is visible from two sides and can be reached via comfortable concrete paths.

Mývatn

The Lake Mývatn area is an inexhaustible trove of natural

Skógarböðin ✉ Vaðlaskógur 605 ☎ 585-0090 🕒 Open Mon.–Fri. 11 a.m.–midnight $ $$$ **www.forestlagoon.is • Mývatn – Tourist information center** ✉ Hraunvegur 8 ☎ 464 4390 🕒 Open in summer 8 a.m.–6 p.m. **www.visitmyvatn.is**

Lake Mývatn.

Turf Houses

A few decades after colonization, birch wood became extremely scarce, making houses difficult to heat. This triggered an architectural change that, over time, led to the evolution of typical Icelandic turf houses. The rooms were small and the combination of the turf's insulating properties and the body heat of the occupants made the temperature inside livable without burning fuel. Sometimes, the living quarters were located in the loft and animals were kept on the lower floor. Their body heat rose into the room above, warming it. Iceland is the only place that, for centuries, has used turf as a building material for the dwellings of both the rich and the poor. Since turf is highly perishable, walls made of this material have to be continuously rebuilt.

treasures. A wide variety of sights and destinations of natural and geological interest surround the lake, which is itself one of the wonders of the country. Overlooking the southern shore is the Skútustaðir area, where visitors can take paths of varying lengths through the area of pseudocraters. The craters are essentially cones of debris, now partially covered by low vegetation and moss that resulted from the interaction of lava with the shallow surface of the lake. The explosions caused by the violent and sudden evaporation of water in contact with magma led to their formation. Skútustaðakirkja, a small, charming church dating from the mid-19th century, stands on the opposite side of the road.

Heading north on the eastern shore of the lake leads to a series of worthwhile attractions. The nature observation point at Höfði offers lovely views of the lake. Access to the Dimmuborgir (Dark Fortresses) area is about 1.8 miles (3 km) farther north. This vast and strikingly unusual-looking lava field was formed when magma flowed over soils rich in surface water and, with extreme heat, the water evaporated suddenly, opening up chimney-like vents in the lava. These magma accumulations sometimes collapsed on top of one another, creating strange shapes that resemble the ruins of ancient castles. Huge bubbles of gas underground later gave way to numerous caves of varying sizes. Icelandic folklore has it that this spooky place is home to supernatural creatures, most notably the trolls Grýla and her husband Leppalúði, and their 13 children, the *jólasveinar*. They were once bogeymen used to frighten disobedient children, but they are now the Yule Lads, who bring Christmas presents to the children of Iceland. Trails of varying lengths allow visitors to explore this gloomy, mysterious area.

About 2.4 miles (4 km) farther north a detour to the east leads to the base of Hverfjall, a volcano that formed 2,500 years ago. The crater is 492 feet (150 m) deep and a steep and slippery path leads to its rim. Farther north on Road 860 is Grjótagjá, a lava cave with a hot spring inside that was used for bathing until the mid-1970s, when volcanic activity in the area brought the water temperature to over 120°F (50°C). Continuing along Road 860 leads back to Route 1, a short distance from the Mývatn geothermal plant and the famous and very popular **Jarðböðin við Mývatn** thermal baths.

Námafjall

Northeast of the lake is Námafjall mountain. On the northern slope is the Hverir area, where the landscape resembles the surface of Mars – with bright ochre colors streaked with crimson-patches–and fumaroles, and bubbling pools of blue-gray mud are surrounded by encrusted sulfur. The marked thermal activity is due to the presence of lava at relatively shallow depths. Paid parking can be found next to the road.

Krafla

From Route 1, the turnoff to the Krafla area (Road 863) is on the opposite side from Hverir. The Kröflustöð geothermal plant is about 4.3 miles (7 km) down the road. About two-thirds along the way

Jarðböðin við Mývatn ✉ Jarðbaðshólar ☎ 464 4411 $ $$$
myvatnnaturebaths.is

The pseudocraters near Mývatn.

INSIDER TIP:
Visit the Ásbyrgi canyon. Local legend has it that the canyon is the hoof print of Sleipnir, the eight-legged steed ridden by Odin.

—ROBERTO LUIGI PAGANI
Author of this guidebook

is a parking lot where visitors will find a continuously functioning hot water shower that is connected to an underground hot spring. Past the plant and up over the hills is the Víti (Hell) crater of the Krafla volcano known for the sapphire and aqua blue lake that lies inside of it.

Dettifoss

The Dettifoss waterfall, located on the course of the Jökulsá á Fjöllum River, is set in a lunar landscape of sand and basalt in the colossal canyon of Jökulsárgljúfur.

At 328 feet (100 m) long and about 145 feet (44 m) high, it is one of the largest waterfalls in Europe, with a water flow rate of up to 7,062 cubic feet (200 cu m) per second. Visitors can approach the waterfall from both sides, but the western side, accessible via a special detour on Road 862, is the most popular. The convenient parking lot is equipped with toilets. From there, visitors can reach the main balcony and then descend to the lower level, if it is not closed due to snow, or take a narrow path to the upper viewing balcony. A short detour between the parking lot and the waterfall leads to Selfoss Falls, with an amphitheater-shaped, 45-foot (14 m) drop. The eastern side of Dettifoss, reachable on Road 864, is less frequented. It takes visitors closer to the precipice of the fall, which makes for a more challenging and dangerous visit.

Hljóðaklettar

The Hljóðaklettar (Echoing Rocks) are located on Road 862, between Dettifoss and Ásbyrgi. Their name reflects the fact that, when standing among the rocks, it is difficult to understand from which direction the roar of the glacier river is coming. These spectacular rock formations include impressive sculpted columns of basalt, pinnacles, and a cave formed under what appears to be a "fold" in the thick basaltic layer. A circular trail about 1.8 miles (3 km) long runs through the area.

Ásbyrgi

This impressive canyon, whose name means "fortress of the gods," was apparently created by a colossal flood that was caused by an eruption, some 8,000 to 10,000 years ago, under the Vatnajökull ice sheet. The canyon is 2.2 miles (3.5 km) long, its average width is 0.6 miles (1 km) and its cliffs reach a maximum height of 328 feet (100 m).

At the center of the horseshoe-shaped canyon is the Eyjan (Island), an isolated rocky massif that towers over the surrounding plain between the two sides of the canyon, separating them for about half the length. Around the middle of the 20th century, several tree species were introduced to the area, and now the canyon is home to a thriving forest. A road leads to trails that allow visitors to explore the last fascinating section of the canyon at its deepest point, where the emerald green pond Botnstjörn is located. **Gljúfrastofa,** the information center for Vatnajökull National Park, which includes Ásbyrgi, is located at the mouth of the canyon. Information on the area's many hiking trails is available here. One local legend has it that the canyon is the hoof print of Sleipnir, the eight-legged steed ridden by Odin but there are no ancient sources for the story, so it is likely a recent romantic invention. Another popular myth is that Ásbyrgi is an important place for the hidden people, the elves.

(continued on p. 245)

Gljúfrastofa ☎ 470 7100 🕒 Open Jan.–Mar. Mon.–Fri. 11 a.m.–3 p.m., Apr.–May daily 10 a.m.–4 p.m., June–Aug. daily 9 a.m.–6 p.m., Sept.–Oct. daily 10 a.m.–4 p.m., Nov.–Dec. Mon.–Fri. 11 a.m.–3 p.m. **www.vatnajokulsthjodgardur.is**

The Dettifoss waterfall, in Jökulsárgljúfur canyon, is among the most powerful in Europe.

THE HIDDEN PEOPLE

In Iceland, fantasy mixes with reality: elves are believed to influence the lives of the citizens, underlining their deep connection to nature.

Elf houses indicate the places frequented by the "hidden people."

Icelandic elves, *álfar* (singular *álfur*), are one of the most frequent cultural elements in the country's traditions, with some surveys even indicating that a large portion of the population believes in their existence. The film *Eurovision Song Contest: The Story of Fire Saga* presents an entertaining caricaturized version of the elves, with actress Rachel McAdams offering them gifts in exchange for favors.

The elves e inhabit the colorful little houses that occasionally grace Icelandic gardens. It is a common misconception that these little houses are a kind of "artificial nest" like birdhouses. In reality, the little houses, in addition to being decorative (somewhat like our garden gnomes), are there to indicate that a particular natural feature such as a hill, a bump, or a boulder is frequented by elves, but the houses are not necessarily lodgings. In fact, Icelandic elves are nothing like the "little people" of British folklore. They are not little at all.

Elves are called the "hidden people", or *huldufólk*. The elves of Icelandic folklore are part of Christian cosmology, not pagan cosmology. They are considered descendants of Adam and Eve just like humans. They are thought to populate our world rather than a separate world like the elves of the pre-Christian Nordic tradition. They also go to church, and in fact, many peculiarly shaped rocks are identified as "elf churches" (*álfakirkjur*). They have the power to make themselves invisible. They are characterized by their beauty and wealth, emanate an aura of light, and dwell in certain rocks.

The Icelandic elf tradition may have replaced of the worship of saints, which was abandoned in 1550 when Danish authorities forced the conversion to Lutheranism. Belief in elves was not mere entertainment; it offered psychological relief in the face of life's sufferings.

The Akureyrarkirkja church is a masterpiece of Iceland's basaltic style.

Tjörnes

This peninsula is characterized by the rock formations on its coastline. On the eastern side, a precipice offers panoramic views of the cliffs where puffins nest during the summer. When the weather is good, the bluish outline of Grímsey Island can be seen from the top of the cliffs on the northern and western sides. The northernmost tip of the peninsula is home to a picturesque lighthouse. Just to the east is the **Mánárbakki Museum**, which includes a period house converted with objects and furnishings from days gone by, and a wood-and-turf house built by the landowner that also illustrates the way of life in the past.

Húsavík

Medieval sources report that Húsavík was where one of the first explorers, the Swede Garðar Svavarsson, spent the winter after sailing around Iceland to determine that it was an island. He initially named it after himself, calling it Garðarshólmi, which means "Garðar's Islet." The toponym was later replaced with Ísland, "Land of Ice," by the explorer Flóki Vilgerðarsson. According to sources, Garðar left a few slaves in the area of Húsavík before returning to Scandinavia, which technically gave it, and not Reykjavík, the distinction of being the oldest settlement on the island. The city gained international fame as one of the primary settings of the Netflix film

Mánárbakki Museum Tjörneshreppi 864 2057/464 1957 Open daily June–Aug. 10 a.m.–6 p.m. or by appointment $ **www.museumguide.is/manarbakki • Húsavík www.visithusavik.is**

Eurovision Song Contest: The Story of Fire Saga (2020). Húsavíkurkirkja church, famous for its architectural beauty, was designed by Rögnvaldur Ólafsson and built in 1907. **Sjóminjasafnið á Húsavík** is an interesting maritime museum, and the **Hvalasafnið á Húsavík (Húsavik Whale Museum)** is home to a rich whale exhibit. In fact, the city is one of the prime spots for whale-watching. Skrúðgarður, a beautiful park on the bank of the Búðará River, offers opportunities for nature walks. Entrance to the park is on Garðarsbraut Street, just south of the church. North of the town, on a terrace above the cliff, is the Geosea spa (*Vitaslóð 1, open 11 a.m. to 11 p.m. from June through August and with reduced hours the rest of the year, $$$, www.geosea.is*).

Grenjaðarstaður

Drive down Road 85 toward the Aðaldalur valley and take Road 845 to reach Grenjaðarstaður, an old turf farm distinguished by its considerable size of about 8,342 square feet (775 sq m). The land where it stands was already occupied during the colonial period. Home to important figures in Icelandic history and also a parish center, the farm was built after the mid-19th century and inhabited until the middle of the 20th century. Now, it is a museum with about 2,000 exhibits. ■

Sjóminjasafnið á Húsavík ✉ Stóragarður 17 (House of Culture) ☎ 464 1860 🕒 Open June–mid-Sept. 10 a.m.–6 p.m., mid-Sept.–May Mon.–Fri. 10 a.m.–4 p.m. $ $ **www.husmus.is • Hvalasafnið á Húsavík** ✉ Hafnarstétt 1 ☎ 414 2800 $ free admission 🕒 Open May–Sept. 9 a.m.–6 p.m. $ $$ **www.hvalasafn.is • Grenjaðarstaður** ☎ 864 3688/464 1860 🕒 Open June–Aug. daily 11 a.m.–5 p.m.

W Visitors to the region can enjoy whale-watching near the tiny village of Hauganes, which looks out over Eyjafjörður Bay.

THE OUTER REGION

Far from the loop of Route 1, this part of the northeast tends to be very sparsely traveled. However, the majesty of its wilderness makes up for the lack of services and the condition of the roads, which are often unpaved.

Heimskautsgerðið, a modern installation that some find reminiscent of Stonehenge.

Many visitors to Iceland come in search of the extreme and although other places are often cited as the best for those seeking complete solitude, there are few places that can compete with the Melrakkaslétta (it means "arctic fox plain") and the Langanes. Both points are cut off from the tourist circuit. Services are extremely limited, and here tourists can truly experience the thrill of being at the edge of the world.

Melrakkaslétta

This peninsula is one of the least visited areas of the country. The small mountain chain, Leirhafnarfjöll (maximum elevation 807 ft, 246 m), that is prominent in the western part, is largely made up of flat land covered by heaths or tundra. The coastal region is spectacular and birdlife is abundant. Road 870 runs along the peninsula from the settlement of Kópasker to the small village of Raufarhöfn on the east coast. Kópasker's economy is primarily based on services provided to neighboring communities and a slaughterhouse. It is also home to a museum dedicated to the 1976 earthquake that struck the area and forced the evacuation of 90 of its 130 inhabitants during a blizzard. About 1.2 miles (2 km) south of the settlement, next to the main road, is the **Snartarstaðir** farm, which houses a museum dedicated to local 19th and 20th-century culture. The lovely Snartastaðakirkja church, which serves the local community, stands on the same grounds.

The northernmost tip of the peninsula is Riftangi, where an old abandoned farmhouse contributes to the area's picturesque atmosphere. Just beyond, about 5.5 miles (9 km) to the east is the Hraunhafnartangi point, home to a charming lighthouse. At the same latitude as Riftangi, it is a contender for the northernmost point in all of Iceland. Thorgeir Hávarsson, protagonist of the *Fóstbræðra saga*, is said to have been killed here and buried at the stone mound just south of the lighthouse, known as Thorgeirsdys.

Farther down the eastern coast, the harbor of Raufarhöfn was mentioned as early as the time of the medieval sagas and may have already been frequented in colonial times. In the late Middle Ages it was popular with German and Dutch merchants. During the period when the Danish had the monopoly on trade and free commerce was prohibited, when Icelanders were forced to buy or sell goods only at predetermined locations and only from licensed Danish merchants, local farmers had to travel to Húsavík or Vopnafjörður to trade. It was not until 1833 that Raufarhöfn was granted the status of a trading port. Three years later, a Danish merchant erected a four-story house there that, at the time, was among the largest in the country. Later, with the explosion of fishing in the early 20th century, the small village grew considerably and, by the 1940s, had become the second most important herring processing center in the country. Some 20 years later it surpassed Siglufjörður, when about 10 percent of the country's total

Snartarstaðir N.-Thingeyjarsýsla Folk Museum ✉ V/Snartarstaði 17 ☎ 464 1860 🕒 Open June 15–Aug. 15 **www.husmus.is**

EXPERIENCE: Chasing the Spectacular Northern Lights

The Northern Lights occur when the Earth's magnetic field is disturbed by solar particles that penetrate the atmosphere's gasses, resulting in a release of photons in a process similar to that of neon lamps. The phenomenon is visible from mid-August to mid-April. In August and April, auroras occur quite late because daylight lasts longer. You may be lucky enough to see the lights from where you are lodging but only if outdoor conditions are ideal, so it is essential to be able to change your location, perhaps by participating in a guided tour. Try the one that starts in the city of the midnight sun, Akureyri, the Northern capital (*guidetoiceland.is*).

The sunset on Eyjafjörður.

herring fishing revenues came from the area. The economic boom came to a brutal end in the late 1960s, when the herring shoals disappeared, and the village was abandoned, becoming the remote and depopulated center it still is today.

A little farther north and off to the west is a curious monument called Heimskautsgerði, a work of art still under construction that resembles prehistoric megalithic sites. Inspired by motifs from the Eddic poems, the monument is a series of stone arches arranged to channel the light of the summer solstice. South of Reufarhöfn, on Road 85 toward Thórshöfn, a detour accessible only with four wheel drive vehicles leads to Rauðanes, a peninsula characterized by peculiar rock formations including an arch and sea stacks.

Thórshöfn

This small town of less than 400 inhabitants is the only one in the area offering services. In the 16th century, it was a trading post frequented particularly by German merchants but, as with Raufarhöfn, the Danish trade monopoly interrupted trade and forced locals to make long, dangerous journeys to carry out their trade. This center was also shaped by the explosive growth of the fishing industry, which is still the town's predominant economic sector. The fairly recent local church, Thórshafnarkirkja, was consecrated in 1999, and is located about 4.3 miles (7 km) north of town, in Sauðanes, is the lovely Sauðaneskirkja, dating to the late 19th century.

Langanes

The atmosphere of the most extreme peninsula in the Northeast, Langanes, is surreal, desolate, remote, and mysterious. The now largely depopulated peninsula consists of a vast area bordered by a mostly unpaved road that is accessible only with four-wheel drive vehicles. The marked feeling of isolation may be the area's main attraction. The cliffs of Skoruvíkurbjarg and the Stórikarl sea stacks are prime viewing spots for seabirds such as gannets. Located on the outermost tip of the peninsula, in the area known as Fontur, is a famous lighthouse. ■

DRIVE: THE EYJAFJÖRÐUR AREA

This area, which has continued to prosper and thrive over the centuries, is home to the residences of important families as well as to a Benedictine monastery. It also offers many naturalistic highlights.

Head south from the town of Akureyri on Road 821 for 4.6 miles (7.5 km) and then turn onto 822 to Kristnes until you reach **Hælið** 1, an exhibit on the history of tuberculosis in Iceland (*$$, open June–Aug. daily 1 a.m.–5 p.m. and Dec. 21–22 2 p.m.–6 p.m., www.haelid.is*).

Continue on 822 until you reach 821 again and continue 0.6 mile (1 km) to **Jólahúsið** 2, the Christmas House, a small center where you can learn about some of Iceland's Christmas traditions. A tower next to the house contains an art installation by an Icelandic artist and the shop offers Christmas-themed gifts from around the world as well as Icelandic handicrafts. Next to the house is a wishing well decorated in mosaic, a work of art dedicated to unborn children.

Continue south on 821 for about 5 miles (8 km) as far as **Grundarkirkja** 3. The church is unique in Icelandic architecture with some elements that are reminiscent of the Russian tradition, particularly the spire. The present church was consecrated in 1905 but ancient accounts mention a church on the site as early as the 12th century. Some of the ancient objects once kept in this church are now on display at the National Museum.

About 5.5 miles (9 km) farther south is **Smámunasafn Sverris Hermannssonar** 4, the Museum of Miscellaneous Objects, dedicated not to preserving special or unique objects but to celebrating the ordinary and its usefulness (*$, open June–mid-Sept. daily 1 p.m.–5 p.m.*). Everyday things such as doorknobs, matchboxes, nails, and keys are displayed and arranged here with a creativity that makes them true works of art. Behind the museum, on the hill, is **Saurbæjarkirkja** 5, one of only five remaining turf churches. It was built in the mid-19th century on the site of a medieval church. To visit the church, ask for the keys at the Smámunasafn museum.

Go back along Road 821 for about 1.2 miles (2 km), turn right and take 829 to reach the lovely **Möðruvellir** 6. Formerly the seat of powerful local lords, the manor farm is mentioned in a number of sagas. The Möðruvallakirkja, built in its present form in the 19th century, has an alabaster altarpiece dating from the 15th century.

Head north on Road 829 until you reach **Munkathverá** 7. According to some accounts, this was the home of Ingjaldur, son of Helgi the Thin, one of the country's most important settlers,

NOT TO BE MISSED:

Grundarkirkja • Smámunasafn Sverris Hermannssonar • Munkathverá • Laufás

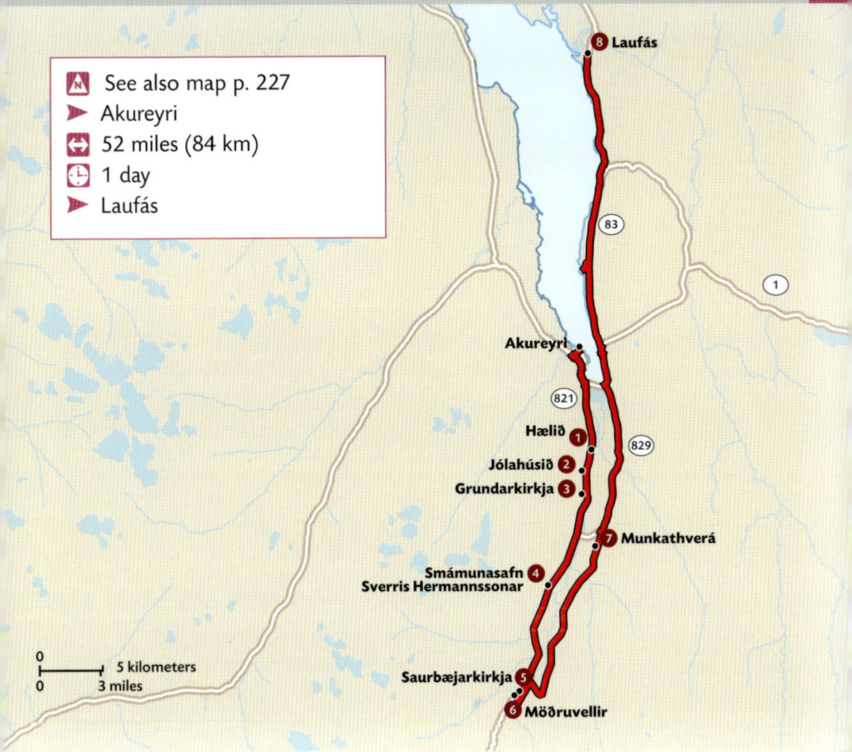

who is said to have erected a large temple here. In 1155, a Benedictine monastery was founded here, which remained in operation until the Reformation. In the medieval period, it was an important cultural center where several ancient manuscripts were written. Jón Arason, the last Catholic bishop of the Icelandic Middle Ages, grew up here. A statue of him by the sculptor Guðmundur frá Miðdal, stands near the church.

From Munkathverá, head north on Road 829 to merge onto Route 1. Continue to the roundabout and take the second exit onto Road 83 for 14 miles (23 km) until you reach the site of **Laufás 8**. Here you will find one of the most beautiful turf houses in the country, which can be visited in its entirety. The site is mentioned in some sagas and was therefore probably inhabited shortly after the colonization period (870–930). The present building dates from the mid-19th century, with some parts from the 16th or 17th centuries, while the furnishings and fittings are generally from the early 20th century. The building was the residence of the pastor who served the adjacent church, which also dates from the mid-19th century. The church's pulpit, carved with the figures of Christ and the evangelists, dates from the 17th century. Outside the church is one of the oldest rowan trees in Iceland, dating from 1855.

From the lush interior to the majestic fjords, a diversified region with a limited amount of tourist traffic

THE EAST

The spectacular Fardagafoss waterfalls near Egilsstadir.

THE EAST

Boasting interesting local history museums, forceful waterfalls, areas of geological interest, islands, mountain peaks, and the most extensive forest in the country, this region has also been the setting for some of Iceland's most famous sagas, such as *Hrafnkels saga Freysgoða*.

The Southeastern region (*Austurland*) was probably the first part of the country to be reached by Europeans. It is a mysterious frontier land. Moisture from the ocean often collects in the mountainous amphitheaters that embrace the fjords, shrouding them in fog. Paradoxically, this is the sunniest part of the country. It is also the only area where herds of wild reindeer can be spotted. The reindeer were imported from Scandinavia in 18th century to diversify the island's economy but their breeding proved unprofitable. Today there are about 7,000 of them.

A number of Roman coins have been found in the area of the fjords; their provenance is still uncertain. In 2018, the results of an archaeological excavation undertaken in Stöðvarfjörður partially rewrote the history of the island's colonization. The excavation revealed the presence of seasonal hunters from Scandinavia about a century before 870 AD, the date considered to be the beginning of the permanent occupation of the island.

Over the centuries, the fjords were the scene of frequent contact with the outside world, including regular visits from foreign fishermen and whalers. The Berufjörður fjord was raided by Saracen pirates in 1627, and Djúpivogur, on the southern shore, was the home of Hans Jónatan, an enslaved African descent who fled Denmark in the early 19th century. In a groundbreaking genetic study conducted in 2018, Jónatan was proven to be the ancestor of hundreds of Icelanders.

In the late 19th and early 20th centuries, many French fishermen frequented the waters of the area, fish being a popular food in Catholic countries on days when abstention from meat was required. Signs of their passage are still visible today, particularly in the village of Fáskrúðsfjörður, where the street signs are in Icelandic and French.

The outermost part of the Eastern region, the part that encompasses the fjords, has historically been isolated from the inland areas because of the peaks that starkly separate the fjords from the great valley of Fljótsdalur. Even today, some small communities remain isolated when snow makes the mountain passes inaccessible and supplies can only arrive by sea. The inland part of the East is dominated by Lake Lögurinn, more correctly called Lagarfljót (which is the name of the river that widens and forms the lake). Along its banks, there are several attractions, including the island's largest forest, called Hallormsstaðarskógur, the region's main town, Egilsstaðir, and the Hengifoss waterfall.

There are also many points of interest in the deep, long valleys that run inland, such as the turf farms of Sænautasel and Bústarfell, the town of Möðrudalur, the highest inhabited place in the country at 1,538 feet (469 m) above sea level, and the famous Stuðlagil canyon. The relatively small influx of visitors makes this region ideal for those who wish to venture off the beaten path in solitude. ■

NOT TO BE MISSED:

The museum of local culture in Egilsstaðir 275–276

Skriðuklaustur 277–278

The Hengifoss waterfall 277

Seyðisfjörður 269–271

The Sænautasel farm 278–279

The San Thorlákur Church in Reyðarfjörður 265–266

The French sailors' museum in Fáskrúðsfjörður 262–264

Langabúð in Djúpivogur 259–260

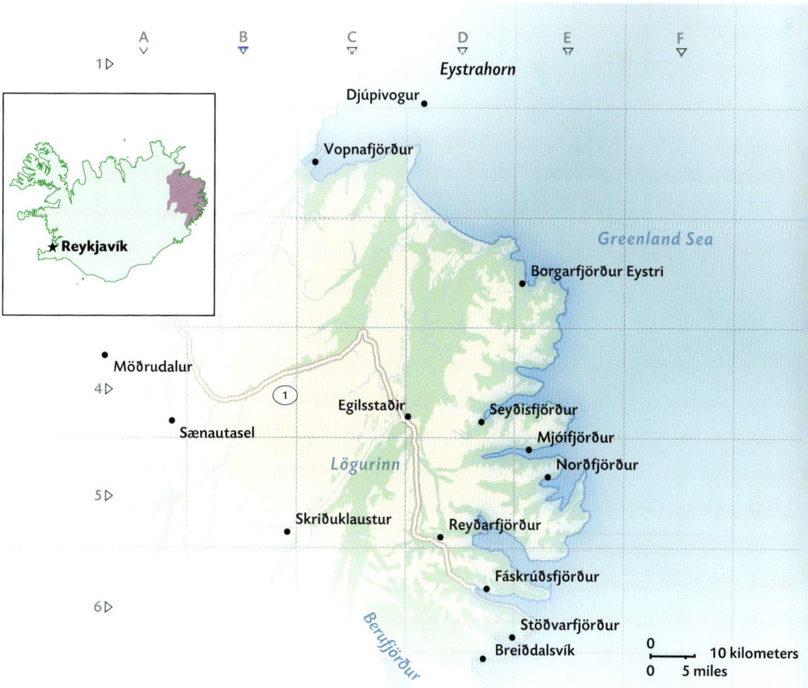

THE MOUNTAINS & THE OCEAN

Characterized by sharp, soaring peaks and impassable mountain ranges, the fjord region is an area of arcane atmospheres, where dense mists from the ocean often gather. Here, local myth and legends mingle with a history far more dynamic and interconnected with that of the rest of the world than one might imagine.

Sheep graze near a farm in Stafafell.

The coastal part of the Eastern region is deeply etched by the inlets of the fjords that define it. Along with the west and northwest fjords, this region is one of the oldest in the country geologically. The area is dominated by basaltic formations that resemble a layer cake. Mountains formed when a series of volcanic eruptions deposited layers of lava on top of each other. These layers were interspersed with thin layers of soil that formed during the periods between eruptions. Erosion wrought by the ice that accumulated during glaciation sculpted the mountains and valleys and exposed layers of rock that are clearly visible. Roman coins have been found in this area. This is also where Hans Jónatan (see sidebar p. 258), the first inhabitant of African descent on the island, lived in the early 19th century. The area was raided by Saracen pirates in the 17th century, and was visited between the beginning of the 19th century and the early 20th century by primarily French fishermen and sailors who left their mark there. The area is also home to Seyðisfjörður, the landing point for the Norræna, the only ferry that connects Iceland to Europe.

Eystrahorn: Door to the Fjords

Mount Eystrahorn rises to an elevation of 2,480 feet (756 m) on the eastern side of Lón Lagoon, which is separated from the ocean by a long shore of black sand. This jagged lava rock formation that emerges from the Krossanesfjall mountain ridge is made primarily of gabbro, a mafic intrusive rock that has worked its way into basalt. The mountain is estimated to be 6 million years old, and several veins of metals, including gold and mercury, have been found there.

Mount Eystrahorn is considered impossible to climb because of its dangerous, unstable, landslide-prone surface. The prime vantage point for viewing the mountain, which is especially popular with photographers, is the nearby Hvalnes Peninsula with its orange lighthouse. This peninsula is where the Saracen pirates who raided Iceland in 1627 landed. Visitors can come down from Hvalnes for a walk along the

Aerial view of Mount Eystrahorn.

beach and a panoramic view of the mountains. About 6 miles (10 km) farther north is Stapavík beach, where waves lap tall sea stacks when the tide rises. Coming from the south, the first inlets are Álftafjörður and Hamarsfjörður, separated from the ocean by large shoals and sandbars.

Berufjörður & Djúpivogurr

The Berufjörður fjord is about 12.5 miles (20 km) long. The landscape around it is characterized by jagged formations that are easily distinguishable from Iceland's typical flattop subglacial mountains. At 3,507 feet (1,069 m) above sea level, Búlandstindur stands out among the mountains in the area; it towers over the Búlandsnes Peninsula on the southern side of the fjord. From the town of Djúpivogur, the mountain looks like an almost perfect pyramid, formed by clearly visible layers of basaltic rock deposited one on top of the other. It was

Hans Jónatan

Born in 1784 in the Danish colony of St. Croix, in the Caribbean, to an African mother and an unknown Danish father, Hans Jónatan was registered as a slave owned by the wealthy Schimmelmann family, a merchant dynasty that had been welcomed into the Danish nobility.

The Schimmelmanns moved to Copenhagen in 1789. When the head of the family died, Jónatan, then 17 years old, was left to the man's wife. Jónatan escaped and enlisted in the Danish Navy. He distinguished himself in the Battle of Copenhagen against the British, earning not only recognition but also his freedom. Not long after, the widow Schimmelmann prevailed in a lawsuit, claiming that she owned Jónatan, and he was enslaved again. However, he managed to escape once more and this time disappeared without a trace.

Today we know that, in 1802, he took refuge in Iceland, where local folk tradition has it that he was much loved for his character. He initially worked as a farmer and then, in 1819, began working as the manager of the Djúpivogur emporium. In 1820, he married a local girl, Katrín Antóníusdóttir, with whom he had three children. He died in 1827.

Jónatan's story stimulated scientific curiosity and in 2018 led to a major genetic study of his descendants (now numbering several hundred). Since African DNA is easily detectable in a mostly homogeneous population like Iceland's, it was possible to reassemble 38 percent of Jónatan's maternal DNA. Having then compared it with that of African populations, it was found to overlap with DNA typical of West Africa, and particularly from the area around Nigeria.

Monument honoring Hans Jónatan by Sigurður Guðmundsson.

in this fjord that Saracen pirates initially landed in Hvalnes in 1627, and began raiding human settlements, after which they continued on to the Vestmannaeyjar islands farther west.

Djúpivogur, on the Búlandsnes Peninsula, is located on the south side of the mouth of the fjord. The relatively small town is known for its ancient harbor. In the summer, visitors can participate in guided tours that depart from the Djúpivogur port to Papey Island, which is about 3 miles (5 km) offshore and visible from the coast. According to the *Landnámabók* (*Book of Settlements*), Christian anchorite monks from Ireland, the so-called *papars*, supposedly lived on this island, but no archaeological finds confirm their presence. However, an excavation carried out between 1970 and 1980 uncovered remains of northern settlements dating back to the colonization period (ninth–tenth centuries).

Overlooking Djúpivogur's small harbor is the historic **Langabúð,** a building that houses the area's

Langabúð Búð 1 478 8220 Open May 15–Sept. 15 daily 11 a.m.–6 p.m., hours vary in winter $ (museum)

tourist information center and a museum dedicated to the Djúpivogur-born sculptor and wood carver Ríkarður Jónsson (1888–1977). Ríkarður studied under Einar Jónsson, an artist to whom a museum in Reykjavík is dedicated. Ásmundur Sveinsson, to whom another museum is dedicated in the capital, was later apprenticed to Ríkarður. The southern wing of the Langabúð dates from the late 18th century, but the building acquired its present form in the middle of the 19th century, with modifications and extensions. Built as a trading post, it is one of the oldest commercial buildings in Iceland.

One of the most curious characters in Icelandic history lived here in Djúpivogur. Hans Jónatan, whom we have already mentioned, was an Afro-Danish slave who fled Denmark and took refuge here in the early 19th century (see sidebar p. 258). In 2021, local authorities erected a monument in Jónatan's memory in front of Langabúð; a column with a glass arrow pointing skyward, with his name and the word *frelsi* (freedom) in the middle of a broken chain.

Breiðdalsvík

Nestled on the shores of Breiðdalsvík Bay, the tiny town of Breiðdalsvík is best known for the beauty of its natural surroundings, with breathtaking mountain views and the broad, lush valley that it sits in, but there is no shortage of cultural attractions here either. The Frysti-

Outside Djúpivogur, you can "Eggin í Gledivik—The Eggs of Merry Bay," granite replicas, mounted on pedestals, of the eggs of the 34 species of birds that nest in the area.

húsið building, which once housed a freezing plant, has been home to the Factory Car Museum, a vintage car museum with several sports and luxury models. The museum has closed in Breidalsvik but will soon move to Garðabær.

Also located in the heart of the small town is **Breiðdalssetur,** home to the University of Iceland's research center that hosts geological and linguistic-themed exhibits. One of the exhibits is dedicated to George Walker, a great 20th-century volcanologist who conducted important research in eastern Iceland and gathered evidence to support the emerging theory of plate tectonics. Another exhibit is dedicated to Stefán Einarsson, who was born in the area in 1887. A professor of Linguistics at Johns Hopkins University in Baltimore Einarsson wrote a book of Icelandic grammar in English (*Icelandic: Grammar, Texts, Glossary*) that is still in print today, as well as the influential *History of Icelandic Literature*, which is also published in English. The center is also responsible for the Drill Core Archive where visitors can view a collection of drill cores taken for scientific and practical purposes. If all the cores present in the archive were put in a row, they would reach a length of more than 25 miles (40 km).

Stöðvarfjörður

At the Stöð farmstead, located at the end of the Stöð fjord at the entrance to the valley, an archaeological excavation completed in 2018 uncovered the remains of a temporary settlement. The settlement dates from about a century before the official beginning of the Viking colonization (ca 870) and led archaeologists to reconsider the chronology of the country's colonization. The findings made it clear that Scandinavian peoples were already aware of Iceland's existence and visited the island in the summer to exploit its resources, fishing and hunting for arctic fox, walrus (which later became extinct) and seal.

For the most part, Stöðvarfjörður is an uninhabited fjord, except for the small town of the same name located on its northern shore. The town got its start in 1896, when Carl Guðmundsson, a local merchant, established a trading station there. The **Brekkan** café-cafeteria serves as the local tourist information center while the visitor center for the municipality of Fjarðarbyggð, which includes much of the eastern fjords, is located inside the building that houses the local arts and crafts

Breiðdalssetur ✉ Gamla Kaupfélagið ☎ 525 5341 🕒 Open June–Aug. Sun.–Thur. noon–4 p.m., Sept.–May by appointment • **Brekkan** ✉ Fjarðarbraut 44 ☎ 475 8939 🕒 Open Mon.–Fri. 11 a.m.–6 p.m., Sat.–Sun. 11 a.m.–2 p.m. $ $$

market, **Salthússmarkaðurinn.** The old church, now called Kirkjubær, was built in 1925. It was converted to tourist lodgings in 1991 but it still has an altar, a pulpit and some pews inside.

The **Steinasafn Petru** is of particular interest. The museum houses the mineral collection of Ljósbjörg Petra Sveinsdóttir (1922–2012), who lived in the area. A mineral enthusiast, for much of her life, she went to remote parts of the region to collect specimens that gradually formed one of the most conspicuous private mineral collections in the world. The collection is displayed in the rooms of what was once her cottage and its garden, a small oasis of plants and flowers surrounded by the barren slopes of the fjord.

Fáskrúðsfjörður

This pretty town nestled on the northern shore of the fjord of the same name, Fáskrúðsfjörður is distinguished by the French influence it experienced the 19th and 20th centuries, due to the large presence of French fishermen who regularly visited the area to fish. As a Catholic

Salthússmarkaðurinn ✉ Fjarðarbraut 43 ☎ 863 2650 🕒 Open in summer • **Steinasafn Petru** ✉ Fjarðarbraut 21 ☎ 475 8834 🕒 Open June–Sept. daily 10 a.m.–5 p.m. $ $ **www.steinapetra.is**

View of the mountains from of the small town of Fáskrúðsfjörður.

country, France was accustomed to eating fish on Fridays, making Iceland's waters with their abundance of fish very appealing. Although there are no confirmed descendants of those sailors, the French heritage and traces of their presence have survived, including bilingual street signs in both French and Icelandic.

A complex of buildings once used by the French has been converted into an elegant hotel, the Fosshótel Austfirðir, where the **Frakkar á Íslandsmiðum** (French in Icelandic fishing areas) museum and tourist information center are located. The complex also includes other restored historic buildings. The French Hospital, for example, was originally built on the other side of the fjord in 1903 by the government of Paris to assist the many French citizens who fished in Icelandic waters. The institute was reconstructed in its current location in the hotel complex using as many elements of the original building as possible. Reconstruction was completed in 2014. Across from the French Hospital is another historic building, the Doctor's House. Entrance to the museum is from the reception area of the Doctor's House building. Upstairs in the house, an exhibition documents the hospital's activities at the time of its use by the French, while the underground corridor connecting

A bilingual street sign in Icelandic and French in Fáskrúðsfjörður.

the Doctor's House to the hospital building is home to an immersive exhibit that documents the living conditions of sailors with the reconstruction of the inside of a French vessel. Access is free for hotel guests. Other historic buildings associated with the French such as the pharmacy (which is now home to hotel rooms) and the Catholic

Frakkar á Íslandsmiðum ✉ Hafnargötu 12 ☎ 475 1170 🕒 Open May 15–Sept. 30 daily 10 a.m.–6 p.m.

chapel, are nearby. Along the side of the mountain, above the complex, is a path ideal for walking that can be reached from the back of the small school sports field, located at the highest point of the village.

About 3 miles (5 km) to the east, on the road that runs along the fjord, stands the Kolfreyjustaðarkirkja church, which was rebuilt in 1991 after the previous building, dating from 1878, was swept away by a storm. The church, now a protected building, was constructed on a very simple model with a small modest structure and no bell tower. Inside, it has an altarpiece by the Danish painter Anker Lund, an engraved baptismal font by the German Wilhelm Bachman, and a chalice and paten that are thought to date from medieval times.

Reyðarfjörður

Reyðarfjörður, located in a vast fjord of the same name, is a midsized center whose economy is particularly dependent on the production of aluminum. The Alcoa Fjarðaál industrial complex was completed in 2007, after years of work that employed thousands of foreign laborers. Kárahnjúkavirkjun, a colossal hydropower plant with a capacity of 690 megawatts was built inland to provide power for the complex. The project was extremely controversial because it included construction of a dam that resulted in the formation of three reservoirs

On the road north of Berufjörður.

Kirkja heilags Thorláks, the Catholic church built in 2017 and dedicated to St. Thorlak (Thorlákur), in Reyðarfjörður.

that covered an immense area of unspoiled land totaling an estimated 1,150 square miles (3,000 sq km). Creation of the industry came at a very high price but the region's economy benefited and flourished. The **Stríðsárasafnið** (War Museum) is located in the town center. It allows visitors a look at the years of World War II, particularly into the period when Allied forces occupied Iceland, with exhibits and films that illustrate the living conditions of Icelanders and the situation in the country during those years.

Just outside the town to the west, on the mountainside, is a convent of Capuchin Friars Minor with an attached wooden church completed in 2017, the **Kirkja heilags Thorláks.** The church, dedicated to Iceland's patron saint, Thorlákur, is a Catholic parish church that serves the Eastern region. It was initially built in Slovakia, then dismantled, shipped to Iceland, and rebuilt onsite over two years, atop a terrace with a lovely view of the fjord and the surrounding mountains. The church played an important role during the years of the construction of the Kárahnjúkar hydroelectric plant, since many of the foreign workers hired came from Catholic countries, in particular from Poland.

Continuing north, a smaller inlet named Eskifjörður breaks away from the main fjord. The small town of the same name lies on its northern shore. Eskifjörður was once a trading post and, during the Danish monopoly period (17th–18th cen-

Stríðsárasafnið ✉ Heiðarvegur 37 ☎ 470 9063 🕒 Open June–Aug. daily 1 p.m.–5 p.m., by appointment in winter **stridsarasafn.fjardabyggd.is** • **Kirkja heilags Thorláks** ✉ Stekkur ☎ 471 1340

Film Productions

Twenty-two years after the Icelandic Film Fund was established in 1979, Iceland's cinematic fortune's changed with the adoption in 2001 of a policy of incentives and tax breaks reserved for foreign productions. Since then, numerous film crews from all over the world (but especially from the United States) have landed on Icelandic shores. Notable blockbusters filmed here include Christopher Nolan's *Interstellar* (2014) with the sublime scenes filmed in the desolate area of Vatnajökull glacier, images that were also immortalized on posters; J.J. Abrams' *Star Wars: The Force Awakens* (2015); and especially *The Northman* (2022), directed by Robert Eggers, who co-wrote the screenplay with Icelandic writer and poet Sjón. The movie, with a star-studded cast that includes Nicole Kidman, Willem Defoe, Alexander Skarsgård, and Björk, is set in 10th-century Iceland and tells the true story of Prince Amleth, a character from Scandinavian mythology said to have been Shakespeare's inspiration for *Hamlet*. Another special foreign film shot on the Island is Ben Stiller's *The Secret Dreams of Walter Mitty* (2013). The movie tells the story of a mournful *Life* magazine employee who, in his search for an exceptional photograph that has been lost, arrives in Iceland. The aerial shots on the west coast are some of the finest ever filmed on the island.

turies), it was one of only six places in all of Iceland to enjoy that status.

The town grew with the development of the fishing industry in the second half of the 19th century, as did many other settlements, and today fishing is still the primary sector of the local economy. The **Sjóminjasafn Austurlands** (Eastern Region Maritime Culture Museum) is located here, in the historic Gamla Búð building, originally constructed in 1816. The building was previously used as a bazaar, a depot, and a fish warehouse. The museum houses various objects related to the processing of fish products and other economic activities that were historically carried out in the area.

Helgustaðanáma is located outside the village, along the northern shore of the fjord on Road 954, the only dirt road that heads east from Eskifjörður. This abandoned mine contains large deposits of Iceland spar, a variety of calcite that is remarkable for its birefringence, meaning its ability to refract the

Sjóminjasafn Austurlands Strandgata 39b, Eskifjörður 476 1605/470 9063 Open June–Aug. daily 1 p.m.–5 p.m. **www.sjominjasafn.com**

rays of light that strike it. Images observed through this calcite appear duplicated. Various European scientists, including Newton, began to study Iceland spar in the 17th century. Beginning in the 19th century, spar was used to construct microscopes and helped advance studies regarding the nature of light waves. In the 1920s, it was replaced by synthetic materials and the Helgustaðanáma mine was abandoned. Today it is a protected area and it is forbidden to collect the countless fragments of ore that are in the piles of debris outside of it. Access to the mine is at one's own risk. Visitors will find information about the history of the place, and the nature and uses of Icelandic spar outside the mine, before the short climb to the entrance.

Norðfjörður

The town of Neskaupstaður, in Norðfjörður, is the easternmost town in Iceland. For a long time, it was one of the communities that could only be reached by sea. It became a trading post in 1895 but gained popularity when it became the only place in the country where socialists came to power during the Cold War years. They ruled from 1946 for the next 52 years. A film, *Litla-Moskva* (*Little Moscow*), by director Grímur Hákonarson (2018) is dedicated to this curious story. A narrow, one-lane tunnel called Oddskarðsgöng was completed in

The coast of the Neskaupstaður Nature Reserve.

1977. About 2,066 feet (630 m) long, it is located high in the hills and connects the town to the rest of the country. Today, the town is connected by another tunnel, Norðfjarðargöng, which opened in 2017 and is 4.6 miles (7.5 km) long.

The processing of fish products is the town's primary economic activity. Of particular interest is **Safnahúsið í Neskaupstað.** The building houses three different museums under one roof: the Natural History Museum, dedicated to Icelandic birds and fish, with a collection that includes several artifacts from the bottom of the sea; the Art Museum dedicated to Tryggvi Ólafsson (1940–2019), a local artist and painter; and the Maritime Museum, which houses a collection related to the fishing industry, boat building, and ancient manual labor methods.

Mjóifjörður

This 11.2-mile (18 km) long fjord is particularly remote and untamed. It is often inaccessible from land in the winter months when snow

Safnahúsið í Neskaupstað ✉ Egilsbraut 2 ☎ 470 9000 ◷ Art Museum and Maritime Museum open June–Aug. Mon.–Fri. 1 p.m.–5 p.m.; Natural History Museum open June–Aug. Mon.–Sat. 1 p.m.–9 p.m., Sun. 1 p.m.–5 p.m. **visitfjardabyggd.is**

The remains of a U.S. Navy ship dating from World War II at Mjóifjörður.

obstructs the mountain pass that connects it to the rest of the country. When this happens the town's only connection to the outside world, and to their supply of resources, is by sea. The Björgvin ferry, which connects the small village of Brekka with Neskaupstaður, operates twice a week from October to May.

The fjord is a popular destination for nature excursions and scenic photos. It offers many memorable sights such as waterfalls, including the Klifbrekkufossar, that plummet over several drops down the slope to the bottom of the fjord. There are a few dozen inhabitants of the micro-agglomeration of Brekka, along the shores of Mjóifjörður. The wooden church Brekkukirkja, dating from 1892, is located here. Inside the church is a 19th century altarpiece painted by the Dane H.W. Holm. A dirt road runs along the north shore of the fjord to Dalatangi, where there is a picturesque lighthouse.

INSIDER TIP:
Choose Seyðisfjörður as the first leg of your trip in Iceland, arriving from the continent by ferry.

—ROBERTO LUIGI PAGANI
Author of this guidebook

Seyðisfjörður

For centuries, Seyðisfjörður was a small isolated community. According to *Landnámabók*, the first settler in the area was a man named Bjólfur, and in 2021 an archaeological excavation uncovered the remains of 10th-century buildings that were probably used for processing fish. Another archaeological excavation that was conducted in 1998 and 1999 at Thórarinsstaðir uncovered the remains of a burnt wooden church dating from the 11th century. The local population is thought to have been less than 200 inhabitants for several centuries. Rapid changes occurred in the late 19th century, when the site of the present town became a settlement of Norwegian fishermen, who constructed several Norwegian-style buildings that still characterize the town's aesthetics today.

Seyðisfjörður quickly became a relatively populous center. It assumed particular importance when technological innovations arrived here before arriving in the rest of Iceland. In 1906, it was reached by the first telegraph cable to connect Iceland to Europe, and in 1913 a central dam, Fjarðarselsvirkjun, was built to generate electricity through the country's first high-voltage, alternating-current plant. Seyðisfjörður became the first town in Iceland to have a grid that distributed electricity to illuminate streets as well as private homes. It was also a base for Allied forces during World War II.

Unusual exhibition on the Road 93 connecting Egilsstasir with to Seyðisfjörður.

The only ferry connecting Iceland with the mainland, the Norræna, lands at this town's harbor every week. The local economy is now primarily based on tourism and the fishing industry is no longer as important as it used to be. The cultural scene is particularly vibrant. The rainbow road leading to the church is one of the most photographed sights in the region. The church itself, Seyðisfjarðarkirkja, built between 1920 and 1922, served as the setting for the television series *Ófærð* (*Trapped*) in 2015.

In December 2020, the town was hit by a landslide caused by heavy rains. It damaged 39 buildings, a dozen of which were completely destroyed, and the entire town had to be evacuated. This landslide was the largest in Iceland's history to hit an inhabited area. Thækniminjasafn Austurlands, the Technical Museum of the Eastern Region, was destroyed in the disaster and an active campaign for funding to rebuild it is currently underway.

Also located in the village is **Skaftfell,** a center for the fine arts i that focuses on the cultural promotion of contemporary art.

The center is home to an artist residency and exhibition space. A

Skaftfell Austurvegur 42 472 1632 Open Tues.–Sun. 5 p.m.–10 p.m. **skaftfell.is**

short distance away, inside the ferry terminal, is **Upplýsingamiðstöð,** the tourist information center. There are several hiking trails of varying difficulty among the steep mountains surrounding the fjord. At the mouth of the fjord, on the southern shore, is a private nature reserve, **Skálanes,** where there is a center for field research and scientific promotion of the area's nature and archaeology. The cliffs at the facility are home to thousands of birds of dozens of different species, including numerous colonies of eiders and terns. Seals and reindeer are also often present, and you may even spot a few whales.

Borgarfjörður Eystri

In the small village of Borgarfjörður Eystri, located in the southern part of the fjord of the same name, is the **Lindarbakki** house,

Upplýsingamiðstöð ✉ Ferjuleira 1 ☎ 472 1551 🕒 Open May–Sept. daily 9 a.m.–5 p.m., Mar.–Apr. Mon., Wed., Fri. 1 p.m.–5 p.m., Tues. 8 a.m.–noon. Always open when cruise ships are in port. **www.sfk.is • Skálanes** ☎ 779 7008 **www.skalanes.com**

A field of blue lupine near the Skálanes Nature Reserve.

construction of which began in 1899. Turf is a highly insulating material that is effective in protecting against subpolar weather. In addition, Icelandic turf houses are built on foundations of volcanic rocks, which are light to transport and are equally insulating. Except for the façade and windows, the entire house is completely covered with a thick layer of grass. Lindarbakki has another peculiarity: it is the only turf house in Iceland that is still regularly inhabited, if only during the summer months. It is a private building but even from the outside, it is particularly photogenic.

The local church, Bakkagerðiskirkja, consecrated in 1901, has a famous altarpiece painted by Jóhannes Kjarval in 1914 that depicts the Sermon on the Mount from the Gospel according to Matthew.

Just south of town is a flat-topped rocky mount called **Álfaborg** (Fortress of the Elves), which according to local folklore is home to these creatures. Its summit is easily accessible and affords sweeping views of the surrounding area. **Hafnarhúsið** is a building that overlooks the small harbor in the village of Borgarfjörður Eystri. It hosts temporary art and photography exhibits.

Lindarbakki Closed to the public; information available on panels outside • **Álfaborg** **www.east.is** • **Hafnarhúsið** 472 1180 **www.borgarfjordureystri.is**

The Lindarbakki Turf House covered in grass, in Borgarfjörður Eystri.

The Álfaborg rock is said to be inhabited by elves.

On Road 94, between Borgarfjörður Eystri and Egilsstaðir, just before entering the fjord and 3.7 miles (6 km) from the town, is the Njarðvíkurskriður cliff. Before the coastal road was built, the path along the slopes was extremely dangerous due to the frequent landslides that claimed many lives, the last of which occurred in 1909. Local folklore blamed the deaths on a monster that lived by the cliff. According to one folktale, the monster was driven back into the sea by a passerby, never to re-emerge. At the spot from which the monster allegedly plunged into the ocean, a memorial cross was erected bearing the inscription "Effigiem Christi qui transis pronus honora. Anno MCCCVI - You who pass, bow down and honor this image of Christ. In the year 1306.". The original cross, which is traditionally thought to be of that venerable age, was replaced by the current one that was erected in 1954. Also on Road 94 is **Kjarvalshvammur,** a cabin where the painter Jóhannes Kjarval completed several of his masterpieces.

Kjarvalshvammur ☎ 470 0750 **visitegilsstadir.is**

The turf house at the museum of Bustarfell.

Vopnafjörður

According to *Landnámabók*, the site of Vopnafjörður was allegedly settled by Eyvindur Thorsteinsson, nicknamed *vopni*, meaning "weapon." It was the setting for the *Vopnfirðinga saga*, which narrates a long feud between families in the area that occurred in the late 10th century. The center became a trading post in the modern age, but at the end of the 19th century, when Iceland experienced a population boom, poorer peasants were forced to resettle on the moors, where they suffered great deprivation. The fjord's port became one of the primary bases from which large numbers of Icelanders migrated to North America, especially to Canada. The **Vesturfaramiðstöð Austurlands,** located in Vopnafjörður, is a volunteer organization dedicated to establishing contacts with the descendants of Icelanders who migrated from the north and east to America after the eruption of the Askja volcano in 1875. There, descendants can take a genealogical survey to help them rediscover their roots. The center also hosts temporary exhibits focused on the migration of Icelanders to the Americas.

Bustarfell, one of the best-preserved turf houses in the country, is home to the **Minjasafnið á Bustarfelli** museum. To reach the museum, drive south on Road 917 and then continue on Road 920 to the turnoff for the museum. The present building was inhabited from the late 18th century until 1966; today it is managed and cared for by the National Museum of Iceland and hosts various events and exhibitions in the summer. Inside, the style and furnishings of the last period in which the building was inhabited have been preserved. ■

Vesturfaramiðstöð Austurlands ✉ Hafnarbyggð 4 ☎ 473 1200
🕒 Open Mon. & Thur. 10 a.m.–5 p.m. or by appointment
www.visitvopnafjordur.com • **Minjasafnið á Bustarfelli** ☎ 855 4511
🕒 Open June 1–Sept. 20 daily 10 a.m.–5 p.m., by appointment in winter
$ $ **www.bustarfell.is**

BEYOND THE MOUNTAINS

The eastern hinterland is a lush region characterized by valleys, both wide and narrow. Its climate is often pleasant during summers and its many unique sights set it apart from the rest of the country. It is home to the largest forest in Iceland, a large lake said to be inhabited by a monster, and a number of remote farms in the valleys and on the peaks that are the setting for masterpieces of local literature.

Much of the hinterland of the Eastern region consists of the Fljótsdalur valley. The valley is named for the great Lagarfljót River that flows into it, just as the Jökuldalur is named for the Jökulsá á Dal River. Some smaller valleys branch off from the main ones, cutting inland. The often harsh and very snowy winters are offset by warm pleasant weather in the summer, something the rest of the country envies. In this part of the country as in others, sagas, legends, and history are inextricably intertwined with the natural landscape.

INSIDER TIP:
Visit the Museum of the Eastern region in Egilsstaðir dedicated to the history, customs, and daily life of the area.

—ROBERTO LUIGI PAGANI
Author of this guidebook

Egilsstaðir

The history of Egilsstaðir is relatively young compared to that of other Icelandic settlements. Although it is remembered as the site of an important local assembly in the 15th century, it only began to develop as a town in the first half of the 20th century, when a local landowner, Jón Bergsson, established a shop and some services for the local community. In the second half of the century, Egilsstaðir became a thriving town and the main center of the Eastern region.

Often wrongly described as a place with few attractions, Egilsstaðir is an extremely pretty town. Located in an area with more stable weather and a milder summer than the coastal areas, it is particularly green and pleasant in the summer. The **Minjasafn Austurlands** (Museum of the Eastern Region), dedicated to the history, customs and daily life of the area is located here. It has a

Minjasafn Austurlands ✉ Laufskógar 1 ☎ 471 1412 🕒 Open Mon.–Fri. 9 a.m.–4 p.m., Sat.–Sun. 10 a.m.–4 p.m. $ $ **www.minjasafn.is**

particularly interesting permanent exhibition on reindeer, which were imported by the authorities in the 18th century to create economic opportunities. Later, however, the reindeer returned to the wild and populated the region's highlands.

In the center of town, at the site of the local church, Egilsstaðakirkja, a rocky elevation, Gálgaás, where death sentences were executed in ancient times. In the southern part of town, visitors can climb towering rock walls for a memorable view of the surrounding region.

Just 2.7 miles (4.5 km) from the town, along Road 93 to Seyðisfjörður, is the parking lot for the Fardagafoss waterfall. Behind it is a shallow cave that can be reached via a narrow walking path. Legend has it that this collapsed tunnel once belonged to a troll who walked through it to reach the sea.

Lögurinn

The Lagarfljót River flows from Vatnajökull glacier to the ocean on the northern coast. For a long stretch, it widens to the point that it looks like a lake known as Lögurinn. Alongside the lake runs Road 931, which is unpaved but not difficult. There are several points of interest on the eastern shore and all around the lake. The first of these is Hallormsstaðaskógur, the largest forest in the country. A number of birch groves that had survived through the centuries were protected in 1905, when reforestation work began. Today, the forest covers an area of 1,828 acres (740 ha) and includes about 90 species of trees that serve as habitat for

Aerial view of the Hengifoss waterfall.

numerous species of birds, such as redpolls, goldcrests, partridges, and crows. In the forest, visitors will find hiking trails, rest areas, an arboretum, and a small town, Hallormsstaður.

At the southern tip of the western shore is Hengifoss Waterfall, whose 420-foot (128 m) drop makes it among the highest in the country. The walking distance to reach it from the parking lot next to the road is 1.5 miles (2.5 km). The waterfall plummets into an amphitheater-shaped gorge. It is characterized by thin layers of clay containing oxidized iron sandwiched between thicker layers of black basalt creating a particular strata pattern. In local folklore, the gorge is populated by elves, and according to one folktale you can hear them singing Christian hymns from among the rocks.

On the way to Hengifoss is Litlanesfoss, a smaller 100-foot (30 m) waterfall closed between two rock walls with soaring columns of basalt.

Skriðuklaustur

Just south of Lake Lögurinn, along Road 933, is **Snæfellsstofa,** one of Vatnajökull National Park's tourist information centers. In 2010 it became the first Icelandic building to be certified as sustainable. It houses an exhibit with information about the area and a small local craft shop. The nearby town of **Skriðuklaustur** is the site of an archaeological excavation, carried out between 2002 and 2012, that brought to light a medieval monastery, and the **Gunnarshús á Skriðuklaustri** building, which houses a museum, a cultural center, and a craft shop. The building was constructed as a residence for the Icelandic writer Gunnar Gunnarsson (see sidebar p. 278), who commissioned it in 1939 after

A burial found at the archaeological excavation in Skriðuklaustur.

Snæfellsstofa ☎ 470 0840 🕒 Open June–Aug. daily 10 a.m.–5 p.m., May & Sept. Mon.–Fri. 10 a.m.–4 p.m., Sat.–Sun. noon–5 p.m., Apr. Mon.–Fri. 10 a.m.–4 p.m., Oct. Tues.–Wed. 10 a.m.–3 p.m. **www.vatnajokulsthjodgardur.is • Skriðuklaustur & Gunnarshús á Skriðuklaustri** ☎ 471 2990 🕒 Open Apr.–May 11 a.m.–5 p.m., June–Aug. 10 a.m.–6 p.m., Sept.–Oct. 15 11 a.m.–5 p.m., hours vary in winter $ $ **www.skriduklaustur.is**

Gunnar Gunnarsson

Born in 1889, when Iceland was still part of the Kingdom of Denmark, author Gunnar Gunnarsson grew up in the eastern part of the country and he published his first book of poems at age 17. After studying at a folk high school in Denmark he decided to write his novels in Danish in order to reach more readers. His books were a success and were translated first into German, and then into other languages.

In 1939 Gunnarsson moved back to Iceland, where he built a beautiful villa in Skriðuklaustur. He lived there for only a few years, however, before moving to Reykjavík, where he took to personally translating his works into Icelandic. He was nominated for the Nobel Prize in Literature six times but never won the prestigious award. Along with Halldór Laxness, he is considered the most important Icelandic author of the 20th century. His Christmas story *Advent* (*The Shepherd of Iceland*) tells the story of a shepherd who climbs into the snowy moors each year during the Advent season to rescue any sheep who may have been lost. It is one of the most famous classics of Icelandic literature and a tradition of the holiday season. *Borglægtens historie*, a 1920 Danish film based on the novel of the same name, was the first film to be shot in Iceland. Other famous novels include *Kirken på bjerget* (*The Church on the Mountain*), *Svartfugl* (*The Black Cliffs*), considered the progenitor of Nordic noir, and *Vikivaki*.

returning from Denmark, where he had lived for decades. Designed by a German architect, the construction was a remarkable undertaking for the time, costing as much as ten single-family homes in Reykjavík and employing dozens of workers.

Follow Road 934 into the innermost region of Fljótsdalur, to the edge of the central highlands, to reach the **Óbyggðasetur/Wilderness Center,** a complex that houses an exhibit dedicated to the country's history and its wilderness territories. The center also offers lodging and guided tours of the surrounding areas.

Sænautasel

Take a short detour of 1.8 miles (5 km) from Route 1, first on Road 901 and then on Road 907 at the intersection to reach Sænautasel. This turf farm and a few others were built on the Jökuldalur moor in 1843. Most were destroyed following the eruption of the Askja volcano in 1875. The municipality rebuilt Sænautasel to its original state in 1992 but part of it col-

Óbyggðasetur/Wilderness Center ☎ 440 8822 🕒 Open May 15–Sept. 30 daily 11 a.m.–6 p.m. $ $$ **wilderness.is**

lapsed in 2009 and was rebuilt the following year. It must have been a farm like this one that inspired the Christmas novella *Advent* by Gunnar Gunnarsson. In the story, a shepherd hikes to the moors during the Advent season to retrieve any sheep that may have been lost. His experience provides a backdrop for reflections on the universal themes of human existence. Apparently, the farm was also the inspiration for one of the settings in Halldór Laxness' novel *Sjálfstætt fólk* (*Independent People*), which won him the Nobel Prize in 1955. In the story, a farmer insists on living on a barren, inhospitable piece of land, so long as he can call it his own.

In the summer, guided tours are available. The farm is divided into an older part, with dirt floors and rock slabs, where visitors can get a close-up view of how families lived in the first decades after the house was built, and a newer part, with wooden panels and floors.

From Road 901, between Sænautasel and Möðrudalur, turn south on a track about 1.2 miles (2 km) long (accessible only with an all-terrain vehicle) to reach what at first glance appears to be a colossal drystone wall, Skessugarður. This wall made of wide basalt rock boulders is 985 feet (300 m) long and up to 16 feet (5 m). The wall formed when a glacier during the last glaciation advanced and then retreated leaving behind a classic moraine accumulation. Later, a flood washed away the sand and lighter debris, leaving behind only the heavier boulders. Local folklore provides a different story about the wall, narrating that two giantesses who had had a falling out erected the wall to divide their properties.

Möðrudalur

Möðrudalur is located along Road 901, which was once a section of Route 1. At 1,538 feet (469 m) above sea level, it is the highest inhabited place in Iceland. It is also where the lowest temperature on record for Iceland was recorded in the winter of 1918: minus 36.4°F (-38°C). The area was occupied very early in the period of the island's colonization, between the 9th and 10th centuries, and for a long time it was an important noble seat.

The writer Gunnar Gunnarsson.

Möðrudalur farm is mentioned in the *Hrafnkels saga* and the *Grettis saga*, but today it is a remote location, an oasis for travelers who want to venture inland or deviate from Route 1. The farm is home to a restaurant, a picturesque building made of wood, stone, and turf, and tourist accommodations. On the opposite side from the restaurant is the local church, Möðrudalskirkja, which was built in 1949 by the local farmer, Jón A. Stefánsson (1880–1971) in memory of his wife who had died five years earlier. The farmer was also a multitalented artist who decorated the church and painted the altarpiece with a scene depicting the Sermon on the Mount, from the Gospel of Matthew.

The church at Möðrudalur farm.

Inland Valleys

Jökuldalur, the valley of the Jökulsá á Dal River, is long and narrow, and very green during the summer. Along the valley are numerous points of interest such as Torfhúsin í Hjarðarhaga (Hjarðarhagi Turf Buildings), two small stone and turf barns used from time immemorial until 1980. These were originally part of a small agricultural complex of seven buildings, which was demolished to make way for Road 1. They were later rebuilt without the more modern elements, thereby restoring their antique character. Entrance is free.

Just west on Road 1 is the parking lot for the Rjúkandafoss waterfall, whose two falls reach a total height of 456 feet (139 m). The waterfall is clearly visible from the road and can be reached via a short path. Turn off of Road 1, into the valley, onto Road 923 to reach the Stuðlafoss waterfall that cascades over basalt columns. To get to the waterfall, follow 923 as far as the Klaustursel farm, then cut across the river to the parking lot.

On the opposite side of the valley, along Road 923, is the **Stuðlagil** canyon, which came to light only a few years ago, after the construction

Stuðlagil ✉ info@studlagilcanyon.com **studlagil.is**

Stuðlagil canyon.

of the Kárahnjúkar dam decreased the water flow of the Jökulsá á Dal River and lowered its water level. This narrow gorge is flanked by tall basalt columns that are among the largest and most symmetrical in the country. The water changes colors according to the seasons; when the ice and snow melt in the spring, or after a heavy rain, the water is cloudy and gray but at other times it takes on a deep turquoise hue.

The easiest and safest way to observe the canyon up close is from Grund Farm. Authorities advise against diving into the river since its waters are glacial and may have rapid, unpredictable underwater currents that can prove dangerous.

The Hafrahvammagljúfur canyon is located at the deepest point in the valley, just before the Kárahnjúkar Dam. Here, a number of hiking trails lead into the canyon, all the way to the dam.

Following the Jökuldalur valley southward on the western side leads to a fork in the road where the valley divides. Road 923 continues on the southern side, from which the Hrafnkelsdalur valley opens up. Aðalból Farm, the home of the main character in the *Hrafnkels saga* (see pp. 282-283), was located here. It is one of the Icelandic farms farthest from the sea; the nearest coastline is on Berufjörður, 37 miles (60 km) away, point to point. ■

HRAFNKELS SAGA FREYSGOÐA

Filled with moral teaching, this is a tale of violence, prevarication, revenge, and pride.

Hrafnkels saga Freysgoða is one of the most famous sagas among those set in the Eastern region. There is still much debate about its origins but a number of historical inconsistencies have led scholars to believe that it is a combination of local legends and literary fiction rather than a record of historical events. The saga's oldest existing manuscript is a fragment from the 15th century, but it is believed to date from the late 13th century.

It begins with a Norwegian, Hallfreður, who moves to Iceland at the time of colonization, around

Panoramic view of the Hrafnkelsdalur valley.

the year 900 AD, together with his 15-year-old son Hrafnkell. After a few years, Hrafnkell settles in an uninhabited valley that he calls Hrafnkelsdalur, where he builds the Aðalból farm. Hrafnkell is a pagan devoted to the god Freyr, for whom he names his favorite horse, Freyfaxi. He solemnly swears to kill anyone who dares to ride the horse without his permission.

Hrafnkell becomes a lord of the land but he is arrogant and refuses to pay fines for the injustices he committed. A young man named Einar, one of Hrafnkell's shepherds, needs a horse to round up sheep that ran away. Since every horse he approaches run away from him except Freyfaxi, Einar mounts the horse and is able to recover all of the animals. At the end of the day, Freyfaxi runs to Aðalból and begins to neigh. Hrafnkell notices the horse is muddy and sweaty and immediately understands what happened, and once he is sure of Einar's guilt, he kills him to uphold his oath.

Hrafnkell, apparently sorry for what happened, decides to make amends to Einar's father, Thorbjörn, offering to provide for him for the rest of his days, but Thorbjörn demands a formal agreement between equals, which Hrafnkell refuses Thorbjörn tries to file a lawsuit against Hrafnkell and gain the support of his brother Bjarni, but Bjarni does not want to be involved in a dispute against such an influential man so Bjarni's son Sámur agrees to take up the cause.

At the general assembly, Sámur and Thorbjörn meet Thorkell Thjóstarsson, a young man from the western fjords, who offers them the support of his brother Thorgeirr, a powerful lord. The assembly found Hrafnkell guilty and gives Sámur the right to kill him and confiscate his property. Sámur, together with Thorgeirr and Thorkell, surprises Hrafnkell and captures him. Against the advice of Thorkell, Sámur offers Hrafnkell two options: he can be killed at once or he can live the rest of his life as Sámur's inferior, with no property or privileges. Sámur takes possession of Aðalból; Hrafnkell chooses to live and he moves away but he never loses heart and over the years, he regains power and influence. He abandones his religious practice and learns to control his temper, earning the respect of many.

After a few years, Hrafnkell got his revenge. After gathering his men and ambushing Sámur, he offers him the same two options he was given years earlier. Sámur chose to live and Hrafnkell returns to Aðalból, his old home, where he regains the rank of local lord. Sámur traveled west to seek the support of Thorkell and Thorgeirr, but they refuses him; they blame him entirely for what happened because he failed to kill Hrafnkell when he had the chance. Sámur returns to Aðalból where he lives as Hrafnkell's inferior for the rest of his days, never getting revenge. Hrafnkell dies of old age as a well-honored lord, leaving behind him a lineage of great men.

Iceland's most remote region, where otherworldly views captivate geologists, photographers, and trekkers

THE CENTRAL HIGHLANDS

■ The colorful volcanic mountains of Landmannalaugar.

THE CENTRAL HIGHLANDS

Once populated mostly by outlaws and fugitives, this region remained largely unexplored for centuries. Today the highlands are one of Iceland's most popular destinations. Dominated by lava and ice, with no paved roads and minimal services, the landscape here is undoubtedly extreme, and visitors should approach it with respect.

The Central Highlands region (Miðhálendið) is the most remote in the country. The vast mountainous area is over 1,640 feet (500 m) above sea level and consists of both hills and plateaus. Crossed diagonally by the fault that divides the North American and Eurasian tectonic plates, it is here that new land emerges from the bowels of the Earth to expand and extend the surface of the island. Temperatures in the interior are noticeably colder compared to the coast, which, when combined with the lack of infrastructure, accounts for the fact that the Central Highlands is an entirely uninhabited region, except for the

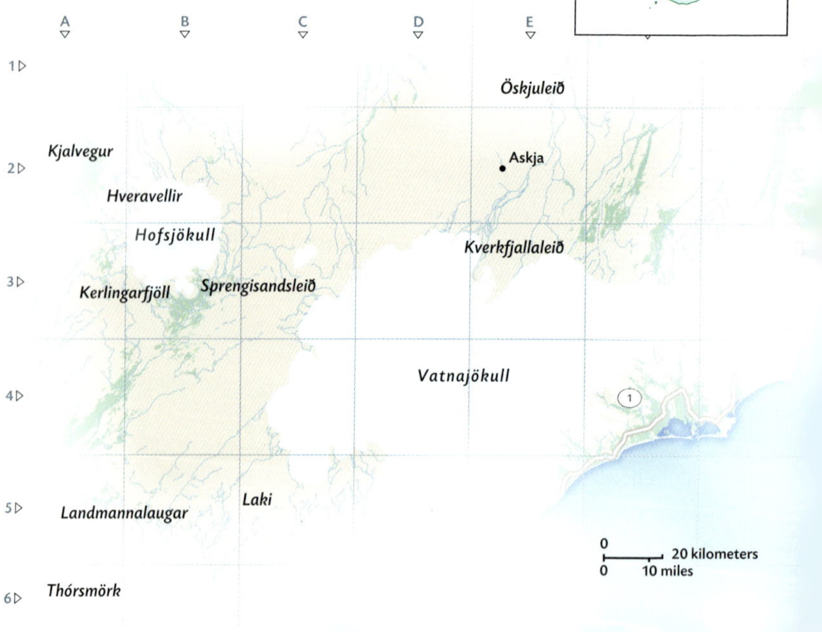

NOT TO BE MISSED:

Landmannalaugar 289–290
Kerlingarfjöll 292–293
Askja 294–296
The Hveravellir hot springs 293
The Laki craters 291

sporadic presence of rangers who are responsible for overseeing the area.

Due to heavy snowfall, access routes are either closed for the winter season, generally between September and June, or marked as impassable, even for modified vehicles. In spring, melting snow turns immense areas into bogs and marshes, making them extremely difficult to navigate. Only during the short summer season is the area partially accessible to tourism.

The difficulty in accessing the area and the desolation that characterizes the highlands are precisely what makes them attractive. The primordial landscape is reminiscent of images of the surfaces of other planets captured by space probes. In fact, it is no coincidence that part of the training of the astronauts of the Apollo 11 mission took place in this very region.

The vastness of the spaces and the colors and shapes of rocks and elevations arouse feelings that make a visit to the highlands a transformative experience. From the Landmannalaugar area, where some of the most popular treks start, through the Kerlingarfjöll area, with its deep yellow rhyolite mountains streaked with ice, to the majestic lake that sits in the Askja caldera, the cosmos of the Central Highlands is wild and merciless in its primeval beauty. The area is accessible only in modified vehicles (equipped with special suspension and wheels) and exploring it safely requires some experience, but there are many tour companies that offer day trips and organize trekking and group tours that allow visitors to take in the beauty and atmosphere of the region.

Only four main routes cross the area. The most popular is Kjalvegur (F35), which connects southern Iceland to the northwest, passing between the Langjökull and Hofsjökull glaciers. Sprengisandsleið (F26), the longest, crosses the region from southwest to northeast. It passes through desert landscapes and when the weather is good, it offers unparalleled views of the glaciers. The Öskjuleið Road (F88) connects the Askja caldera to Route 1. It is extremely challenging but a few tour agencies accompany groups here from populated centers. The F88 Road leads to Herðubreið Mountain, 5,518 feet (1,682 m) high, one of the most photogenic in the country, and to the Askja caldera, one of the most poignant views Iceland has to offer. The Kverkfjallaleið, Road F902, goes from Möðrudalur to the Kverkfjöll, a mountain range covered in ice that is sculpted with impressive caves. ■

IN THE HEART OF THE ISLAND

Some of the country's most popular trekking areas are located in the southern part of the Central Highlands. Frequent guided tours leaving from the capital make the area more accessible to those who want to experience Iceland's more otherworldly side.

The famous Laugavegur trail and Lake Álftavatn in the Fjallabak Nature Reserve.

The silences and solitude experienced in many places in Iceland's majestic nature create the alienating feeling of being on another planet. The Central Highlands take this feeling to the extreme. Barren mountains with no evident traces of human life are painted in an unexpected palette of yellows, reds, oranges and greens, often interspersed with spots of the candid white of snowfields and ice patches that survive the summer temperatures.

Landmannalaugar

Landmannalaugar is an area located in the Fjallabak Nature Reserve, reachable on rough, unpaved roads that are accessible only with a four-wheel drive vehicle. Landmannalaugar, whose name means "the people's pools," belongs to the municipality of Rangárthing ytra in southern Iceland. The natural geothermal pools, located near Landmannalaugar, are fed by hot spring water from the Torfajökull volcanic system. The area lies on the edge of the Laugahraun lava flow, formed in 1477, and consists of a wide, flat gravel valley crossed by a glacial stream, the Jökulgilskvísl. Visitors can cross the stream to reach the site or leave their car in the parking lot and continue on foot. The lodge and campground in the Landmannalaugar area are open in the summer. The area is surrounded by rhyolitic mountains, including Mount Barmur, where hues of yellow ochre alternate with the bright green of moss and the white of ice patches that survive the summer temperatures in the mountain folds.

The campground is the starting point for hiking trails, including the famous Laugavegur trail. Popular destinations include Brennisteinsalda (2,805 feet, 855 m), a mountain streaked with black, red, and orange, surrounded by fumaroles at its base. It can be reached by the trail that climbs the front of the lava flow west of the campground on the well-known Laugahringur trail. The trail is a loop that takes about two hours to complete. It comes out in the valley, just south of the local campsite across the narrow Grænagil Ravine (Green Ravine). The fragments of glassy rock that line the walls of the ravine contain a small amount of iron that gives the walls a greenish hue. Glassy rocks make Mount Bláhnúkur (3083 feet, 940 m), towering south of the ravine, a blue-black color. About 0.6 mile (1 km) south of the campground, arduous hikers can also undertake the trek to Mount Skalli, and then continue farther south to descend the bright

Laugavegur

Laugavegur, the most popular and frequently traveled hiking trail, begins at Landmannalaugar and leads to Thórsmörk. About 34 miles (55 km) long, it usually takes four or five days to complete. The huts on the trail are extremely basic and should be booked well in advance. Hikers will find Hrafntinnusker (3,700 feet, 1,128 m), a mountain dominated by the colors of rhyolite with large quantities of obsidian along the trail, as well as Álftavatn, a lake that is an oasis in the untamed highlands, home to several species of birds, ducks, and swans.

Landmannalaugar – Information center Open June–Sept. 8 a.m.–7 p.m. & 8 p.m.–10 p.m. **www.fi.is**

yellow Uppgönguhryggur ridge to Hattver. The valley is named for a slab of rock, Hattur (Hat), that sits precariously on an elevation jutting out from Mount Suður-Skalli.

Cross the Jökulgilskvísl River (when conditions permit) and climb the elevations to the east to reach Grænihryggur, a mountain ridge with a deep green color created by the presence of iron. Located on the F208 is Sigöldugljúfur, a canyon known for the plentiful waterfalls that cascade down its sides, and Ljótipollur, a crater created by a phreatomagmatic explosion that occurred in 1477. The red streaks on its steep sides are the result of the presence of oxides. Inside the crater is Ljótipollur, a lake that covers an area of about 0.2 square mile (0.5 sq km) and is about 33 feet (10 m) deep. Lake Frostataðavatn lies just to the south on the same road; it covers an area of 1 square mile (2.6 sq km) and is bordered, in part, by a picturesque lava flow.

Take the F228 road from the west via the F26 or F208 road to reach Veiðivötn, a region of about 50 lakes. The lakes lie in two rows of eruptive fissures that are part of the Bárðarbunga volcanic system. The 33-mile (53 km) journey starts from Landmannalaugar and is quite challenging.

Thórsmörk

According to the *Landnámabók* (*Book of Settlements*), the Thórsmörk valley, north of the Eyjafjöll mountain range was settled by Ásbjörn Reyrketilsson. Historically, farmers in the Fljótshlíð region took their livestock to graze in this area, critically damaging the vegetation in the early 20th century. Subsequently, grazing was prohibited in the valley. Its flora has thrived ever since, in part because of the special microclimate created by the surrounding mountains, which protect the area from the precipitation that rain and snow clouds would bring.

Thórsmörk ☏ 893 1191 **www.fi.is**

Laki

About 18–25 miles (30–40 km) point to point, north of Kirkjubæjarklaustur and west of the edge of the Vatnajökull glacier, is **Lakagígar,** a volcanic fissure named after Laki, a mountain that dissects it. When the volcanic system erupted in 1783, a 15-mile (25 km) fissure opened at Laki forming some 135 vents that are known as Lakagígar

Fimmvörðuháls

Another popular hike is Fimmvörðuháls. It goes from Skógafoss waterfall to Thórsmörk across the area between the Eyjafjallajökull and Mýrdalsjökull glaciers, and has numerous waterfalls along the way. The landscape varies widely, from the green of the valley floor to the lunar landscapes in the mountains. It is about 15 miles (25 km) long in total.

Thórsmörk's waterways and green elevations fascinate excursionists from all over the world.

(Laki Craters). The area is quite famous for its brightly colored mosses that radically contrast with the dark colors of the rocks. The craters are accessible with an all-terrain vehicle on the rough and challenging F206 road, starting from Hunkubakkar, just south of Kirkjubæjarklaustur, at the turnoff leading to the Fjaðrárgljúfur canyon, and continuing for about 30 miles (50 km). Along the way is the Fagrifoss waterfall, which plummets over a 260-foot (80 m) drop. The drop is unique in that it is not entirely vertical; instead, it flows over the slope below, giving the waterfall the appearance of a veil. ■

Lakagígar ☎ 575 8400 **www.vatnajokulsthjodgardur.is**

THE INLAND ROUTES

The inland routes, including Kjalvegur and Sprengisandsleið, are the only roads that cross Iceland from one side to the other. They are unpaved roads and cart tracks that lead to the most remote, isolated places in the country.

The Kerlingarfjöll geothermal area.

Geologically speaking, the interior is the youngest part of the island. It is characterized by primeval landscapes that offer a glimpse of what the Earth might have looked like in its early days.

Kjalvegur

The F35 Road is called Kjalvegur, in honor of Kjölur, a 2,300-foot-high (700 m) mountain pass in the area between the Langjökull and Hofsjökull glaciers that the road crosses in its central section. Kjalvegur connects south and northwest Iceland for a distance of about 75 miles (120 km). The road begins shortly after the famous Gullfoss waterfall and comes out to the north on Road 731, a short distance from

Route 1, between Blönduós and Skagafjörður. Attractions found along the route include Hvítárvatn Lake, located on the eastern side of Langjökull glacier. The lake has a surface area of 11.5 square miles (30 sq km) and a maximum depth of 285 feet (84 m). About 15 miles (25 km) farther north on the west side of the road is the turnoff to Kerlingarfjöll (Road F347), a mountain range that formed about 10,000 years ago. The mountains stand out in the surrounding area for the ochre hues caused by the rhyolite that forms them. The area was declared protected in 2017.

The name of the mountain chain, "Giantess Mountains," comes from a legend in which one of the rock formations is said to be a giantess who was turned into stone by the sun.

The geothermal resort of Hveravellir with its hot spring pool is located about 18.5 miles (30 km) north of the turnoff for Kerlingarfjöll. The oasis was home to the famous outlaw Fjalla-Eyvindur (1714–83), who was exiled into the wilderness with his wife for 20 years after the couple was convicted of nomadism, theft, and allowing their son to die.

INSIDER TIP:
If you love hiking in unadulterated nature, the inland routes in the heart of Iceland will not disappoint you.

—ROBERTO LUIGI PAGANI
Author of this guidebook

Sprengisandsleið

Sprengisandur is a vast highland that extends between the Vatnajökull and Hofsjökull glaciers; its maximum elevation is 2,625 feet (800 m) above sea level. The highland is crossed by Sprengisandsleið, the F26 Road, which is about 155 miles (250 km) long. The road leads north, where it becomes Road 842, and then comes out on Route 1 at the Goðafoss waterfall. In the northern part, other branches lead to Eyjafjörður (F821, Eyjafjarðarleið) and Skagafjörður (F752, Skagafjarðarleið). The southern part of the road runs for a stretch along Lake Thórisvatn, a reservoir that formed when a dam was constructed in 1971. It is the largest lake in the country, with a surface area of 33 square miles (86 sq km) and a maximum depth of 357 feet (109 m).

At roughly the halfway point, south of Hofsjökull glacier, is Thjórsárver, a 1,600-square-foot (150 sq m) protected area notable for its vegetation, which is lush

Sprengisandsleið ☎ 842 4377 (Nýidalur ranger)

despite being at about 2,000 feet (600 m) above sea level, quite an elevation for Iceland. It is home to 663 plant species, and 47 types of birds, including about one-third of the world's population of pink-footed geese (*Anser brachyrhynchus*), that nest here.

The Aldeyjarfoss waterfall is located near the point where the F26 Road ends and the 842 begins. Its 65-foot (20 m) drop is surrounded by columns of basalt. Heading north, the first two farms you will find on the road were the setting for the acclaimed 2015 movie *Rams*.

Öskjuleið

Askja is a large volcanic caldera, about 31 miles (50 km) wide, whose highest point reaches 4,973 feet (1,516 m). The area was relatively unknown until 1875, when a devastating eruption caused a massive migration of Icelanders, particularly from the north and east, to the Americas. The ash that was spewed during the eruption poisoned the land and killed the livestock, leading to a subsequent famine.

Öskjuleið, the challenging F88 Road that leads to the site, starts as a turnoff from Route 1, between

A car speeds along the deserted Sprengisandsleið road.

Mývatn and the turnoff to Möðrudalur. Hrossaborg, a 1,640-foot (500 m) wide tephra and scoria crater that formed about 10,000 years ago is located on the western side of the road, just past the junction of Route 1 and F88. A pass carved out by glacial meltwater leads to the crater, where the view of the surrounding area is spectacular.

About 37 miles (60 km) farther south along the road is the Thorsteinsskáli hut, the starting point for Herðubreið, a 5,518-foot-high (1,682 m) table mountain with extremely steep slopes. This peculiarly shaped tuya was formed when, after a subglacial eruption, the lava cooled suddenly and accumulated vertically instead of flowing and expanding into a lava field. A long trail that starts at the campsite at Thorsteinsskáli in Herðubreiðalindir leads to the base of the mountain. The Drekagil canyon hut is located at the end of the trail, at the foot of the Dyngjufjöll Mountains. The site, which was designated as a base camp for NASA training missions is now home to a campground and ranger station. Crossing the canyon is possible, when the level of the creek that runs through it is not high enough, to

Óskjuvatn, the crater lake situated in the main caldera of the Askja volcano.

run into the gorge. Its rock formations resemble monstrous figures and in fact, its name means "Dragon Gorge." From Drekagil, drive along the F894 Road to the parking lot and then continue on foot to the rim of the Viti crater to reach Öskjuvatn (literally "Askja Lake"), the lake that lies in the caldera. With a surface area of about 4.6 square miles (12 sq km) and a maximum depth of 721 feet (220 m), it extends behind the Viti crater, surrounded by mountains. Ódáðahraun is located north of Askja. A vast, desolate lava field of about 1,700 square miles (4,400 sq km), its oldest part dates back 10,000 to 12,000 years, while the most recent part was formed in 2014–2015 when Bárðarbunga erupted. The Apollo 11 astronauts trained for their moon landing here as well as in the area around Askja.

Kverkfjallaleið

Kverkfjöll is a mountain range with peaks of 5,787 feet (1,764 m) located on the northeastern edge of the Vatnajökull glacier that partially covers it. The mountains' volcanic nature causes the ice cap to melt and ice caves to form periodically. Unlike the caves formed on the south side of the glacier, these caves are unstable and have a tendency to collapse, making them inaccessible. Most of the meltwater is channeled into the bed of the Jökulsá á Fjöllum River. The area can be reached by taking the F905 Road from Möðrudalur as far as Kverfjal-

Askja ☏ 842 4357 (active in summer) **www.vjp.is**
Kverkfjöll ☏ 842 4369 (active in summer) **www.vjp.is**

laleið, then the F902, for a total of 65 miles (105 km). Only experienced drivers in off-road vehicles should tackle this extremely challenging route. The Sigurðarskáli campsite is located a short distance from the southern end of the road.

Also along the F910 Road, at an elevation of 2,099 feet (640 m), is the Hvannalindir oasis, a lush area separated from the rest of the country by wide spaces whose desert nature made cattle grazing impractical, thus preserving the oasis from the damage grazing causes. The oasis is home to 32 varieties of plants and some 30 species of birds. There is also a small station manned by rangers, who offer walking tours of the area. ■

A pink-footed goose.

A farm at the foot of the Kverkfjöll glacier.

TRAVELWISE

Leftovers from a bakery in Stykkishólmur are sold on the honor system.

Page 298: The window of a turf house in Keldur.

TRAVELWISE

PLANNING YOUR TRIP

When to Go

Due to its particular location near the North Pole and the Gulf Stream that laps its shores, Iceland's summers and winters are certainly cold but not extreme, especially in the southern part of the island. Choosing when to go will have an impact on how much of the Icelandic landscape you will be able to visit. In fact, during the winter months, the days are very short and some roads (including main roads) are impassable with any means of transportation because of weather conditions, ice, and snow. Visitors have to be somewhat flexible because itineraries can vary depending on precipitation. During the months between October and April, there are fewer visitors, prices are lower, and the whitewashed Icelandic landscape has its own undeniable charm.

Summer offers the most opportunities, not only because road conditions are better, but also because the vast majority of tourist activities are open exclusively during the summer months, or at any rate, may operate with limited hours in other seasons. This leads to higher prices for accommodations and transportation. It is fundamental to keep in mind that, given the island's location, days seem to be never-ending, with the sun out for up to 20 hours a day, so if you are photosensitive, remember to bring an eye mask for sleeping and sunglasses to protect your eyes during the day. If seeing the breathtaking views of the Northern Lights is an imperative part of your trip, the best time to go is in the months between October and March. The lights can be seen even later, in April, or earlier, in August, but not as frequently. If watching whales near the fjords is a must for you, summer is when sightings are most frequent even if whales are present in these waters year-round.

What to Take

Icelanders know well that the island's weather is unpredictable; there is a saying that if the weather in Iceland is not to your liking, just wait five minutes and it will change. Onion layering is the best way to dress, even in the summer months and on the coast, where year-round temperatures are milder than in the north and inland. Even with the effects of the Gulf Stream, the average temperature in the summer months remains between 50°F and 58°F (10 °C and 14 °C). It is important to have appropriate footwear that allows you to move safely and comfortably through Iceland's natural landscape, unless your visit is limited to Reykjavík, but even there, especially in the cold seasons, it is best to have shoes that provide a good grip on ice and snow. In the winter, thermal underwear and a heavy windproof jacket are fundamental.

If you forget some item of clothing you need for exploring the wilderness, the shops on the island should be able to provide it; there is no shortage of retailers that sell everything you need for outdoor excursions. Likewise, should you forget a book to spend the evening hours with after a long day of exploration, you will have no trouble finding many bookstores in town that are stocked with books in English, and sometimes even French and German. Icelanders are avid readers.

Documents & Visas

Those arriving in Iceland from countries that are party to the Schengen Borders Agreement do not need to obtain a visa to enter Iceland. A passport or identity card for expatriation that is valid for the duration of the trip is sufficient. For stays longer than three months, you must apply for a long-term visa, which allows you to remain in Iceland for up to another 90 days. Icelandic authorities suggest applying well in advance, no later than 14 days before the three-month stay granted by the Schengen area ends. In addition to the documents listed on the official government website (*www.island.is*), the receipt for payment of the fee (12,200 Icelandic kroner, about $86) must also be enclosed. These can either be sent by mail or deposited in person at the reception desk of the relevant offices (Dalvegur 18, Kópavogur).

You can find the information necessary to prepare your trip at the Visiting Iceland website (*www.is.usembassy.gov/u-s-citizen-services/local-resources-of-u-s-citizens/visiting-iceland/*).

Embassies

The U.S. Embassy in Iceland is located at Engjateigur 7, 105 Reykjavik. U.S. citizens who have an emergency and need to reach the U.S. Embassy during normal working hours, 8 a.m. to 5 p.m. Monday through Friday excluding U.S. and Icelandic holidays, can call the U.S. Embassy switchboard at (354) 595-2200.

The Embassy of Iceland in the United States is located in Washington, D.C., at 2900 K St. NW, #509. Phone: +1 202-265-6653.

Locations of Icelandic consulates in the U.S. include Dallas, Seattle, Minneapolis, Los Angeles, Boston, Atlanta, New Orleans, Houston, Charleston (SC), San Diego, Detroit, Anchorage, Norfolk, Chicago, Denver, Phoenix, Portland (OR), Salt Lake City, San Francisco, San Juan (PR), and Miami.

Customs

Sums of cash exceeding 10,000 euros or the equivalent in other currencies must be declared both when entering and when leaving the country.

The importation of alcohol into Iceland is quite restricted: the amount of spirits (anything with 22 percent alcohol by volume) is limited to 1.05 quarts (1 L); wine is limited to 0.8 quarts (0.75 L) and beer to 3.15 quarts (3 L). However, spirits, wine, and beer can be brought into the country in a number of different combinations. Consult the Skatturinn Iceland Revenue and Customs website for the complete list of types and quantities (*www.skatturinn.is/english/individuals/customs-matters/travelling-to-iceland/duty-free-imports/*). The minimum age for bringing alcoholic beverages into Iceland is 20 years, and 18 years for tobacco. The amount of tobacco that can be imported into the country is limited to 8.8 ounces (250 g) of tobacco or 200 cigarettes.

Up to a maximum of 6.6 pounds (3 kg) of foodstuffs can be imported, with a maximum value of up to 25,000 Icelandic kroner (about $175). Importation of raw, salted, or dried meat, raw eggs, and unpasteurized dairy products is prohibited.

A 100-day supply of personal prescription medications can be imported without a customs declaration.

Further information regarding other product categories is available on the Iceland Revenue and Customs website (*www.skatturinn.is/english/individuals/customs-matters/travelling-to-iceland/duty-free-imports/*).

Insurance

The U.S. Department of State recommends you check to see that your health insurance plan includes coverage overseas and repatriation by air. Their website also provides a list of overseas insurance providers (*www.travel.state.gov*). Basic insurance policies may not cover activities such as trekking so be sure you choose the plan that is most appropriate for the type of trip you are planning. Also, remember that if you need to claim compensation, you must provide receipts or medical bills and if you have to report a theft, you will need to fill out a police report.

HOW TO GET TO ICELAND

By Plane

Iceland Air (*www.icelandair.com*), the national airline, offers direct flights from several airports in the United States. International flights land at the Leifur Eiríksson International Air Terminal in Keflavík (KEF; 425 6000, *www.isavia.is/en/keflavik-airport*). It is located 30 miles (48 km) from Reykjavík and is well connected by buses that run from early morning. It takes about 45 minutes to arrive in the city. The frequency of departures is adjusted according to flight schedules. Taxis are also available but are quite expensive; fares can be over 15,000 ISK, or about 105 dollars, each way.

There are also other airports on the island, but they are used mostly for local flights. Akureyri and Egilsstaðir are technically minor international airports but flights out of Iceland from these airports are seasonal and are limited to Spain, the Netherlands, Denmark, Switzerland, and Germany.

By Ferry

For those who want to bring their own means of transportation to Iceland, traveling by ferry is a good choice, but it is not a direct solution. In fact, except for tour cruises, the only connection by sea is via Denmark. The ***M/S Norröna*** (+298 345900, *www.smyrilline.fo*) departs once a week. The crossing to Iceland takes two days in the summer and three in the winter. During the summer, the ferry departs from Hirtshals on Tuesday morning and docks in Seyðisfjörður (on the opposite shore from Reykjavík) on Thursday morning. From September through May, it departs on Saturday afternoon, travels by sea all day Sunday, docks for six hours at the port of Tórshavn on the Faroe Islands on Monday morning, and finally arrives in Iceland on Tuesday morning. The ferry is similar to a cruise ship, with a movie theater, bistro, and gym available to travelers.

Visitors can ship cars and other vehicles to Iceland without being a passenger on board.

GETTING AROUND

By Plane

Iceland's national airline **Iceland Air, Eagle Air** (562 2640, *www.eagleair.is*) and **Norlandair** (473 1121, *www.norlandair.is*) offer the most flights between Iceland's major locations with several flights connecting the capital (at Reykjavík Airport - RKV, not to be confused with nearby Keflavík) to other cities on the island on a daily basis. Furthermore, the regional airports are well connected by special shuttle buses that connect most of the cities with their terminals.

By Bus

Strætó (540 2700, *www.straeto.is*) is Iceland's primary company for land transportation. Its characteristic yellow buses operate in Reykjavík as well as on long-distance routes around the country. To buy tickets in the city, you can either download the Klapp app (*www.klappid.is*) or buy a Klapp card. Tickets to the rest of the island can often be purchased aboard the bus. You can pay with a credit or debit card, with cash (but drivers may not have change), or through the Strætó app. Prices are calculated by zone: the capital represents a single zone (490 ISK), and the ticket price is multiplied by the number of zones you cross. On some routes, the so-called "pre-order service" is obligatory, meaning you have to buy your ticket before boarding. You can find a complete, updated list on the service website.

The bus routes that span the entire island make it possible to "circumnavigate" it, depending on the season (in winter, the number of runs decreases significantly) and the weather. It is important to consult the timetables for the pertinent season (available on the service's website) for weather conditions that could lead to changes in your route (*www.wet.is*).

During the summer, the so-called Highland Buses will take you to the starting points of the hiking trails at Thorsmörk and Landmannalaugar. The service is primarily offered by **Trex** (587 6000, $$$, *www.trex.is*), which also provides round-trip passes from Reykjavík. Tickets for these routes must be booked at least 24 hours in advance. The buses have Wi-Fi and toilets on-board.

Multiple companies offer organized tours, customized to meet every need including day trips and excursions that mostly depart from the capital. You can find a complete list of these operators on the Icelandic Tourist Board website (*www.ferdalag.is*).

By Ferry

A number of ferry lines and tour boats connect the smaller islands and fjords to the coast during the summer. They offer sightseeing tours that allow visitors to appreciate Iceland's nature, fauna and flora, and to enjoy the view of the coasts from the water.

Ferry travel may also be impacted by the season and the weather so it is important to check conditions well in advance. Car transport is available on all the main routes but remember to book in advance and to bring your car registration, insurance, and driver's license, which you will need in order to bring your car to Iceland without paying taxes.

There are connections between Reykjavík and the island of Viðey (*www.elding.is*), between Stykkishólmur, Flatey and Brjánslækur (*www.seatours.is*), to the islands of Grímsey (*www.samskip.is*) and Hrísey (*www.hrisey.is*), and the to Vestmannaeyjar Islands.

A complete list of operators on these routes and tours can be found on the Iceland Tourism Board website (*www.ferdalag.Is*).

By Train

There is no railway in Iceland.

By Car

To rent a car in Iceland, you must be at least 20 years old and have had your driver's license for at least one year, unless you are renting a vehicle such as minivan or a 4x4, in which case the minimum age goes up to 23.

Icelanders drive on the right. Speed limits are 30 miles an hour (50 km/h) in urban centers, 50 miles an hour (80 km/h) on gravel or unpaved roads, and 55 miles an hour (90 km/h) on paved roads. Your low beam lights must always be on, even during the day.

Vehicles must be equipped with the appropriate tires for the season (regular tires, snow tires, or studded tires, which are permitted only from November 30 to April 15).

The maximum blood alcohol level permitted is 0.05%; exceeding this level will result in fines and the revocation of your license. Using a smartphone or mobile phone while driving is illegal unless the device is hands-free.

The main road is the Hringvegur (officially Thjóðvegur 1), also known as the Ring Road because it runs along the perimeter of the island. This completely paved road is always very busy around Reykjavík and also becomes very busy along its entire length in the summer when it serves as the main route for the many tourists who come to discover the island.

As already mentioned in the section regarding speed limits, not all Icelandic roads are paved. Unpaved roads can be navigated with a normal car, but particular caution and prudence are advised, whereas F-Roads (from *fjall* for "mountain") are rough, challenging roads that lead to the heart of Iceland. They are open only in the summer for a short period of time. Four-wheel drive or off-road vehicles suitable for rough terrain and for fording potentially dangerous waterways are best for traveling these roads.

If you are renting a vehicle, advise the rental agency of your intention to tackle these roads. Use the Safetravel app for real-time information about road conditions with a free SMS service (*www.safetravel.is*), and the Epic Iceland guide for information about F-Roads (*www.epiciceland.net*). Never underestimate the risks associated with traveling these routes, even in suitable vehicles. Plan your route in advance and evaluate the information about the roads and conditions available at the above-mentioned sources.

Driving off road, which would disturb the flora and fauna, is absolutely forbidden and is punishable with a heavy fine. In spring, look out for the flocks that graze in the fields along the roadside.

Self-service gas stations are located in all towns and on major roads but always be sure you have enough fuel to reach the next station, because in some more remote areas they may be fewer and farther between. Make sure you have a credit or debit card to pay with as many stations do not accept cash.

The installation of charging stations has made it possible to travel with electric vehicles, and the updated list of locations available on the Visit Iceland website will make it easier for you to organize your trip (*www.visiticeland.com*).

A camper is another possible means of transportation on wheels during the summer months. Many campsites are closed in winter. Camper travel is extremely independent since rest areas do not require a reservation. Remember that, in order to protect the flora and fauna, camping or stopping outside designated areas with your camper is forbidden and carries a hefty fine. Four-wheel drive campers are perfect for those who are planning excursions into rougher areas.

By Taxi

Taxis are available in all of Reykjavik and in the larger towns on the island. Transportation by taxi can also be organized outside of urban areas but it must be planned well in advance and it can be very costly.

By Bicycle

Bicycle tourism can be particularly challenging in Iceland. Frequently, the weather is inhospitable and the unpaved roads can be very tough for anyone who is inexperienced with nature and its elements. Expect the unexpected and avoid the roughest routes unless you are an expert cyclist.

Fortunately, most buses allow you to load your bike for a small fee (usually around 2,000 ISK) if the weather should take a turn for the worse.

There are well-maintained cycling routes around Reykjavík and some of the other major centers including Akureyri. The Hringvegur bike trail is paved so it is comfortable to travel on but there is no dedicated bike path so you will find yourself pedaling alongside the cars.

When renting your bicycle, remember that the price does not always include using it for long distance. Ask about the rental agency's policies in advance. The majority of rental services are located in Reykjavík. A thorough list can be found on the Icelandic Mountain Bike Club website, a comprehensive resource for tourism on two wheels (*www.fjallahjolaklubburinn.is/english*).

PRACTICAL ADVICE

Addresses

Addresses in Iceland are composed of the street name, street number, postal code, and city, but often, the address includes GPS coordinates because many smaller localities are not named in the typical way.

Postal Service

Pósturinn (*www.posturinn.is*) is the national postal service of Iceland. They have many offices throughout the city as well as in the smaller towns and islands where you can buy stamps.

Telephone

Use the country code 00354 to call Iceland from outside the country. Local numbers have seven digits. As of 2017, European SIM cards can use international roaming services without incurring additional charges. Operator contracts apply in the E.U. To call abroad from Iceland, dial 00 followed by the country code, area code, and local number.

Units of Measurement

Iceland uses the metric system.

Electricity

Iceland operates on a 230V supply voltage and 50Hz with two associated plug types, both of which will require a travel adaptor to accommodate a U.S. plug.

Etiquette & Local Customs

Contrary to what many think about people from the northern part of the world, Icelanders are very friendly, informal, and, above all, slow-paced. Remember not to get impatient if, for example, service at the bar is very relaxed.

Formal titles are not necessary but politeness and courtesy are. Remember to greet with *Góðan daginn* when you arrive, *Bless* when you leave, and *Takk* to express thanks.

Holidays

Many businesses in Iceland (bars, restaurants, museums) may be closed on public holidays, particularly around Christmas and the New Year.

January 1 – New Year's Day
January 6 – Epiphany
Maundy Thursday, Good Friday, Easter, Easter Monday (dates vary)
Third Thursday in April – First day of summer
May 1 – Labor Day
First Sunday in June – Fishermen's Day
June 17 – Icelandic National Day
December 24 – Christmas Eve
December 25 – Christmas Day

December 26 – St. Stephen's Day
December 31 – New Year's Eve

Alcoholic Beverage Regulations

The minimum age for drinking and buying alcoholic beverages is 20 years old.

Media

Iceland's national public-service broadcasting organization, Ríkisútvarpið (or RÚV) has three radio channels (Rás 1, Rás 2, and Rondó) and two television channels (RÚV Sjónvarpið and RÚV 2). There are also a number of channels operated by private companies.

There are two major national newspapers: the *Fréttablaðið*; ("The Newspaper" in English), which is distributed free of charge, and the *Morgunblaðið*, meaning "The Morning Newspaper." The best-known and oldest magazine is the *Iceland Review*, an English language quarterly devoted to Iceland and its culture.

Currency

Iceland's currency is the *krona* or *krónor* in the plural (ISK). Currency can be exchanged at the Keflavik airport or at the Tourist Information Center in Reykjavík, as well as at banks and private offices in the cities. Major credit cards (Visa, MasterCard, and American Express) are accepted (indeed, preferred) in many places, even in the smaller towns. Hotels usually accept traveler's checks as well.

Business Hours

In high season, from June to August, shops, supermarkets and museums are generally open every day from 10 a.m. to 5 or 6 p.m. In Reykjavík and other larger centers on the island, some stores may stay open longer, a few even until 8 or 10 p.m. In the off-season, opening hours are limited and closing days are more frequent.

Banks follow the traditional 9 a.m. to 4 p.m. schedule, Monday through Friday; post offices are open a little longer–from 9 a.m. to 6 p.m. Monday through Friday.

Religion

The official religion of Iceland is Lutheranism, practiced according to the National Church of Iceland (Thjóðkirkjan). About 70 percent of the population belongs to this church while just over 10 percent of the population is Christian of other denominations. Another 10 percent of the population is atheist. A small percentage, which has increased in recent years, professes to belong to Ásatrúarfélagið, a religious organization founded on ancient Norse paganism.

Bathrooms

Reykjavík has many public bathroom facilities, but there are fewer in the less urbanized parts of the island (although more are being installed as tourism increases), so breaks along your route should be well organized.

Smoking

Smoking is prohibited in all indoor public places (bars, restaurants, museums) and in accommodation facilities. Icelanders are very serious about preserving the natural environment, so be sure not to abandon your cigarette butts on the ground.

Time Zone

Iceland is in the Greenwich Mean Time zone (GMT) and does not recognize daylight saving time. It is five hours ahead of New York, four hours when daylight saving time is in effect.

Tipping

Prices include everything so tipping is not necessary.

Traveling With Children

Iceland's unique nature and wide-open spaces make it a fun, natural destination for children. Except when in the more treacherous areas such as on the cliffs and fjords, children can be left free to explore. There are no tourist attractions designed specifically for children, but the wonders of nature offer a myriad of curiosities and marvels for the most inquisitive of little explorers, as do the island's museums where small ethnographic exhibits and displays offer information about the island's fauna and geology. Generally, entrance fees for children under 12 are either reduced, often to half price, or free. Excursions in some areas of the island, particularly where the conditions are icy and the roads are rough, may not be suitable for children under 10.

Travelers With Limited Mobility

Unfortunately, beyond its urban areas, Iceland is not always a friendly destination for travelers with limited mobility, but the government has begun to take significant actions to correct this. Many accommodation structures in major cities offer accessible rooms, and public transportation in Reykjavík and Akureyri is generally accessible, with ramps and platforms, but outside the cities, public transportation and accommodations are not necessarily accessible. Travelers with limited mobility may have to depend on private operators for transportation and should contact their accommodation in advance for information about room accessibility. A good source of information is Thekkingarmiðstöð Sjálfsbjargar, the National Confederation of People with Disabilities (*www.sjalfsbjorg.is*).

Pets

An import permit issued by the Icelandic Food and Veterinary Authority is necessary to bring cats, dogs or other pets into the country. In order to obtain the permit, pets must fulfill testing and vaccination requirements. A complete list of requirements, specified by animal and breed, is available on the authority's website (*www.mast.is/en/import-export/import-of-live-animals*).

Tourist Information

Ferðamálastofa, Iceland's tourist board (*www.ferdamalastofa.is*), provides interesting data and statistics relating to the number of travelers and air traffic conditions. Visit Iceland, the country's official tourism website, is the result of a collaboration between public authorities and private groups. Here, travelers can find information and tips about current events and possible itineraries (*www.visiticeland.com*).

EMERGENCIES

Iceland is generally a safe country with a low crime rate, but common sense rules for traveling safely still apply. Carry your money and valuables where you can see them, do not leave your bags unattended, and avoid dimly lit streets at night.

Carry photocopies of your passport or other important documents when traveling, and use credit and debit cards to avoid carrying too much cash. Police are usually courteous and helpful.

Help!	*Hjálp!*
Police	*Lögreglan*
Police officer	*Lögreglumaður*
Emergency	*Neyðartilvik*

Emergency Telephone Numbers

112 is the single emergency number in Iceland.

Health

No particular vaccinations are required to enter Iceland.

Pharmacies are usually open 10 a.m. to 6 p.m. Monday to Friday and 10 a.m. to 4 p.m. on Saturdays. Few are open at night. In an emergency, medical care is available at health care centers (Heilsugæslustöð). For information, call 585 1300 or check the website at *www.heilsugaeslan.is.* Most of the health care staff speaks English. Health care centers may be more difficult to find outside of urban areas.

If you find a tick when hiking, particularly in the spring when herds are grazing, check the exposed parts of your skin and scalp; if possible, wear a hat and long pants and check children. If however you get bitten by a tick, remove it as soon as possible with tweezers, grasping the body close to the skin and pulling gently at a right angle, being careful not to break the insect's abdomen. If the affected area of skin becomes infected, seek medical attention.

Citizens of E.U. countries can use their European Health Insurance Card (EHIC) to avoid having to pay for basic emergency medical treatment but travel insurance is necessary to ensure full coverage.

A bit of terminology:

hospital	*sjúkrahús*
doctor	*lækni*
dentist	*tannlæknir*
pharmacy	*Apótek*
medicine	*lyf*
ambulance	*sjúkrabíll*

What to Do If you Have a Car Accident

If you have an accident in Iceland, you must file a report describing the dynamics of the accident, and if the two parties do not agree or if there are injuries, you have to call the 112 emergency number to request the intervention of law enforcement and/or an ambulance.

Every car must have emergency lights and a reflective warning triangle to use in case of an accident

FURTHER READING

Fiction

The Saga of Oddr the Archer by Anonymous (13th century)
The Tale of Ragnar Lodbrok by Anonymous (13th century)
The Saga of Egil Onehand and Asmund Berserkerbane by Anonymous (14th century)
Gunnar's Saga by Anonymous (15-16th century)
Paradise Reclaimed by Halldór Laxness (1962)
Summer Light, and Then Comes the Night by Jón Kalman Stefánsson (2005)
A Traveler's Guide to Icelandic Folktales by Jón R. Hjálmarsson (2008)
Icelandic Fairy Tales by Angus W Hall (2016)
The Darkness Knows: A Detective Konrad Novel by Arnaldur Indriðason (2017)

Reykjavík: A Fresh Portrait of Iceland's Capital by Pall Stefansson and Sólveig Jónsdóttir (2021)

Outdoor Life & Nature

Iceland in Motion by Olivier Grunewald (2012)
Here Is Iceland, a Children's Book by Margrét Tryggvadóttir (2017)
Birds by Hjörleifur Hjartarson, Rán Flygering (2020)

Travel

Letters from Iceland di W.H. Auden (1937)
Takk. Lost in Iceland by Epi (2019)
The Planet Island by Giorgio Manganelli (2006)

History & Culture

The Book of Icelanders (Íslendingabók): Norse Text, Translation, and Word List by Ari Thorgilsson (12th century)
The Saga of the Volsungs by Jesse Byock (2012)
The Passenger. Iceland by VV.AA. (2018)

HOTELS & RESTAURANTS

Iceland offers an array of accommodations that range from the most luxurious hotels to the simplest of campsites. Note that many businesses, whether hotels, restaurants, or other, may close for the winter season (between September and May).

Hotels

The range of accommodations in Iceland is large and diverse, but the increasing flow of tourists, especially in the summer season, makes last-minute arrangements extremely difficult, particularly in rural areas where distances between accommodations can be extremely long. It is always advisable to make reservations well in advance, whether in hotels, guesthouses, or even campgrounds. Not finding available accommodation once you arrive at your destination can be a difficult problem to solve. The services that are available tend to vary; some facilities offer restaurant service, bars, and conference rooms while others are extremely basic, particularly in remote areas. Family-run guesthouses are quite common, particularly in rural areas, and offer a cheaper option than hotels. Internet connection is generally available everywhere.

Restaurants

There are many restaurants throughout the territory, most of which are of good quality. They offer a wide variety of appetizers, but remember that Icelandic dishes are generally unique, and tend to be quite filling. Water is always free and there is never a cover charge. Often, the price difference between the price of street food and a complete meal at a restaurant is so small that eating in the restaurant may be preferable.

Organization & Abbreviations

The hotels and restaurants are listed by chapter and place-name, in alphabetical order and then according to price. Hotels are listed before restaurants. The number of rooms indicated includes suites. "Nonsmoking" means either nonsmoking rooms or a general ban throughout the hotel and in restaurants, which does not usually extend to outdoor areas. Abbreviations used are AE (American Express), MC (MasterCard), V (Visa); L (lunch) and D (dinner).

REYKJAVÍK & THE SOUTHWEST

HILTON NORDICA $$$$$

SUDURLANDSBRAUT 2,
108 REYKJAVÍK
TEL 444 5000
hilton.reception@icehotels.is
www.hilton.com

Ten minutes by car from Reykjavík, the hotel's rooms are spacious and some have ocean views, perfect for relaxing after a long day of exploring. The hotel's restaurant, **Vox,** offers a fusion of international classics and Icelandic cuisine.

P All major cards

BUS HOSTEL REYKJAVÍK

$$$

SKÓGARHLÍÐ 10,
105 REYKJAVÍK
TEL 535 0350
info@bushostelreykjavik.com
www.bushostelreykjavik.com

A friendly place for budget conscious travelers is a good way to describe this hostel. Breakfast is not included. Double rooms and shared dormitories are available.

All major cards

FOSSHÓTEL REYKJAVÍK

$$$

THÓRUNNARTÚN 1,
105 REYKJAVÍK
TEL 531 9000

Located in the center with a nice view of the city and the port, the hotel has a restaurant (**Haus Restaurant**) that is open for lunch and dinner as well as a bistro. For hiking enthusiasts, it is a great starting point for the Laugavegur Trail.

320

All major cards

LIGHTHOUSE INN

$$$

NORDURLJOSAVEGUR 2,
251 SUDURNESJABÆR
TEL 433 0000
lighthouseinn@simnet.is

At just 30 minutes by car from the volcano, this family-run hotel was built by the three brothers who own it. The substantial use of wood throughout the hotel creates a truly Nordic mountain atmosphere. Breakfast included.

P All major cards

FISKMARKAÐURINN/ THE FISH MARKET

$$$$

AÐALSTRÆTI 12, 101 REYKJAVÍK
TEL 578 8877
info@fiskmarkadurinn.is
www.fiskmarkadurinn.is

This restaurant, which opened in 2007, offers very innovative combinations such as sushi made with Icelandic fish and herbs. Great for both dinner and for an aperitif with friends.

L

All major cards

SOMETHING SPECIAL

MATUR OG DRYKKUR

$$$

GRANDAGARÐUR 2,
101 REYKJAVÍK
TEL 571 8877
info@maturogdrykkur.is
www.maturogdrykkur.is

Located in a late 1960s building that was once a fish-salting plant, this restaurant offers a very unique ambience. The special attention given to historical recipes and the fact that all of the dishes and their ingredients are prepared on-site make this an interesting gastronomic stopover.

Thurs.–Sun. 6.30 p.m.–11 p.m.

All major cards

CAFÉ BRYGGJAN

$$

MIÐGARÐUR,
GRINDAVÍK
TEL 426 7100
info@bryggjan.com
www.bryggjan.com

Truly, a place for fishermen, the café was originally a company that produced fishing nets. In the 2000s, it added first a café and then a res-

taurant, the Netagerðin Dining Hall. Aside from the few concessions made to tourism with a few pizzas and a hamburger, the menu is for the most part local, including the beers. There is often live music on Friday.
Café 7 a.m.–11 p.m., restaurant L and D
All major cards

KAFFI LOKI

$$
LOKASTÍGUR 28, 101 REYKJAVÍK
TEL 466 2828
bookings@loki.is
www.loki.is

That theirs is like the food that Icelandic mothers and grandmothers cook is the promise that the owners make ... and keep. Homemade rye bread, lamb, fresh and smoked fish, and salted butter all served with a view of Hallgrímkirkja.
8 a.m.–10 p.m.
All major cards

MESSINN

$$
LÆKJARGATA 6B, 101 REYKJAVÍK
TEL 546 0095

The specialty of this easygoing place is fish, in particular their so-called *fish pans*, fish and vegetables brought to the table directly in sizzling pans. Perfect for sharing.
MC, V

RÖSTIN RESTAURANT

$$
SKAGABRAUT 100, 250 SUÐURNESJABÆR
TEL 422 7220/893 8909
www.gardskagi.com

In the evening, it is hard to beat the view from this restaurant. Located on the second floor of the Garðskagi Museum, it offers a panoramic view of Snæfellsjökull glacier at sunset. Vegetarian and gluten-free dishes are available.
Thurs.–Sun. 12 a.m.–9 p.m.
All major cards

SÆGREIFINN/SEA BARON

$$
GEIRSGATA 8, 101 REYKJAVÍK
TEL 553 1500

The place is small and rustic but the food is warm and hearty. Fish is the specialty and the soups are noteworthy. The perfect place to look out on the Old Port while keeping warm.
All major cards

PRICES

HOTEL
An indication of the cost of a double room in the high season is given by **$** signs.

$$$$$	Over $200
$$$$	$150–$200
$$$	$100–$150
$$	$70–$100
$	Under $70

RESTAURANTS
An indication of the cost of a three-course meal without drinks is given by **$** signs.

$$$$$	Over $65
$$$$	$45–$65
$$$	$35–$45
$$	$25–$35
$	Under $25

THE SOUTH

SKÁLATJÖRN GUESTHOUSE

$$$$

801 SKÁLATJÖRN
TEL 899 6685
info@skalatjorn.is
www.skalatjorn.is

These small apartments, each with its own kitchen, are part of an owner-managed complex that also includes a goat farm, where guests can familiarize with the animals if they like. The Eyjafjallajökull volcano is visible from here.

7 P All major cards

SELFOSS HI HOSTEL

$$

AUSTURVEGUR 28, 800 SELFOSS
TEL 771 1969
selfosshostel@gmail.com
www.selfosshostel.is

An hour away by car, the hostel is an excellent starting point for exploring the Golden Circle. It offers 8-bed dorm rooms as well as single and family rooms, in addition to an outdoor hot tub. The hostel also organizes tours with a variety of activities.

P All major cards

SOMETHING SPECIAL

FJÖRUBORÐIÐ

$$$$

EYRARBRAUT 3A, 825 STOKKSEYRI
TEL 483 1550
info@fjorubordid.is
www.fjorubordid.is

The name of this restaurant means "on the beach," perfect for its position and its menu, which is based primarily on lobster, but also includes vegetarian dishes. Its signature dish is the soup that many say has inspired more than one sailor to brave the storm.

Thurs.–Mon.
All major cards

FRIÐHEIMAR

$$$

REYKHOLTI, BLÁSKÓGABYGGÐ, 806 SELFOSS
TEL 486 8894
fridheimar@fridheimar.is
www.fridheimar.is

The entire menu is based on the many varieties of tomatoes that grow in the greenhouse, where lunch is served. When we say the entire menu, we mean it, even drinks and desserts!

Noon–4 p.m. MC, AE

GAMLA FJÓSIÐ

$$

HVASSAFELL, 861 HVOLSVÖLLUR
TEL 487 7788
www.gamlafjosid.is

With a name that means "The Old Barn," this simple, typically furnished family-run restaurant offers a menu with ingredients that are made or grown on-site or locally sourced. The bread is homemade, the vegetables are grown locally, and the meat comes from farms where animals graze freely.

All major cards

KAFFI KRÚS

$$

AUSTURVEGUR 7, 800 SELFOSS
TEL 482 1266
kaffikrus@kaffikrus.is
www.kaffikrus.is

In the heart of Selfoss, the café offers an international menu that includes vegetarian dishes as well as hot beverages. The espresso is not bad at all.

Sun.–Thurs. 11 a.m.–9 p.m., Fri.–Sat. 11 a.m.–10 p.m. V

THE SOUTHEAST

HÓTEL KRÍA

$$$$

SLÉTTUVEGUR 12-14, 870 VÍK
TEL 416 2100
hotelkria@hotelkria.is
www.hotelkria.is

Very close to the Hringvegur with an exceptional view of the mountains, this modern hotel is a great place for a stopover on a complete tour of Iceland. The name refers to the arctic terns that nest nearby.

72 + 1 suite P
All major cards

HÓTEL DYRHÓLAEY

$$$

ÁS, 871 VÍK
TEL 487 1333
dyrholaey@dyrholaey.is
www.dyrholaey.is

From all sides of this family-run hotel, visitors will have spectacular views of the nature that surrounds it; the south-facing rooms look onto the Mýrdalur, those on the north face the Búrfell Mountains and to the east, the view is of cultivated fields. Breakfast included.

150 P All major cards

VÍK CAMPING

$

KLETTSVEGUR 7, 870 VÍK
TEL 487 1345
vikcamping@vikcamping.is
www.vikcamping.is

Located about 0.6 mile (1 km) from one of the southernmost little towns on the island, this large campground can host up to 250 guests in tents, campers, and cabins. It offers campers all the services they need: hot and cold water, electrical current, bathrooms, showers, Wi-Fi, and picnic tables. Guests can also rent cottages but the cottages are managed by Airbnb so they are more expensive.

May–Oct.

SOMETHING SPECIAL

KJARR

$$$

KLAUSTURVEGI 2,
880 KIRKJUBÆJARKLAUSTUR
TEL 546 1400
info@kjarrrestaurant.is
www.kjarrrestaurant.is

The food in this recently opened restaurant is made from very locally sourced ingredients, some of which come from less than 350 feet (100 m) away. The food is simple and genuine and the ambience is warm and relaxed.

May–Oct. 12 a.m.–10 p.m.
All major cards

KAFFI HORNIÐ

$$

HAFNARBRAUT 42,
780 HÖFN Í HORNAFIRÐI
TEL 478 2600
info@kaffihornid.is
www.kaffihornid.is

This café/restaurant is well known for its menu, based on shrimp and lobster from a few miles away. Their extensive menu offers a bit of everything including fish, meat, vegetarian dishes, pizza, and ice cream made by a nearby dairy.

11.30 a.m.–9 p.m.
All major cards

THE WEST

ICELANDAIR HOTEL HAMAR

$$$$

HAMRI, 310 BORGARNES

TEL 433 6600
hamar@hotelhamar.is
www.hotelhamar.is
Surrounded by nature, the hotel's large rooms often have a nice balcony with a view on the golf course connected to the hotel, considered one of the best on the island. Guests also have the use of a hot tub.
54 All major cards

BJARGARSTEINN MATHÚS

$$$
SÓLVELLIR, GRUNDARFJÖRÐUR
TEL 438 6770
bjargarsteinn.business.site
This restaurant is located on the beach and offers a limited menu dedicated entirely to fish and crustaceans served in a variety of ways. The chef, who says he has quite a sweet tooth, also has an eye for desserts.
Thurs.–Sun. 6 p.m.–9:30 p.m.
All major cards

KRAUMA

$$$
DEILDARTUNGUHVER,
320 REYKHOLT
TEL 5556066
krauma@krauma.is
www.krauma.is
The restaurant is connected to a thermal station and serves typical cuisine made with fresh, local ingredients. The atmosphere could only be one of relaxation, given the location, and offers a special view of the hot springs.
70 + 70 (outdoor)
11 a.m.–10 p.m.
All major cards

SJÁVARPAKKHÚSIÐ

$$$
HAFNARGATA 2,
340 STYKKISHÓLMUR
TEL 438 1800
info@sjavarpakkhusid.is
The view of the port is particularly beautiful, as is the location in a century-old building with modern décor. The menu varies according to the season and to available local ingredients (fish, vegetables and beer), a sign of the owners' attention and sensitivity.
30 + 30 (outdoor)
Apr.–Nov. All major cards

SKIPPER GASTROPUB

$$
THVERVEGUR 2, 340 STYKKISHÓLMUR
TEL 552 8004
skipper@skipper.is
www.skipper.is
Hamburgers are the boss in this pub, which is also a great place for a drink before or after dinner. Small happy hour dishes are also available.
6 p.m.–10 p.m.
All major cards

THE WESTERN FJORDS

HÓTEL BREIÐAVÍK

$$$$
BREIÐAVÍK / LÁTRABJARG, 451 PATREKSFJÖRÐUR
TEL 867 1575
breidavik@patro.is
www.breidavik.is
This structure offers a number of possibilities including cottages, rooms with or without a private bathroom and even a place for sleeping bags or your own tent in equipped outdoor spaces. Breakfast is included. Many people come to Latrabjarg to see the puffins.
38 All major cards

FINNA HÓTEL
$$$
BORGARBRAUT 4, 510 HÓLMAVÍK
TEL 451 3136
finnahotel@finnahotel.is
The hotel is located in the center of the small town, making it easy for visitors to reach the thermal station. The spacious rooms may have private or shared bathrooms. The terrace offers a beautiful view of the fjords.
17 All major cards

CAFÉ RIIS
$$
HAFNARBRAUT 39, 510 HÓLMAVÍK
TEL 451 3567
caferiis@caferiis.is
www.caferiis.is
The bistro is located in the oldest building in town, something the owners are very proud of, together with the dishes they serve, created with fresh local ingredients. Pizzas are available but the classic menu is already very extensive.
Mon.–Fri., L and D; Sat.–Sun. hours are on their Facebook and Instagram pages All major cards

FLAK
$$
EYRARGATA, 450 PATREKSFJÖRÐUR
TEL 456 0145
www.flakflak.is
A youthful venue in its approach and its décor. A good place for a hot dinner of fish soup or a beer with friends and maybe a game of darts. There are often events and live music.
Only Sat. 7 p.m.–1 a.m.
All major cards

SIMBAHÖLLIN
$
FJARÐARGÖTU 5, 470 THINGEYRI
TEL 899 6659/869 5654
www.simbahollin.is
It would be hard to find a place with more atmosphere than this café, an old 1915 grocery store that has been restored, keeping as much of the original as possible. Its specialty is Belgian waffles with homemade rhubarb jam.
Jun. 1–Aug. 31, 12 a.m–6 p.m.

PRICES

HOTEL
An indication of the cost of a double room in the high season is given by **$** signs.

$$$$$	Over $200
$$$$	$150–$200
$$$	$100–$150
$$	$70–$100
$	Under $70

RESTAURANTS
An indication of the cost of a three-course meal without drinks is given by **$** signs.

$$$$$	Over $65
$$$$	$45–$65
$$$	$35–$45
$$	$25–$35
$	Under $25

THE NORTH

HÓTEL KEA
$$$$$
HAFNARSTRÆTI 87-89, 600 AKUREYRI
TEL 460 2080
kea@keahotels.is
www.keahotels.is
In the center of Akureyri, overlooking the town's famous church,

the hotel's rooms are particularly beautiful and elegant with a clearly Nordic minimalist style. There are many locales nearby and the hotel itself has a bar and restaurant. Breakfast included.
104 P All major cards

HÓTEL SIGLÓ

$$$$$

SNORRAGATA 3, 580 SIGLUFJÖRÐUR
TEL 461 7730
siglo@keahotels.is
www.keahotels.is

In what was once the herring capital, this classically designed hotel, reminiscent of Icelandic fishermen's houses, is actually a great mix of comfort and luxury. The hotel's three restaurants provide an array of meal choices.
68 P All major cards

NAUSTIÐ

$$$

ASGARDSVEGUR 1,
640 HÚSAVÍK
TEL 464 1520
naustidfood@gmail.com

This fish restaurant, which inevitably offers lamb dishes in the spring, proposes many dishes, sandwiches, and other food for takeout but we suggest you enjoy the conviviality of the locale.
Mar.–Sept.
All major cards

EYR BRYGGJAN

$$

STRANDGATA 49, 600 AKUREYRI
TEL 440 6600
bryggjan@bryggjan.is
www.bryggjan.is

The historic, 140-year-old building that houses this restaurant is the oldest in the area. It went from an industrial structure to a welcoming locale with some elegant features. The terrace is open in the summer.
D Wed.–Sat.
All major cards

TORGIÐ

$$

GULA HÚSIÐ VIÐ HÖFNINA, 580 SIGLUFJÖRÐUR
TEL 467 2323
torgid@torgid.net

It is impossible to miss this restaurant, which is located in a lovely little house with yellow walls. The specials change daily and there is a buffet at lunchtime during the week. The dishes are very rich, perfect at the end of a day of walking.
L every day, D Wed.–Fri.
All major cards

BAUTINN

$

HAFNARSTRÆTI 92,
600 AKUREYRI
TEL 462 1818
bautinn@bautinn.is
www.bautinn.is

Located in an early-20th-century building, the restaurant serves good food at reasonable prices in a warm, pleasant atmosphere. Most of the dishes are not very traditional but they are definitely rich and tasty.
Mon.–Thurs. 11.30 a.m–9.30 p.m.; Fri. 11.30 a.m–10 p.m.; Sat. 12 a.m–22 p.m.; Sun. 12 a.m–9.30 p.m.

THE EAST

HÉRAÐ – BERJAYA

$$$$$

MIDVANGUR 1-7, 700 EGILSSTAÐIR
TEL 444 4000/471 1500

herad@icehotels.is
www.icelandhotelcollectionby
berjaya.com
An elegant hotel decorated in light tones, it is also notable for its restaurant, **Lyng,** which specializes in traditional reindeer recipes. Its proximity to Fardagafoss and Hengifoss makes it a great starting point for amazing excursions.
60 + Electric car charging station All major cards

HÓTEL VALASKJÁLF

$$$
SKOGARLONDUM 3,
700 EGILSSTAÐIR
TEL 471 2400
valaskjalf@701hotels.is
www.valaskjalf.is
The hotel offers lodging, a bar for an aperitif, and a restaurant (open only in the summer), and organizes tourist activities in the area.
39 All major cards

BERUNES – HI HOSTEL & CAMP

$$
BERUNES, 765 DJÚPIVOGUR
TEL 869 7227
berunes@hostel.is
www.berunes.is
This old farm was remodeled to become a particularly vivacious hostel that hosts a well-known, excellent restaurant. Lodging options range from independent cottages to your own sleeping bag.
65 June–Sept.
All major cards

CAFÉ SUMARLÍNA

$$
BÚÐAVEGUR 59,
750 FÁSKRÚÐSFJÖRÐUR
TEL 475 1575
sumarlina@simnet.is
www.sumarlina.is
There are a few traditional dishes but the menu is prevalently pizza of all sizes with a variety of toppings, hamburgers and some international fried treats. The café's desserts and hot beverages make it a good place for a snack.
Mon.–Fri. 11 a.m.–9 p.m., Sat.–Sun. 4 p.m.–9 p.m.

LANGABÚÐ

$
DJÚPIVOGUR ICELAND
TEL 478 8220
The café offers homemade sweets and cakes as well as a limited selection of savory dishes, including soups. Enjoy a hot drink after your visit to the museum and the buildings of Langabúð.
Every day May–Oct.

VIÐ VOGINN

$
VOGALAND 2, 765 DJÚPIVOGUR
TEL 354 478 8860
vidvoginn@simnet.is
www.vidvoginn.is
At breakfast, lunch, snack time and dinner, this café-restaurant serves rather traditional cuisine for every meal in a colorful atmosphere with special touches and a great view of the port. The menu has icons that indicate local foods.
11 a.m.–8 p.m.
All major cards

ENTERTAINMENT

Travelers to Iceland often focus on nature but there are also many opportunities for socialization and entertainment. Icelanders are particularly fond of reading and music, and the concerts and festivals offer a variety of music to a variety of audiences. Even a drink with friends in a pub can be a great occasion to dive into the spirit of the island.

Music Festivals

The unique live events visitors can enjoy will definitely include folk music inspired by the legends and customs of the far North, as well as rock and metal that is well loved here.

Iceland Airwaves Festival
www.icelandairwaves.is
This multi-genre festival featuring international stars and new Icelandic talent is held in early November in Reykjavík in several venues in the city (all within a few minutes' walk of each other).

Dark Music Days
www.darkmusicdays.is
This contemporary Icelandic music festival held at the end of January in Reykjavík gives special attention to creative, experimental music.

Thjóðhátíð
www.dalurinn.is
Concerts, bonfires, and fireworks are the highlights of this open-air festival held in Vestmannaeyjar on the weekend preceding the first Monday of August.

Siglufjörður Folk Festival
www.siglofestival.wpcomstaging.com
Artists experienced in Balkan music, American folk, Mexican songs, and traditional Icelandic and Norwegian songs perform a mix of different types of folk music at this review that is held in July.

Reykjavík Blues
www.blues.is
This blues festival in the capital takes place for a few days in the first two weeks of April.

LungA Art Festival
www.lunga.is
More than a music festival, this is a celebration of art in its various forms. Held in Seyðisfjörður, a village of 700 inhabitants in mid-July, it draws a vibrant audience of fans to enjoy the creative work of young talents.

Aldrei fór ég suður
www.aldrei.is
A warehouse made available to the musicians is home to this free rock festival that is held during Easter at Ísafjörður.

Eistnaflug
Two days dedicated to heavy metal in the little town of Neskaupsstaður at the beginning of July.

Menningarnótt
www.menningarnott.is
Literally "Culture Night," it takes place the first weekend after August 18 (or August 18 itself if it falls on a Saturday). The celebrations involve many public and private spaces, with performances and events.

Bars, Cafés & Brewpubs

Whether you want to enjoy the endless days during the summer or warm up in the cold winter, sitting in a local is always a good choice and a good way to enjoy the Icelandic welcome. Always remember to check opening hours; some may vary significantly between high and low season.

Mál og menning
Laugavegur 18, Reykjavík
www.husmalsogmenningar.is
Between bookshop, bar, and live music stage, the choices are many in this small venue. The singalong sessions are very popular, too. Open until midnight on weekends.

Askur Taproom
Fagradalsbraut 25, 700 Egilsstaðir
Tel 470 6070
askur@askurtaproom.com
www.askurtaproom.is
This pub has a good selection of local beers as well as evenings with live music, games, and a huge screen for watching sports.

Smiðjan brugghús
Sunnubraut 15, 870 Vík
Tel 571 8870
www.smidjanbrugghus.is
Beer, hamburgers, ribs, and hot wings are the specialties in this pub.

Beljandi Brewery
Sólvellir 14, 760 Breiðdalsvík
Tel 470 0000
info@breiddalsvik.is
www.breiddalsvik.is
Open every night in summer and almost always closed in winter, this pub serves only local beer.

Segull 67
Vetrarbraut 8-10, 580 Siglufjörður
Tel 863 2120
segull67@segull67.is
www.segull67.is
Tasting tours are offered at this brewery.

Dokkan Brugghús Brewery
Sindragata 14, 400 Ísafjörður
Tel 788 1980
www.dokkanbrugghus.is

Kaldi Bar
Laugavegur 20b, 101 Reykjavík
Tel 581 2200
www.kaldibar.com
Thick stone walls create a very special atmosphere in this cocktail bar in the capital.

Kaffibarinn
Bergstaðastræti 1, 101 Reykjavík
Tel 888 1193
kaffibarinn@gmail.com
One of the first bars in the city, it stays open almost all night on Friday and Saturday with music and DJs. It has become a bit touristy, but it is still fascinating.

Röntgen
Hverfisgata 12, 101 Reykjavík
rontgen@rontgenbar.is
www.rontgenbar.is

Veður Bar
Klapparstígur 33, 101 Reykjavík
arnar@vedurbarinn.is
www.vedurbarinn.is

Skúli Bar
Aðalstræti 9, 101 Reykjavík
Tel 519 6455
info@skulicraftbar.is

Bókakaffið
Austurvegur 22, 800 Selfoss
Tel 482 3079
bokakaffid@bokakaffid.is
Coffee and books are a favorite combination for Icelanders and this café-bookshop (with a branch in the capital as well) is a good place to have a hot drink while paging through your book.

Akureyri Backpakers
Hafnarstræti 98, 600 Akureyri
Tel 571 9050
www.akureyribackpackers.com
This bar and restaurant in the hostel are a great place to meet other travelers.

Kaffi Rauðka
Gránugata 19, Siglufjörður
Tel 461 7733
www.kaffiraudka.is
This rather large venue has a stage for live music. It is only open in the summer and at Christmas, with concerts and events, and Christmas dinner.

Tíu sopar
Laugavegur 27, 101 Reykjavík
Tel 888 25380
vinstukan@gmail.com
www.tiu-sopar.is
Fun, young wine bar with small dishes that are perfect for an aperitif.

Activities

In Iceland, the amount of opportunities to enjoy wide-open spaces and uncontaminated nature almost obliges visitors to take part in at least one of the many related activities that the island offers. It can be a relaxing moment in the spa after a long walk or a hike through the glaciers; the possibilities are endless. Not only agencies organize activities; often hotels and museums do also.

Spas & Thermal Stations

With the natural hot springs that Iceland's volcanoes, geysers, and geothermal phenomena create, it is no surprise that one of the favorite pastimes on the island are spa days. These are often very different from what we are used to, with pools that follow the hot springs, creating real natural spas. Modern spas have only recently arrived in Iceland but the benefits of thermal waters have been recognized for centuries, and Icelanders have always loved these sources of warmth and relaxation.

Vök Baths
Vök við Urriðavatn, 701 Egilsstaðir
Tel 470 9500
hello@vokbaths.is
The water in this center is so clean that it is certifiably drinkable, the only one in Iceland. You can have a glass of it at the bar.

Hvammsvík Hot Springs
Hvammsvík, Kjósarhreppur, Mosfellsbær
Tel 510 5900
info@hvammsvik.com
www.hvammsvik.com

Sky Lagoon
Vesturvör 44-48, Kópavogur
Tel 527 6800
info@skylagoon.is
www.skylagoon.is
Overlooking the ocean, this spa offers a seven-step program that alternates hot water, cold water, and steam to reinvigorate your body and spirit.

Geosea Geothermal Sea Baths
Vitaslóð 1, 640 Húsavík
Tel 464 1210
geosea@geosea.is
www.geosea.is
This may be the northernmost center of the whole island, facing the Arctic Circle. From here, you can glimpse whales in the ocean in the distance and the Northern Lights in the sky.

Forest Lagoon
Vaðlaskógur, 605 Akureyri
Tel 585 0090
info@forestlagoon.is
www.forestlagoon.is

Laugarvatn Fontana
Hverabraut 1, 840 Laugarvatn
Tel 486 1400
fontana@fontana.is
www.fontana.is

Secret Lagoon Hot Spring
Hvammsvegur, 845 Flúðir
Tel 555 3351
www.secretlagoon.is
Open since 1891, it's the oldest in Iceland.

The Beer Spa
Ægisgata 31, 621 Árskógssandi
Tel 414 2828
bjorbodin@bjorbodin.is
bookings@bjorbodin.is
The name says it all. In addition to its normal spa, here you can dip into tubs of beer, water, hops and yeast. There are seven tubs that can hold up to two people at a time.

Activities to Discover Iceland

In Iceland, there is no shortage of activities related to exploration and nature. Some are quieter and suitable for those who prefer to travel comfortably, while others are more adventurous and adapt for those looking for a little adrenaline. In many cases, a number of professionals in the sector offer a variety of packages suited to what you want to do. We strongly recommend you use these tours especially for hikes that may take you to difficult areas: having an expert guide with you is always the best option. Information on the level of difficulty in some places and on some trails is available on the Visit Iceland tourism promotion website (*www.visiticeland.com*, particularly in the Safe Travel section).

Flyover Iceland
Fiskislóð 43, 101 Reykjavík
Tel 527 6700
www.flyovericeland.com
A truly captivating virtual reality experience. Enormous screens, moving chairs, fans, music, and even odors make you feel like you really are a bird flying over Iceland.

Zipline Iceland, Vík
Víkurbrat 5, Vík í Mýrdal
Tel 6988890
zipline@zipline.is
www.zipline.is
In a secure harness, you will hurtle along four zip lines, the longest of which is almost 800 feet long (240 m), as you watch the hills and plains rush by below.

Eldhestar – Horse riding
Vellir, 816 Ölfus
Tel 480 4800
info@eldhestar.is
www.eldhestar.is
These tours on horseback vary in difficulty and length, lasting from a few hours to more than one day.

Iceland Bike Farm
Mörtunga 2, 880 Kirkjubæjarklaustur
Tel 847 1604
info@icelandbikefarm.is
www.icelandbikefarm.is
A real farm that offers lodging to the many cycling enthusiasts that either travel with organized tours or move around independently.

Midgard Adventures
Dufthaksbraut 14, 860 Hvolsvöllur
Tel 578 3370
adventure@midgard.is
A family-run business that offers tours around the area of Hvolsvöllur as well as lodgings and a bar/restaurant at their base camp.

Icelandia
www.icelandia.is
This group connects a number of tour operators that offer top-level experiences.

Ice Explorer
Jökulsárlón, 781 Höfn
Tel 866 3490
ice@explorers.is
www.explorers.is
Guides specialized in ice caves and Vatnajökull glacier hikes.

Glacier Adventure
Hali, 781 Höfn
Tel 571 4577
info@glacieradventure.is
Guides lead small groups to Iceland's mountain peaks, glaciers and ice caves in the Vatnajökull area.

From Coast to Mountains (Ingólfshöfði tours)
Hofsnes
Tel 894 0894
info@FromCoastToMountains.is
www.fromcoasttomountains.com

Fjallhalla Adventures
Miðholt 23, 801 Reykholt
Tel 547 9999
info@fjallhalla.is
fjallhalla.is
Specializing in tours for small groups, they offer adventures with a variety of activities in all of Iceland.

Mountaineers of Iceland
Tel 580 9900
ice@mountaineers.is
Snowmobile and Super Jeep tours of the Langjökull glacier.

Sleipnir Tours
Stálhella 2, 221 Hafnarfjörður
Tel 565 4647
info@sleipnirtours.is
www.sleipnirtours.is
They have the largest vehicles for exploring the glaciers, and offer excursions along the Golden Circle as well.

Arctic Adventures
Skutuvogur 2, 104 Reykjavík
Tel 562 7000

Elding – Whale-watching
Tel 519 5000
elding@elding.is
www.elding.is
Offering many boat tours including one to view the Northern Lights.

North Sailing – Húsavík
Tel 464 7272
info@northsailing.is

Inside the Volcano – Thríhnúkagígur
Tel 519 5609/540 1313
info@insidethevolcano.com
For a hike that actually takes you inside the crater of a dormant volcano!

Troll Expeditions
Tel 519 5544
info@troll.is
www.troll.is

Borea Adventures
Tel 456 3322
info@borea.is
www.borea.is
Offering a choice of tours by kayak and other non-motorized means that allow visitors to avoid noise and enjoy nature without disturbing it. In the summer, there are two boats that go to the Hornstrandir Nature Reserve.

West Tours
Aðalstræti 7, 400 Ísafjörður
Tel 456 5111
info@westtours.is
www.westtours.is
Activities and hiking in the Hornstrandir Nature Reserve, to Hesteyri and to the Vigur Islands, by land and by sea.

Westfjords Adventures
Thórsgata 8a, 450 Patreksfjörðu
Tel 456 5006
info@wa.is
www.westfjordsadventures.com
Offering a wide variety of guided and unguided tours with vehicles ranging from jeeps to bicycles.

Campgrounds

Camping enthusiasts will be in their element in Iceland, where they will find many facilities for those who want to travel independently, whether it be by camper or with just a tent and a backpack. Campgrounds in Iceland usually offer all the necessary amenities including electrical connections, toilets, showers, Wi-Fi and more (stove and kitchen, lockable lockers, etc.). You will need to reserve or at least inquire in advance about availability; finding yourself with nowhere to stay overnight can be a problem in Iceland, where the distances between one site and another can be long. Driving on Iceland's unpaved roads is advisable only when you are adequately rested. In many cases, reservations can be made on the Parka website (*parka.is*). Keep in mind the season when you plan your travel since many campgrounds may close or operate with reduced availability in the cold winter months.

Laugardalur, Reykjavík
Tel 568 6944
info@reykjavikcampsite.is
www.reykjavikcampsite.is

Víðistaðatún, Hafnafjörður
Tel 565 0900
info@lavahostel.is
www.lavahostel.is

Stykkishólmur Camping Ground
Tel 438 1075
mostri@stykk.is
www.visitstykkisholmur.is

Húsafell
Tel 435 1551
info@hotelhusafell.is
www.husafell.com

Tungudalur, Ísafjörður
Tel 894 1500
gih@gih.is
www.gih.is

Heydalur, Mjóafirði
Tel 456 4824
heydalur@heydalur.is
www.heydalur.is

Ásbyrgi
Tel 842 4364
asbyrgi@vjp.is
www.vatnajokulsthjodgardur.is

Vaglaskógur
Tel 860 4714
vaglaskogur-camping.business.site

Egilsstaðir
Tel 470 0750
camping@egilsstadir.is
www.campegilsstadir.is

Borgarfjörður eystri
hshelgason@gmail.com
www.borgarfjordureystri.is

Kirkjubær II, Kirkjubæjarklaustur
Tel 894 4495

Skaftafell National Park
Tel 470 8300
skaftafell@vjp.is
www.vatnajokulsthjodgardur.is

LANGUAGE GUIDE

Vowels

Á á sounds like the "ow" as in *cow*
E e sounds like the short "ai" sound in *air*
É é sounds like *yeah*, but shorter
i sounds like the "i" in *win*
Í í sounds like the "ee" in *we*
J j said as a "y" at the beginning of words. Elsewhere it is aspirated before the "y" sound
O o sounds like the "o" in *hot*
Ó ó sounds like "oh"
Ú ú sounds like the "ew" sound in *yew*
Ei and ey sound like the "a" sound in *case*
Æ æ sounds like "eye"
Ö ö sounds like the "ur" in *murder*

Consonants

Þ; þ sounds like "th", used at the beginning of a word
Ð; ð sounds like "th", used in the middle or at the end of a word
f sounds like "f" in English except between vowels, when it sounds like a "v"
g sounds like a hard g. In between vowels and at the end of a word sounds like a soft German "ch" at the back of the throat. It is not pronounced between accented vowels. It is said as an Icelandic j between a vowel and j. After a vowel and before a t or s it is a hard German "ch"
j sounds like a "y"

Greetings

Hi *Hæ*
Goodbye *Bless!*
Good morning *Góðan dag(inn)*
Good evening *Góða kvöldið*
Good night *Góða nótt*
Yes *Já*
No *Nei*
Thank you *Takk (fyrir)*
Sorry! *Afsakið!*

Lodgings

Hotel: *hótel*
Apartment: *íbúð*
Have you got a double/single room:
Áttu laust einstæklingsherbergi/ tveggja manna herbergi?
For tonight/tomorrow:
Í kvöld/annað kvöld
For one night/two nights/ three nights:
Í eina nótt/tvær nætur/thrjár nætur

Shopping

May I have... *Gæti ég fengið...?*
Have you got... *Eigið thið...?*
How much does this cost?
Hvað kostar...?
Can I pay with my credit card?
Get ég borgað með korti?

Restaurants

Have you got a table for two?
Eigið thið borð fyrir tvö?
Can we sit outside/on the terrace?
Getum við setið úti?
Can I see a menu in English?
Get ég fengið matseðil á ensku
Can I order? *Má ég panta?*
I've already ordered, thanks.
Ég er búin/n að panta, takk
Can I have the check?
Get ég fengið reikninginn?

Trips and signs

Bus *Strætó*
Car *Bíll*
Ferry *Ferja*
Service station *bensínstöð*
One ticket, please.
Get ég fengið miða í..., takk

INDEX

Page numbers in **bold** type indicate illustrations. Categories are in **CAPITAL** letters.

ILLUSTRATIONS CREDITS

2-3, Gavn Helier/Jon Arnold/Photolibrary; 4, Viola Signorini/Pierluigi Sacco; 12, Bill Perry/Shutterstock; 14-15, umberto Sirito; 16, Viola Signorini; 17, Daria Medvedeva/Shutterstock; 19, andrada bursuc/Shutterstock; 20, Hatairat Assavavutipong/Shutterstock; 21, lev radin/Shutterstock; 22, Kirill Chernyshev/Shutterstock; 23, Palmi Gudmundsson/Shutterstock; 24, Christian Riedelsheimer/Shutterstock; 25, John Penney/Shutterstock; 26, Raadsig/Wiki Media Commons; 27, Wikidata; 28, Jóna Thórunn/Wiki Media Commons; 29, Rob Oo/Wiki Media Commons; 30 been.there.recently/Shutterstock; 31, Universal History Archive/Shutterstock; 33, Wikidata; 34, Wiki Media Commons; 35, Wiki Media Commons; 37, Unknown author/Wiki Media Commons; 38, Wiki Media Commons; 39, Wiki Media Commons; 41, Felix Lipov/Shutterstock; 42, Wiki Media Commons; 43, Wiki Media Commons; 44, Wiki Media Commons; 45, Anders Peter Photography/Shutterstock; 46, Ruben M Ramos/Shutterstock; 47, Jennifer Boyer/Flickr; 48, Wiki Media Commons; 49, canyalcin/Shutterstock; 50, Magnussen, Friedrich/Wiki Media Commons; 51, Amehime/Shutterstock; 52, Nagel Photography/Shutterstock; 53, Christian Wilkinson/Shutterstock; 54, Alla Khananashvili/Shutterstock; 55, Shadowgate/Flickr; 56, Featureflash Photo Agency/Shutterstock; 57, Christian Bertrand/Shutterstock; 58 e 59, Kvikmyndamiðstöð Íslands (Icelandic Film Centre); 60, Guenter M1/Shutterstock; 61 top, Wiki Media Commons; 61 bottom, Wiki Media Commons; 62, Andriy Blokhin/Shutterstock; 63, Viola Signorini; 64, Viola Signorini; 66, Viola Signorini; 67, Chamille White/Shutterstock; 68, SasinTipchai/Shutterstock; 69, CHANUN.V/Shutterstock; 70, MyImages - Micha/Shutterstock; 71, lowpower225/Shutterstock; 72, Fanfo/Shutterstock; 73, Pom Bakery/Shutterstock; 74, Bernhard Richter/Shutterstock; 78, Wojciech Strzelecki "Wojtrix"/Wiki Media Commons; 80, Viola Signorini/Pierluigi Sacco; 81, Wiki Media Commons; 82, Bill Perry/Shutterstock; 85, Lyciz Mill/Shutterstock; 87, Truba7113/Shutterstock; 88, Viola Signorini/Pierluigi Sacco; 89, Michal Piec/Shutterstock; 90, RPBaiao/Shutterstock; 91, Kutna Hora, Czech Republic/Wiki Media Commons; 92, Dan Shachar/Shutterstock; 93, Andreas Wolochow/Shutterstock; 94, Brian Logan Photography/Shutterstock; 95, vvoe/Shutterstock; 96, Eugene Ga/Shutterstock; 98, Palmi Gudmundsson/Shutterstock; 100, Peter Gudella/Shutterstock; 102, Rudy Balasko/Shutterstock; 103, Danillo Evangelista/Shutterstock; 105, Jose Arcos Aguilar/Shutterstock; 106, Umberto Sirito; 107, Blue Planet Studio/Shutterstock; 109, Johann Ragnarsson/Shutterstock; 111, 4H4 PH/Shutterstock; 112, Johann Helgason/Shutterstock; 114, VisualProduction/Shutterstock; 118, I Wei Huang/Shutterstock; 120, VicPhotoria/Shutterstock; 122, Viola Signorini/Pierluigi Sacco/Shutterstock; 123, Viola Signorini/Pierluigi Sacco/Shutterstock; 125, teddiviscious/Shutterstock; 126, Jon Gretarsson/Wiki Media Commons; 130, Cecilia Heisser / Nationalmuseum/Wiki Media Commons; 132, Christian Schwier/Shutterstock; 134, Jacob Boomsma/Shutterstock; 136, Viola Signorini/Pierluigi Sacco; 137, trabantos/Shutterstock; 140, Isabel Baldovi/Shutterstock; 142, Luigi Morbidelli/Shutterstock; 144, Tommy Larey/Shutterstock; 146, Viola Signorini/Pierluigi Sacco; 150, Nick Fox/Shutterstock; 151, Viola Signorini/Pierluigi Sacco; 152, Viola Signorini/Pierluigi Sacco; 154, Viola Signorini/Pierluigi Sacco; 157, Pascal Riemann/Shutterstock; 159, Johannes Bluemel/Shutterstock; 161, Jules_Kitano/Shutterstock; 163, Adellyne/Shutterstock; 165, Viola Signorini/Pierluigi Sacco; 166, Gestur Gislason/Shutterstock; 168, Klara Kla Dvorakova/Shutterstock; 169, Viola Signorini/Pierluigi Sacco; 173, VIKVAD/Shutterstock; 174, biletskiyevgeniy.com/Shutterstock; 176, Jacob Boomsma/Shutterstock; 178, Daniel Doerfler/Shutterstock; 179, Viktor Hladchenko/Shutterstock; 180, Umberto Sirito; 183, Nur Ismail Photography/Shutterstock; 184, Viola Signorini/Pierluigi Sacco; 185, Jaroslav Jaroslavsson/Shutterstock; 186, Ivan Kurmyshov/Shutterstock; 188, Brian Gratwicke/Flickr; 189, Davis Dorss/Shutterstock; 191, Viola Signorini/Pierluigi Sacco; 192, Javen/Shutterstock; 194, Wiki Media Commons Commons; 196, Tomasz Wozniak/Shutterstock; 198, Wiki Media Commons Commons; 199, Wiki Media Commons Commons; 200, Photostravellers/Shutterstock; 202, Giedriius/Shutterstock; 204, Jiri Vondrous/Shutterstock; 206, Marti Bug Catcher/Shutterstock; 207, Florian Baron/Shutterstock; 208, Alexey Stiop/Shutterstock; 209, Wirestock Creators/Shutterstock; 211, Gestur Gislason/Shutterstock; 212, Julia Bjornsdottir/Shutterstock; 213, Diego Delso/Wiki Media Commons Commons; 214/215, Pavel Svoboda Photography/Shutterstock; 215, Giedriius/Shutterstock; 216, Kiran Photo/Shutterstock; 217, Kamila Koziol/Shutterstock; 218, Bill Kennedy/Shutterstock; 219, Belinka/Shutterstock; 220, Bengt A. Lundberg/Wiki Media Commons Commons; 222, Jan Jerman/Shutterstock; 224, Shlyahov Sergei/Shutterstock; 228, Filip Fuxa/Shutterstock; 231, Viola Signorini/Pierluigi Sacco; 232, Woodophotography/Shutterstock; 235, Gabrielle photographs/Shutterstock; 236, Elsmore Media/Shutterstock; 237, Viola Signorini/Pierluigi Sacco; 239, Viola Signorini/Pierluigi Sacco; 241, africa2008st/Shutterstock; 243, Viola Signorini/Pierluigi Sacco; 244, Panther Media GmbH/Alamy Stock Photo; 245, Checco2; 246, Viola Signorini/Pierluigi Sacco; 247, Noah Jordan/Shutterstock; 249, Matt Koz/Shutterstock; 252, Oleg Senkov/Shutterstock; 256, Viola Signorini; 257, Rawpixel.com/Shutterstock; 259, Pjt56/Wiki Media Commons Commons; 260, Viola Signorini/Pierluigi Sacco; 262, Umberto sirito; 263, Erdrokan/Wiki Media Commons Commons; 264, fukez84/Shutterstock; 265, Wiki Media Commons Commons; 267, Ralf Broskvar/Shutterstock; 268, Little Blind Chicken/Shutterstock; 270, Viola Signorini/Pierluigi Sacco; 271, Silaghi Octavian/Shutterstock; 272, sergioboccardo/Shutterstock; 273, Pjt56/Wiki Media Commons Commons; 274, Dickelbers/Wiki Media Commons Commons; 276, tbate54/Shutterstock; 277, Wiki Media Commons Commons; 279, Spm/Wiki Media Commons Commons; 280, Lor Chick/Shutterstock; 281, Gianfranco Vivi/Shutterstock; 282, Christian Bickel fingalo/Wiki Media Commons Commons; 284, Oleg Senkov/Shutterstock; 288, Greshnov Kirill/Shutterstock; 291, inspi_ml/Shutterstock; 292, Stefano Rulli/Shutterstock; 294-295, Alex Marakhovets/Shutterstock; 296, Uhryn Larysa/Shutterstock; 297 top, Samta N/Shutterstock; 297 bottom, Henner Damke/Shutterstock; 298 e 299, Viola Signorini/Pierluigi Sacco

National Geographic

TRAVELER

Iceland

FIRST EDITION

Since 1888, the National Geographic Society has funded more than 14,000 research, conservation, education, and storytelling projects around the world. National Geographic Partners distributes a portion of the funds it receives from your purchase to National Geographic Society to support programs including the conservation of animals and their habitats.

Piazzale Luigi Cadorna, 6 - 20123 Milan, Italy
www.whitestar.it

Licensee of National Geographic Partners, LLC.

ISBN: 978-8-8544-1971-1

Printed in China
24/JPM/2

First edition: Iceigeo, Milan (coordination: Lorenzo Sagripanti; translation: Alexa Ahern, Cynthia Anne Koeppe; layout: Simona Scolari; editing: Graziella Del Ciuco, James Schwarten)

MIX
Paper from responsible sources
FSC® C178000

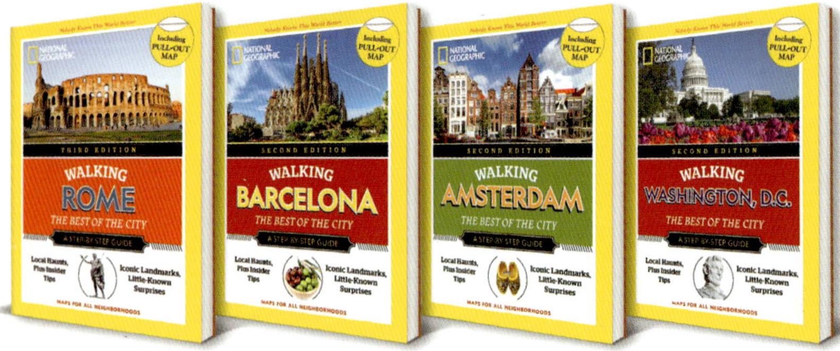

THIRD EDITION
WALKING ROME
THE BEST OF THE CITY
SECOND EDITION
WALKING BARCELONA
THE BEST OF THE CITY
SECOND EDITION
WALKING AMSTERDAM
THE BEST OF THE CITY
SECOND EDITION
WALKING WASHINGTON, D.C.
THE BEST OF THE CITY